Learning Later, Living Greater

LEARNING LATER, LIVING GREATER

*The Secret for Making the Most
of Your After-50 Years*

Nancy Merz Nordstrom, M.Ed.
Jon F. Merz

SENTIENT PUBLICATIONS

First Sentient Publications edition 2006

Cover design by Kim Johansen
Book design by Timm Bryson

Library of Congress Cataloging-in-Publication Data

Nordstrom, Nancy Merz.
Learning later-living greater : the secret for making the most of
your after-fifty years / by Nancy Merz Nordstrom & Jon F. Merz.-- 1st ed.
p. cm.
ISBN-13 978-1-59181-047-6
ISBN-10 1-59181-047-7
1. Older people--Education. 2. Elderhostels. 3. Adult education. I.
Merz, Jon F. II. Title.
LC5457.N67 2006
374.1824'4--dc22
2005033898

Printed in the United States of America

10 9 8 7 6 5 4 3 2 1

SENTIENT PUBLICATIONS, LLC
1113 Spruce Street
Boulder, CO 80302
www.sentientpublications.com

To the pioneers of the learning in retirement movement, and to all the lifelong learners who have followed in their footsteps. Thanks to your dedication and hard work, the later years of future generations will be greatly enhanced.

To my children for your unwavering support and enthusiasm.

To Maurie for the joy and the laughter you have brought into my life.

—Nancy Merz Nordstrom

Contents

PART SIX. REPRISE—TO BOLDLY GO

PART SEVEN. RESOURCES

Introduction

Early on a warm August morning in 1993, I awoke to find myself a widow at age forty-eight, with four children, the youngest just fifteen, still living at home.

Three years later, after the fog caused by my husband's unexpected death had lifted, I returned to school. It had been more than twenty-five years since I was last a student.

When I walked across the academic threshold at age fifty-one, I felt and acted old. In short, I *was* old! Over the course of two years, I underwent a complete rejuvenation—a higher-quality rejuvenation than any spa or resort could ever hope to provide. In fact, I felt as though I had found the fountain of youth. I emerged from my studies full of zest, joy, and enthusiasm. I was more alive than I had been in years. Henry Ford's comments, "Anyone who stops learning is old, whether they are twenty or eighty. Anyone who keeps learning is young," certainly applied to me.

Being back in school did for me what therapy, grief counseling, and the passage of time could not do. It gave me back not just a life, but an enhanced life—a life with increased self-esteem, focus, and vitality. In a way, I had been given a second chance, and I felt it was critically important to make the most of that chance. I also felt that I wanted to leave some kind of legacy about how one can remake a life when the unexpected happens, not only for my own descendents, but for all those who would walk that same road.

The opportunity to do that came shortly after my schooling was completed. I joined the Elderhostel organization, the world's first and largest educational travel organization for older adults. Their mission to be the "preeminent provider of high-quality, affordable educational opportunities for older adults," was the perfect fit for me as an advocate of how lifelong learning can change and enrich your life. Elderhostel believes that "learning is a lifelong process and sharing new ideas, challenges, and experiences is rewarding in every season of life." These were exactly my feelings.

As the director of the Elderhostel Institute Network (EIN), I found myself immersed in lifelong learning. Sometimes known as continuing learning, it's learning for the sheer joy of learning, or learning not dictated by academic requirements. For the purposes of this book, however, we'll use the term lifelong learning.

Time and time again, I spoke with people whose lives, like mine, had been changed by the power of this incredible tool. It was a wonderfully validating experience for me, proving over and over that lifelong learning in any form, and at any age—but especially in older adults—could transform lives.

Lifelong learning in the later years provides the perfect opportunity for people to take part in all the things they have never had time for. Here is an opportunity for people from all walks of life, who have been busy working and raising a family, to do what they always wanted to do—to learn, travel, and socialize, all the while expanding their knowledge and wisdom.

It doesn't matter what form your work life took or how far you climbed the corporate ladder—or how much you ignored it—lifelong learning is not exclusive. Anyone and everyone is welcome to indulge!

Yet every working day, I also realized that many people knew little or nothing about this vehicle for enhancing their later years. Of course, everyone is, to some extent, a lifelong learner. Reading books, newspapers, and magazines; taking up a hobby; or doing crosswords is considered informal learning. But what I'm talking about here is more formal types of lifelong learning: noncredit courses in classrooms, educational travel programs, and learning that takes place through meaningful community service.

The Elderhostel Institute Network, as the largest and most respected educational network for older adults in North America, provides resources that ultimately help approximately 100,000 people through formal non-credit classroom programs. But there are millions more out there—including people who have already retired, the soon-to-retire baby boomers, and even younger generations who know little or nothing about these and other types of learning programs, not to mention the incredible value lifelong learning brings to our later years.

Hence this book. It's a breezy, upbeat look at three different paths of lifelong learning: in the classroom, through educational travel, and in the community. I hope that it will spur you on to learn more, to delve deeper into the value of lifelong learning in your after-fifty years, and to seek out the opportunities that await you.

Imparting the message about the value of lifelong learning has become my passion. I want to tell you to throw out all your old memories about what being in school was like. As an older adult returning to school—for credit or just for fun—it's an entirely new and very different experience.

And I want to reassure you that your past academic attainments have no bearing whatsoever on your joining a lifelong learning program. Forget degrees and all the credentials that society confers on us. All you need is the desire to keep your mind active and alert and an innate curiosity about the world around us.

Gone are the talking heads, rote memorization, and test taking. In their place are facilitators eager to learn as much from you as you are from them, welcoming the give and take of lively discussion enriched with life's experiences. There really is no greater way of learning than by sharing in and absorbing the many different viewpoints expressed in a spirited discussion. So if your previous academic experiences were negative, forget them. If they were positive, know that lifelong learning for you as an older adult will far surpass them.

Philosopher John Dewey said it best, I think: "Education must be reconceived, not as merely a preparation for maturity (whence our absurd idea that it should stop after adolescence) but as a continuous growth of the mind and a continuous illumination of life...real education comes after we leave school, and there is no reason why it should stop before death."

In writing this book, I'm hoping to awaken in you in some small way what was awakened in me: the value of lifelong learning to you as an older adult.

Although this book focuses on what is called *noncredit* lifelong learning, *for-credit* lifelong learning is equally valuable, and many books are available that address for-credit lifelong learning opportunities. Colleges welcome degree-seeking students of any age. It remains for you to decide which route is right for you. Lifelong learning, no matter what its form, is an incredibly important tool for helping you find life satisfaction.

Life, especially in the after-fifty years, is all about choices and opportunities. Having choices and opportunities are what make life worth living. It gives us a reason to get up in the morning. Every day we are given new choices and opportunities. It's the way we select them that gives our life meaning.

So make the choice and take this opportunity to find out what lifelong learning is really all about. My hope is this book will do that for you. Then, if you decide lifelong learning has a place in your life and you seek out opportunities in your community, I can just about guarantee that a year from now your life will be richer, fuller, and far more satisfying.

An old Chinese proverb says, "Learning is a treasure that will follow its owner everywhere." Great treasures await you in the world of lifelong learning.

Nancy Merz Nordstrom
Summer 2005

PART ONE

To Boldly Go

Chapter One

To Boldly Go

Don't be afraid to take a big step.
You can't cross a chasm in two small jumps.
—David Lloyd George

Do you want more out of life? Do you want to make the most of your after-fifty years?

Then fasten your seat belts—we're about to shift into warp speed and explore a world you may never have known existed.

For most people, the image of retirement is one of early-bird specials, golf games, and retirement communities in the Sun Belt. It's early-to-bed nights sprinkled with bingo and grandchildren. We're used to images like this because of the way retirement is portrayed in the media. It's how most of our predecessors chose to live in their later years.

But for those of us who took part in reshaping the country during the 1960s, those of us who have worked our entire lives to produce an outstanding quality of life, and those of us who have endeavored to improve our society's cultural mores, retirement is about to be redefined.

In fact, let's start right now by not even calling it *retirement* anymore. From now on, we'll call it the *third age of life* (the first age being our childhood and the second age being our working and family years). Remember those three-stage rockets that powered our quest to reach beyond our planet out to the moon? Well, like them, our own third age of life will propel us to explore realms never before seen and will enrich our lives in ways we never imagined.

Forget going quietly into that good night; we're about to turn our third age into the best years of our lives!

Recent Statistics

How can we do this? By taking control of our destinies. After all, recent studies show a huge upswing in longevity; people are living longer than ever before. Half of all the people who ever lived to age sixty-five are alive today.[1] By the year 2030, between 20 and 25 percent of people in the United States will be over fifty.[2] That means most of us have a good twenty or thirty years left of life once we leave the working world. That's plenty of time to take control.

According to an American Association of Retired Persons (AARP) study conducted in 1999, 80 percent of us plan to continue working, but in new and different ways. Only 16 percent of us plan a retirement like that of our parents. And 4 percent are undecided about their plans.[3] If only 16 percent of retirees want the same lifestyle as their parents choose, where does that leave the rest of us who yearn for a more exciting and challenging third age?

Put simply, we have a choice.

We can join that 16 percent and allow the popular portrayal of retirement to continue—we'll wile away our hours cooling pies on windowsills and sipping lemonade on our porches while we contemplate "the good ol' days."

I was born in 1926 and grew up in the shadow of the Great Depression. Very few people went to college; most were lucky to graduate from high school what with having to go and get any jobs they could just to help out the family at mealtimes. After I graduated from high school, I was lucky enough to get a job as a secretary. I fell in love, got married, and spent many years raising my three wonderful children. But even still, I longed for more, so I went back to work. My desire to stay active followed me into retirement; I joined a lifelong learning group. With all the choices of subject matter, there is so much to be learned! The social environment is great. I get to meet all sorts of new friends, which is a true bonus. What I like best are the classes. They're relaxed and informal, making them all the more enjoyable. There are no tests and no pressure, just the fun of learning. The more you know, the more you want to know.

—Martha Jancewicz, Norwich, Connecticut

Or we can take charge of our lives and boldly begin a new phase of exploration. We'll indulge in lifelong learning. We'll give back to our communities. We'll raise the quality of life in our society once again.

Our minds will lead; our bodies will follow.

A wise older woman once said that the ideal life, after leaving the forty-hour workweek, should be composed of one-third work, one-third play, and one-third giving back. What a wonderful philosophy!

Taking Action with Lifelong Learning

So how can we put that philosophy into action?

Within these pages you'll discover the world of lifelong learning. By first effecting change within yourself—by choosing the challenge and excitement of personal discovery that later-life learning offers—you'll be better positioned to then effect change in our society, whether at the town, city, state, or even the national level. Lifelong learning is a real door-opener.

We've made big changes before. Throughout our lives, we've met incredible challenges and persevered. From the turbulent years of our youth, through the years we struggled to raise a family and succeed at our chosen careers, into our mid-life crises, we've seen it all. Now, in our third age, we are perfectly positioned to redefine the role of older adults in our society. The experiences and wisdom we've gained become the very tools we'll use to reshape what it means to be an elder.

Traditional cultures of the past held older adults in high esteem. Today, however, they are viewed as burdens, often seen as a useless drag on society—interested in taking, not giving. Nothing could be further from the truth. According to a 2002 study undertaken for Civic Ventures,[4] Americans aged fifty and older now devote more time than ever before to bettering their communities. It makes perfect sense: we have the time and energy to do so, now that the pressures of raising a family and laboring in the job market are behind us. But our society as a whole still does not take that into consideration in picturing older adults.

This has to change.

And we can do it! More than seventy-six million of us are standing on the brink, ready to pass into the third age of life. Others of you are already there. With little effort, working together we can blow the tired stereotypes of retirement and older adults right out of the water. And instead

We retirees are no longer content with only golf and bridge or any of the other old stereotypes that have plagued the older generations. Alzheimer's? Who has time for that when there is so much out there waiting to be learned and explored? Lifelong learning has become my tonic of life!

—Gloria Grenz, Pocatello, Idaho

we'll become treasured resources, guiding other generations and society as a whole.

The pioneers of modern-day lifelong learning—most from the Greatest Generation—are still working hard to effect this change. But there just aren't enough of them to change the mindset of an entire society.

They need our help.

Our sheer numbers, combined with our proven zest for adventure and challenge, will make our work easy. And all it takes is one simple step: getting involved with lifelong learning.

About This Book

Before we take a closer look at what you'll find within these pages, you should keep in mind two very important points about lifelong learning.

First, the lifelong learning programs we discuss in this book are *not* for-credit programs. This is not a book about how to gain credits toward a degree. Many such books are available, and most colleges and universities welcome older learners into their degree programs.

Second (and this is *extremely* important), the level of your previous academic experience doesn't matter. Not one bit! High school through college educated, anyone and everyone is welcome to participate in lifelong learning. All you need to indulge in lifelong learning is a desire to keep your mind active and alert and an urge to learn for the sheer joy of learning.

Each chapter of *Learning Later, Living Greater* begins with a powerful first-person account of lifelong learning in action. These stories are told by people who used the excitement and challenge of personal discovery to effect change and empower their third age. It's happening to thousands of people every day, all around you. Read the stories and use them to motivate you on your own personal lifelong learning quest.

The rest of Part One introduces lifelong learning. If you're thinking about including the adventure and thrills of this bold new frontier in your life, you'll want to know exactly what it is and how it can dramatically enhance your own third age experience.

In Part Two, "It Ain't Over Till It's Over," you'll explore the latest information on brain research and how it relates to lifelong learning. New and exciting research in the 1990s—the Decade of the Brain—showed that keeping your brain active and involved, even as you age, may help prevent Alzheimer's disease.[5]

Most surprising of all, this research has shown that the brain will continue to adapt, grow, and in some ways improve with age provided you continue to challenge it. We'll also look at the mind/body connection and how the impact of lifelong learning on your mental state can have astounding benefits for the rest of your body as well.

Finally, we'll take a look at lifelong learning in the after-fifty years. It's a very special time with its own unique challenges and opportunities.

Part Three, "Health Clubs for the Brain," delves into the world of lifelong learning in the classroom. You'll find answers to questions like: What are lifelong learning programs? Who belongs? What are the benefits? What is the curriculum? Where are the programs? You'll even discover how to start your own program if you can't find one in your community. Then, come along and explore the other lifelong learning options available in your community, as well as around the world. There's a huge international lifelong learning movement out there, just waiting for your involvement.

In Part Four, "Up, Up and Away!," you'll discover how to add an entirely new facet to your vacations by involving yourself in educational travel. It's lifelong learning with wings, and there are no boundaries to the worlds you can discover. Find out what these learning adventures are all about and who takes part. You'll also get acquainted with the largest educational travel organization for older adults operating in the United States.

In Part Five, "Rebels with a Cause," you'll discover how lifelong learning enhances society. Using the knowledge, skills, and wisdom you have developed over a lifetime of full-time work and personal experience, you'll be able to meld old and new interests into meaningful volunteer activities that will benefit society. With a renewed sense of purpose, you will be well positioned to take on the role of community advocate or leader—making it a better place for all generations.

Part Six is entitled "Reprise—To Boldly Go." In this part, you will peer into the future of lifelong learning, an uncharted frontier. As the lifelong learning movement gains momentum, thrilling and innovative things will happen. Here's your chance to get a sneak peek at the coming wave of excitement. This part ends with a wrap-up of all that we've talked about—a summary that will help get you focused and on track.

Part Seven is the "Resource" section. It contains an illuminating self-exploration exercise—a sort of lifelong learning compass. Figure out if lifelong learning is for you, and if so, in what direction you want to start. It's a fun little exercise designed to help you get the most out of your lifelong learning quest. In this section, you'll also find contact information for the many resources mentioned throughout the book.

Sprinkled throughout each section of the book, you'll also find related interviews with experts in the field. Their expertise and knowledge about lifelong learning is enlightening and can help answer some of your questions.

Finally, at the end of each chapter is a page entitled "Charting My Journey." Be sure to make notes here about what you've just read. Doing so will help you clarify your thoughts about lifelong learning. You will use your notes to complete the exercise at the back of the book.

Remember, you're not alone. There are more than seventy-six million other people out there just like you. And they're facing the same decision: Do you choose the static rocking-chair world of your parents' retirement? Or do you use *Learning Later, Living Greater* to fuel your journey to discover the secrets of lifelong learning and make your after-fifty years the very best time of your life?

Up until now, not many people really grasped the concept of lifelong learning. It was more like a secret—a whisper on the winds of change. But no longer.

Maybe retirement once meant being able to do only certain things. Maybe retirement meant acting a certain way because that's the way it was done. Not anymore.

As you'll discover here, your third age is about an incredible array of choices and opportunities available to give your life new meaning and adventure.

It's a great time to become a lifelong learning explorer—to boldly go!

Learning Later, Living Greater My Way!

Charlotte Yacker

Charlotte Yacker is a member of the Osher Lifelong Learning Institute (OLLI), sponsored by the University of Massachusetts at Boston. OLLI was formerly known as the Life Enrichment Through Studies Program (LETS).

On September 20, 1998, life dealt me a devastating blow: the sudden death of my son. Just three days prior, I had chaired the first planning meeting for the development of the Life Enrichment Through Studies (LETS) Program at the University of Massachusetts at Boston. These two events which happened almost simultaneously, along with other personal turmoil, temporarily sidelined my involvement with the LETS program.

But the quest that had led me to develop an organization devoted to fostering older adult learning at the UMass, Boston campus demanded that I somehow find the strength to return to it. So, three months later I again immersed myself in the planning and development of LETS by making presentations to alumni and various other groups to ensure that the program would be developed and then allowed to grow and prosper.

My own involvement and participation has been a personal boon. It helped me deal with the indescribable pain brought on by the death of my son, as well as a subsequent serious illness. It has also given me enormous satisfaction in being an integral part of the program—a program that offers incredibly fulfilling benefits to everyone who participates. I can personally testify to the immeasurable benefits derived from my own participation. And no matter to what degree or in what capacity members are involved, their own lives will be greatly enhanced and made far, far richer by lifelong learning at LETS.

I would urge anyone looking for new learning experiences, those interested in developing new friendships with like-minded persons, and anyone hoping to enhance their later years to take advantage of opportunities available in lifelong learning participation.

Charting My Journey

• • • •

(These pages, found at the end of each chapter, are for your notes.)

Charting My Journey

• • • •

An Introduction to Lifelong Learning

Chapter Two

You don't grow old: when you cease to learn you are old.
—Reuel L. Howe

So what is this thing called lifelong learning? Is it another infomercial about earning a degree in gunsmithing? Will a Z-list celebrity shout its merits at you from the television?

Not a chance.

In fact, lifelong learning isn't necessarily a *thing* at all. It is a belief—a philosophy—that espouses one simple truth: lifelong learning is the process of maintaining an active mind and youthful spirit through continuous interaction with peers and experts in all fields of interest. Distilled even further, it's an opportunity to make your own unique contribution to society, to meet new people, and to explore new ideas.

Lifelong learners embark on their adventures in several different ways. They can take informal classes on just about any conceivable topic. They can learn and relax simultaneously through educational travel. Or they can give back by using their own skills and experiences to help enrich the lives of others in their community. The hat trick of lifelong learning, exploring, and serving is the hallmark of excellence that makes this philosophy so attractive to individuals and society as a whole.

Lifelong learning does mean different things to different people. As unique and individual as we all are, lifelong learning gives us methods for enhancing that individuality even further. One person might explore lifelong learning as a way of keeping their social roster active during their post-work years. Another may relish the chance to study obscure topics that they never had time for while they were working. Still another may find educational travel to be the only way to travel. Each of these people will define lifelong learning differently. And given their experiences, they'll all be right.

But they'd also have a shared commonality, and that is the fact that lifelong learning enables them to expand their intellectual, social, spiritual, and physical horizons beyond any previous expectations.

Whoever said retirement was only about golf and early-bird dinner specials?

> Lifelong learning is a maturation process, not simply to continue or elongate what was life, but a process that creates something altogether new—in this very moment—while at the same time points to the many exciting things to come.
> —Harriet Leckich, Gulfport, Misssissippi

A Brief History of Lifelong Learning

Education has always played an important role in helping shape our personal destinies. Success in many fields is measured by how much time we spent hitting the books prior to graduation. Many of today's top power brokers make no secret of the fact that the choice of higher education institutions can help someone forge a brilliant career in their chosen profession.

But until recently, formal education had been the domain of youth. Certainly there are some who stay in school much longer, pursuing advanced degrees, but overall, by the age of about twenty-two, many adults end their educational journeys.

Not everyone agrees with this ideology. As far back as 1854, Henry David Thoreau was arguing for a different philosophy when he wrote:

> It is time that we had uncommon schools…that we did not leave off our education when we begin to be men and women. It is time that villages were universities and their elder inhabitants the fellows of universities, with leisure—if they are, indeed, so well off—to pursue liberal studies the rest of their lives.

Then, in the late 1800s, there was an attempt to bring closer attention to the idea of lifelong learning. The Chautauqua movement, which was known as "colleges for one's home," brought individual study to adults of all ages throughout the United States. Unfortunately, this movement's initial momentum soon faded away and it would be some time before lifelong learning actually established a true foothold in the granite of educational philosophy.

Until that happened, the best options available to mature adults were either to return to school in pursuit of a degree or to simply audit a class, most often without any type of interaction with other students or the professors. Finally, in the 1960s, educational philosophy began to change; people once again began looking at ways they could maintain a healthy mind long after traditionalists spoke of ceasing active learning.

Lifelong learning gained momentum. Institutes devoted to enriching mature adults through a wide variety of courses, adventures, and community service options opened. And people began to notice—so much so, in fact, that lifelong learning is now no longer limited to just the United States. For instance, France's own initiatives began in 1972. Shortly thereafter, the International Association of Universities of the Third Age (U3As) was established. The idea quickly spread through Europe, spurring countries like Belgium, Switzerland, and Britain to begin their own organizations devoted to lifelong learning. Since then, Canada, New Zealand, and Australia have also reaped great benefits from the establishment of lifelong learning programs. And as you read this, Japan, Mexico, and other countries are getting on board as well.

You can now find lifelong learning opportunities on a global scale: at colleges and universities, senior centers and adult communities, libraries, churches, shopping places, and public spaces. Every day, the concept of lifelong learning grows by leaps and bounds as more people age and realize how much more enriching their life experiences will be with the added value of continued learning and adventure.

What's the Big Deal About Lifelong Learning?

While there are many positive aspects to embracing lifelong learning, we can—like for the hat trick we explored earlier—look at three main benefits.

Body

Prior to the 1990s, a decade of important brain research, scientists thought that getting older was automatically accompanied by a decline in our mental functions.

This is not true! In fact, recent research shows that it is entirely possible to grow *new* brain cells as old ones age, provided we undertake enriching and challenging learning activities.[1]

But don't take our word for it. Dr. Paul Nussbaum, a well-known researcher, international consultant on health and aging, and the author of *Brain Health and Wellness,* feels that active learning—lifelong mental stimulation—appears to offer a vaccination against neurodegeneration. Among the ingredients of this learning vaccine are that learning, as a physiological and psychological event, must now be considered a health-promoting behavior; and that the brain requires environmental enrichment at any age.[2]

By stimulating your brain with lifelong learning, you will naturally enjoy other physiological benefits as well. Exposure to new ideas and thinking might prompt new physical activity that can help stave off illness and disease. A healthy brain means a healthy body!

Mind

Intimately connected with the physical, the mental side of lifelong learning is amazing. Imagine being able to explore whatever you want. What would you read about? What would you want to try? And as your mind devoured this new brain food, it would naturally want to eat even more. Your thoughts, beliefs, and personal philosophies might expand so much that you find yourself on a brand-new journey of self-discovery. You might also discover new talents—and the increased self-esteem gained from this discovery would be priceless.

Lifelong learning has also helped many people weather the storms of personal crisis. The care and support that members of a program give each other is tremendously valuable. Knowing we have friends is sometimes enough to help us during the dark hours.

Ironically, our after-fifty years are a time when most of society expects us to slow down and let life continue going by without our active participation. Imagine how wonderful it would feel not only to maintain an incredibly active mind, but also to boldly explore avenues of life you didn't have a chance to delve into when you were younger.

Rather than dread getting older, people might actually look forward to these years as a time when they can set off on adventure after adventure, exploring the amazing universe around us all.

Spirit

Lifelong learning lifts your spirit. Those who indulge enjoy an incredible amount of social activity. Social interaction is extremely important, as research has shown that interacting with our peers in a friendly setting helps us live longer. Over the last twenty years, scientists have documented the fact that being involved in social activities not only enhances lives but adds years to life as well.

According to findings published in the August 1999 edition of the *British Medical Journal*, people who spent time in social activities—volunteering, running errands, or getting together with friends (lifelong learning could well be included here!)—fared just as well as those who spent the time exercising.[3]

The journal goes on to say, "social engagement was as strong as anything we found in determining longevity. It was stronger than things like blood pressure, cholesterol or other measures of health." This study is not the only one to come to this conclusion. Back in 1982, the *Journal of Epidemiology* published results of a study done at the University of Michigan over a nine- to

I love the adventures lifelong learning gives me. Fascinating courses that blend the old with the new, coupled with the interaction I enjoy with my peers, makes my life so much more than what it was. I can relive the Civil War in Missouri; follow in the footsteps of Lewis and Clark; explore the untold history of Russia, Europe, or the United States; and visit all sorts of exotic locales from the comforts of my armchair. I've learned high-tech computer skills, studied elder law, learned how to steer my own investments to maximum benefit, bettered my nutrition, and even explored new forms of exercise. I've found my singing voice for old wartime sing-a-longs, studied the beginnings of ragtime, and learned to appreciate jazz. I've found myself drawn to Shakespearean poetry and obscure writers I'd never heard of, and I've begun to appreciate the various artistic movements of the late nineteenth century. Even now, I'm taking courses that make me a more complete human being. And I love every moment of it. Lifelong learning is quickly proving to be a vital part of my life.

—June Glaser, Jefferson City, Missouri

twelve-year period. That study showed that men who reported more social relationships—movies, church, classes, or trips with friends or relatives—were significantly less likely to die during the study period. Socially active women also benefited, although not quite as dramatically.[4]

People become involved in lifelong learning as much for the socialization as they do for the education. Social activities are a very big component of lifelong learning—participants make new friends and some have even found new spouses!

Social activities surround lifelong learning programs. And they make a wonderful addition to your social calendar, no matter who you are. But don't confuse these activities with stereotypical senior citizen events. All of these activities have a strong educational component. Just look at a few of the many events lifelong learning explorers take part in:

- walking and hiking clubs
- theatre trips
- field trips
- book clubs
- current events groups
- weekend getaways
- theme festivals
- chess clubs
- theme dinners
- card groups
- bird clubs
- special interest groups

Participants in lifelong learning programs are as busy as they want to be, taking courses, developing new friendships, helping in the community, going on field trips, and just plain having fun. These activities bring new focus to their lives and open the eyes of society at large about what it means to be an older adult.

Lifelong learning's core values of learning, exploring, and serving—coupled with benefits for the body, mind, and spirit—make it a powerful tool for personal transformation and enhancement.

Learning Later, Living Greater My Way!

Eva Shatkin

Eva Shatkin is a member of QUEST: A Community for Lifelong Learning in Manhattan, sponsored by the City College of New York, Center for Worker Education.

Late one night in September 2004, I heard the distressing news that two members of my family were seriously ill. I managed to distract myself from brooding on that by immersing myself in a book. After a few hours, I turned off the light to get some sleep. But I was unable to. For the rest of the night, I dozed fitfully; I was unable to throw off the gloom enveloping me.

At five o'clock in the morning, I arose and busied myself with my usual morning routines. Then I worked on the presentation of a new course I had proposed to teach jointly with a retired doctor. We planned to examine the problems of bioethics at this juncture of scientific knowledge.

I headed off to school, partly still concerned about the health of my family and partly absorbed with the course I wanted to teach. Once I was there, I listened to the variety of topics others were preparing to teach during the upcoming semester. It was amazing to learn of the subjects that members of my peer learning group wanted to open up for exploration. Each of the participating coordinators was thrilled about what they were proposing to do. If two exciting courses were given at the same time, which one would I prefer to attend? It was going to be a difficult decision.

Before I knew it, and much to my astonishment, the day had passed, and my mind had gotten so caught up in the excitement of the upcoming semester that the gloom that had enveloped me the night before was completely forgotten. I returned home invigorated and found a message on my answering machine letting me know the two sick family members were much better. I felt as though my lifelong learning activities had helped me avoid becoming depressed over a situation I could not control.

Recently, during our semester break, my daughter came up from North

Carolina for a rare visit. We enjoyed many great conversations and made a point to go out together exploring the rich resources my city offers. At the airport on the day she was leaving, she suddenly asked, "What are you going to do when I'm gone?"

My response? "I have a life."

Yes, I have a life that serves me as a stimulus, a distraction from sorrow and aging, a working existence among peers whom I count as dear friends. That's a lot to be grateful for. I enjoy members of my family when they can interrupt their busy lives to see me, but I am not dependent on them for what to do with the blessed years I have been given.

Charting My Journey

• • • •

Charting My Journey

• • • •

PART TWO

It Ain't Over
'til
It's Over

Chapter Three

The Latest Brain Research

Just as iron rusts from disuse, even so does inaction spoil the intellect.
—Leonardo da Vinci

A recent AARP study showed that over 90 percent of adults age fifty and older planned to continue learning. Why? For three simple reasons: they want to know what's going on in the world, they want to continue their personal and spiritual growth, and they have so much fun learning about something new.[1]

This study shows that we're not going to abandon our ability and desire to learn just because we're no longer working full time. We understand that lifelong learning is vital to keeping ourselves active and involved in life.

The New Research

Is lifelong learning really critical to remaining healthy and active? You bet. Consider this: one of the biggest revelations to come out of the 1990s was that the human brain undergoes significant physiological change when it is exposed to new learning and new experiences.

Research undertaken at Harvard, Duke, and Johns Hopkins Universities, to name just a few, is now showing that keeping our brains stimulated through lifelong learning and other activities will dramatically help us retain mental alertness as we age. Moreover, the brain's physical anatomy actually responds to these enriching activities and is therefore changed for the better.

No, you won't suddenly grow a big head, so don't throw out all your old hats. What scientists have discovered is that the brain can grow new connections. Think of it this way: all that old wiring inside your head might lose some of its insulation over the years if you do nothing. But by engaging in lifelong learning, you not only preserve that older wiring with better insulation, but you also grow new cells and pathways, thereby enhancing your response times, thought processes, and reflexes. And the electrical upgrade isn't even expensive! Of all the findings during the congressionally mandated Decade of the Brain, this startling new discovery appears to be the most important.

Scientists used to think that the number of neurons—those building blocks of nerve cells—were fixed and never changed. New evidence suggests otherwise. The number actually fluctuates throughout our lives, depending on our activity levels. Armed with this knowledge, we no longer have to worry as much about a gradual decrease in our mental acuity. As long as we keep challenging our brain—those "little gray cells" as Agatha Christie's Hercule Poirot was so fond of saying—it appears they will continue to grow and thrive. And the more complex the task or activity, the more synapses are firing in your brain. This leads to increased circulation in your head, which is highly beneficial. Scientists are studying the possibilities that such activities could help stave off Alzheimer's and Parkinson's diseases in some people predisposed to those illnesses.

Just like our hearts, our brains need to be nurtured. Lifelong learning is one very important way to ensure that care.

Here are some of the highpoints of recent brain research.

Doctors Fred H. Gage, of the Salk Institute in San Diego, and Peter S. Eriksson, of the Göteborg University Institute of Clinical Neuroscience, have collected data showing that the brain of adult humans—even older adults—regularly regenerates neurons in the hippocampus (the section of the brain responsible for learning).[2,3]

The research of Dr. Marian Diamond, University of California, Berkeley, with rats shows the positive relationship between an enriched environment (cages with toys and other rats) and brain development in rats. "The enriched rats had a thicker cerebral cortex [responsible for higher nervous functions], than the rats [in impoverished environments"].[4]

Doctor Paul Nussbaum—a clinical neuropsychologist, professor at the University of Pittsburgh School of Medicine, and the director of the Aging Research and Education Center in Pittsburgh, Pennsylvania—says that based on new knowledge about the brain, he recommends that habits of mental stimulation be maintained throughout life.[5]

His vision for learning in later life—which he views as an excellent way to keep older adults fully integrated in society—parallels what this book is all about: that lifelong learning can help keep third age adults, with their capacity for continued learning, useful to society. Those of us over fifty represent a vast resource for teaching, civic involvement, and meaningful service.

Ron Kotulak, author of *Inside the Brain: Revolutionary Discoveries of How the Mind Works*, which is based on his Pulitzer prize–winning series for the *Chicago Tribune*, says, "Education has both a biological and behavioral positive effect. Biologically, it works by laying down significantly more connections between brain cells. Behaviorally, it works by providing knowledge that empowers one to articulate needs and overcome potential barriers."[6]

> I've found that learning about different religions is very enlightening. Ignorance breeds bigotry. Simply put, the more knowledge we have, the more we realize how many things we do have in common with people all around this amazing world of ours. Perhaps, thanks to learning, bigotry will begin to diminish and someday actually disappear.
> —Lucy Kline, Brevard, Florida

In a study of more than one thousand people ages seventy to eighty, Dr. Marilyn Albert, associate professor of psychiatry and neurology at Harvard and director of gerontology research at Massachusetts General Hospital, found that the higher the education level, the more likely people were to engage in mentally stimulating activities.[7] Her study also uncovered four main factors that seemed to help older adults maintain their cognitive abilities:

- Education, which appears to increase the number and strength of connections between brain cells
- Strenuous activity, which improves blood flow to the brain
- Lung function, which makes sure the blood is adequately oxygenated
- The feeling that what you do makes a difference in your life

> The experiences in life are proportional to one's courage to learn, change, grow, lead, serve, transform, accept, challenge, and leave a profound legacy.
>
> —Mission Statement, Mississippi Gulf Coast Lifelong Learning Institute

Doctor Yaakov Stern, a clinical neuropsychologist at Columbia University, found that people who had less than an eighth-grade education had twice the risk of getting Alzheimer's as those who went beyond the eighth grade. And when people with low education levels also worked at mentally unstimulating occupations, they had three times the risk of developing dementia.[8]

Charles Gilbert and other researchers at The Rockefeller University discovered that the brain can repair itself and construct memory, and in so doing can change thought patterns and learn new skills. Both repair and memory depend on stimulation or mental activity, something that as a society we have tended to ignore. Doctor Gilbert says, "We need to recognize the importance of challenging our minds as a vital component of health, and of mental health."[9]

What happens to people's intellectual abilities as they age was the subject of the Seattle Longitudinal Study, started in 1956 by Dr. K. Warner Schaie. Doctor Schaie, the director of the Gerontology Center at Pennsylvania State University, studied more than five thousand people aged twenty to ninety and older. He found that intellectual ability varies widely, but as he said, "There are very few toddling, senile millionaires. It takes education and resources to make and keep that kind of money. Couch potatoes, on the other hand, are the quickest to slip into intellectual limbo. The danger starts when people retire, decide to take things easy, and say they don't have to keep up with the world anymore."[10]

Dr. Schaie found that in mental testing, bridge players did very well while bingo players did not. Crossword puzzle workers did better on verbal skills, and jigsaw puzzle players tend to maintain their spatial skills. There are many ways to exercise the brain, but you have to do something. "Inactive people tend to show the most decline. The people who are almost too busy to be studied are the ones who do very well."

In the longitudinal study, seven factors stood out among people whose intellectual abilities were still sharp:

- A high standard of living marked by above-average education and income
- A lack of chronic disease
- Active engagement in reading, travel, cultural events, education, clubs, and professional associations
- A willingness to change
- Marriage to a smart spouse
- An ability to quickly grasp new ideas
- Satisfaction with accomplishments

Last, according to Michael Merzenich, a pioneering neuroscientist at the University of California, San Francisco, science is finally awakening to the fact that the brain reorganizes itself during learning. "It's something that people don't realize. They don't think about the power that they have within themselves to change their brains."[11]

The studies discussed in this chapter point out the value of incorporating lifelong learning into our lives. And age is not a barrier. Albert Einstein, Claude Monet, Arturo Toscanini, Claude Pepper, Hume Cronyn, and Pablo Casals, among others, were all productive and vibrant well into old age.[12]

Studies aside, these individuals certainly prove that creativity does not end at a certain age. We now know, thanks to the new research, that creativity can grow and thrive well into our later years.

Lifelong learning programs are perfect for developing this creativity. Within these programs, old and new talents and skills can be rediscovered or developed, and allowed to shine. The increased self-esteem that results from these activities is priceless. Belonging to a lifelong learning program is a powerful tool in our quest to become the person we were always meant to be.

In the words of Dr. Paul Nussbaum, "Every time your heart beats, 25 percent of that blood goes right to the brain. But while exercise is critical, it may be education that is more important. In the twenty-first century, education and information may become for the brain what exercise is for the heart."[13]

Lifelong learning is certainly too important to ignore!

Interview with an Expert

Deanna Baxter Eversoll, Ph.D.

Deanna Baxter Eversoll, Ph.D., is chair of the ASA national "Mind Alert" selection committee for Annual Awards and Training Sites for Brain-based Learning Projects, an editorial board member for the LEARN Newsletter, a leadership council board member for ASA—LEARN, project director of the Osher Lifelong Learning Institute at the University of Nebraska, and past director of the University of Nebraska SAGE Program for Older Learners.

Scientists have long been studying the brain. How does that research differ today?

I can answer that question in two words—advanced technology.

Because neuroscientists can now actually see the brain at work with thermograph pictures, many of the old assumptions about how the brain functions have been proven to be *false* assumptions.

Startling new findings have been discovered as to how the brain ages. The three-and-a-half-pound brain has as many neurons as the Milky Way has stars and as many connections as there are atoms in the world. And we now know that neuron loss is not significant as the brain ages and the brain is physically capable of rewiring itself throughout life.

How important are these findings to the baby boomers?

We are living longer and more of us are living this longer life. The baby boom generation—born between 1946 and 1964—has 10,800 turning fifty each day. Therefore, all ages must understand what this demographic shift means to all of society. Our founding fathers in 1776 had a life expectancy of thirty-five, and in 1998 our life expectancy is averaging seventy-six.

What do you consider the single most important thing people can do to keep their brains healthy?

The new findings clearly show that education is a key factor that correlates with psychological and physical wellness in later years. Like the body needs healthy food, so does the brain—*and* this healthy brain food is *education*. Education sets the groundwork for an approach to life's problems that stimulates the brain in active ways to enhance both the body and the mind.

What we once thought was inevitable—significant memory loss with age—is not inevitable. A significant portion of our loss is the result of lack of brain exercise through significant problem-solving activities and the lack of interest in continuing to learn and be curious about the world around us.

How can research about the body help the mind?

One great improvement is delaying the frailty of the physical body. It used to be that people got old in their sixties. Today, that's been delayed for many until their eighties. The mind learned what could be accomplished by eating wisely and exercising regularly and initiated actions to make the body healthier. We certainly never think about not feeding the physical body once it reaches mature size, but instead we look for constant enhancements. We now need to apply this same strategy as we use the new findings about our brains to boost our mental powers and delay frailty of our minds.

How do our social contacts improve our mind?

There is a saying that goes: A friend is someone who reaches for your hand and touches your heart. In reality, a friend is someone who reaches for your hand and touches your brain. This is the central headquarters of our thinking and feeling processes, and bright, energetic, thoughtful friends challenge us to make new mental connections and truly learn.

Any recommendations on how to choose our friends?

The best of all worlds is to have friends who are diverse in their approaches to life. It is important to realize that friends improve our mental powers when they agree and also when they disagree. When they disagree, they force us to consider alternate thoughts and acknowledge their emotional feelings on a topic. On the other hand, when they agree, they let us pursue the what-ifs of the ideas we have in common and help us enhance already-formed concepts.

Does the younger generation benefit the most from this research?

Definitely not! Too many Americans look forward to retirement as a period when they can tune-out, turn-off, and lie back and let the world go by. We know that is not a positive psychological state for teenagers, and it is equally destructive for grandparents. Lifelong doses of education are found to be the best prescription for preventing mental capacity decline—even for delaying such destructive diseases as Alzheimer's. This is a challenge for all ages of our society.

What are your recommendations for our readers?

I want to remind them of how powerful their minds really are in determining what they do to shape their futures. We are all born learners, but unless we use the potential of what we know to act, we have not really learned the lesson. True learning translates into action, and we should measure our success by how well we listen, read, write, and actively solve problems.

Any final thoughts?

I want to urge all ages to embrace the new brain research findings with enthusiasm. I also want to challenge them to look to education as a powerful tool for achieving wellness throughout their lifetimes. The positive outcomes will not only benefit them personally, but also in turn benefit the communities in which they live.

We all know the old saying, you can't teach an old dog new tricks. Let's replace it with one that says, use it or lose it—have you hugged your brain today?

Learning Later, Living Greater My Way!

Jerry Gordon

Jerry Gordon is a member of the Osher Lifelong Learning Institute sponsored by the University of California, Riverside

A decade ago, when I was fifty-six, my job ended, and I was not prepared for the sudden departure from a daily routine. I soon realized, however, that I was a very lucky man, as I now had the time and opportunity to extend my breadth of knowledge and nourish my brain through lifelong learning.

I began by enrolling in an intensive university extension workshop in managing a not-for-profit organization; for the next two years, I served as an unpaid executive director for a new social service agency that still exists. Also during that time, I participated in a conservancy program, where I learned how to maintain trails and create diversions for rain runoff, and I even learned the names of plants. Furthermore, my wife and I participated in several Elderhostel programs on both the East and West Coasts. From Yiddish culture to classical music, plus a dose of the environment on a remote location of Catalina Island, I extended my breadth of knowledge.

Currently, I am responsible for arranging an intellectual lecture series for nearly one hundred retirees through university extension. Based on my successful experience, I was asked to create a radio interview program on our local National Public Radio (NPR) station, which requires me do further research before the recording sessions. Most of the topics have been new to me, and the response from the listening audience has been favorable.

For two years, I have participated in the Osher Lifelong Learning Institute at the local university, where I was given the tools to write my memoirs; I continue to work on my memoirs and will likely do for the rest of my life. I have also taken classes in Native American issues, political philosophy, American drama, and world drama. The options are always stimulating.

I am a lecturer and guide at a historical hotel; the hotel required nearly a year of study and classes before we were allowed to lead our own tours. This experience has become an important part of my life, as I later became one of the teachers in the program, helping to prepare new docents. I continue to collect new information, new insights, and new stories to tell my guests.

Learning goes on all the time. I am involved from early in the morning to late at night, and for some reason I rarely have a chance—nor do I have a desire—to watch television. I must be missing something on the tube, but I'm too busy to find out what it is.

There you have it—an inside look at my stimulated brain. It has been a wonderful decade, and I look forward to many more learning opportunities as long as my "sponge" has room to absorb more. There will always be a learning opportunity waiting to be pursued, and I hope to continue the quest. There is no choice.

Charting My Journey

• • • •

Charting My Journey

· · · ·

Chapter Four	# The Mind/Body Connection

In the province of the mind, what one believes
to be true either is true or becomes true.

—John Lilly

The belief that our thoughts and actions can influence our health—the mind/body connection—is not a new concept. Over the years, in certain circles, this notion was an accepted fact. Research in the latter half of the twentieth century, however, has shown that this long-held belief is actually true.

But what does it really mean? It's probably safe to say that wishing for a gold Rolls Royce won't suddenly make one appear in your driveway. But there is significant evidence to suggest that coordinating the interaction between our minds and bodies can result in amazing things. Lifelong learning plays a major role in this because it helps balance both your mind and body. And when things are in balance, you feel better and have the ability and desire to create a rich and satisfying life.

Technically, the study of the mind/body connection goes by several intimidating labels certain to demolish anyone playing Scrabble with you. Among these names are such polysyllabic nightmares as psychophysiology, neuropsychology, and psychoneuroimmunology. We'll opt for a much shorter abbreviation of the last one: PNI.

Background

In the 1960s, one of the early pioneers in the study of modern-day PNI was psychiatrist George Solomon. He observed that depression seemed to make rheumatoid arthritis worse.[1] He then began investigating the impact of emotions on immune function in general. His research was responsible for the development of the new field of PNI.

Then in the late 1960s and early 1970s, cardiologist Dr. Herbert Benson began studying the effects of meditation on blood pressure. He developed the term "the relaxation response,"[2] which today is recognized far and wide. Finally in the mid 1970s, psychologist Dr. Robert Adler's studies demonstrated that cognitive and emotional cues could affect immune response.[3] Thanks to his research, PNI was finally recognized as a legitimate medical specialty.

Since these early discoveries, researchers everywhere have been studying PNI. Over the ensuing years, PNI has demonstrated its value in three different research areas: physiological research, epidemiological research, and clinical research.

> I take three or four lifelong learning courses each semester. I facilitate an eight-week, year-round history course. And I serve on all the committees. This takes thirty hours a week. The best part? It feels like a real vacation and I've never been happier.
>
> —David Gee,
> Chesterfield, Missouri

Research Today

Today, one of the most widely recognized authorities on the study of PNI is neurobiologist Dr. David Felton, who heads up the Department of Neurobiology and Anatomy at the University of Rochester Medical Center in New York. Dr. Felton has been awarded several prestigious grants, including a genius grant from the MacArthur Foundation for his work in the growing field of PNI.

In 1981, Dr. Felton and his team of researchers made an important discovery. They found a hardwire connection between the body's immune system and the central nervous system, which is controlled by the brain.[4]

Simply put, using special stains, the team was able to trace nerves to various locations throughout the body. They then discovered a network of nerves leading from the brain to cells in the immune system.[5] This was the long elusive scientific proof that the mind/body connection was real! Hard evidence showed that the brain has the ability to send signals to immune system cells.[6]

Thanks to that discovery, we now know that the immune system, instead of hanging around waiting to kill bacteria, is working all the time.

It's critical to every function in our bodies.[7]

Dr. Felton says about his discovery, "Our grandmothers knew all along that our minds and our bodies were connected, even if the scientific community didn't. We've simply provided irrefutable data showing that it's true."[8]

Today, the study of PNI is extremely important: scientists, medical and mental health practitioners, and consumers are all actively exploring the possibilities associated with PNI. In fact, Harvard University established a mind/body clinic in Boston in the 1970s, and more have been founded around the world since then.

The National Institutes of Health (NIH) allocate research money on a regular basis to fund PNI study. In FY1999, ten million dollars was directed to conducting research in the behavioral sciences and establishing more mind/body medical centers.[9]

How Does the Mind/Body Connection Work?

The human brain and body work together. Neuro-pathways from your brain are communicating all the time with your cells and muscles. Messages travel back and forth at blistering speeds. This merging of the mind and body creates a holistic connection that is critical for health and wellness.

Sometimes this connection can be compromised. We feel out of balance. Maybe we get cranky or irritable. Depression might even set in. Whatever our reaction, the first step toward regaining our balance is to identify the culprit. And these days, the most common culprit is stress.

Stress is something we all live with in varying degrees every day of our lives. Medical research has shown that stress can dramatically affect different systems in our bodies, including the endocrine or hormonal system, and the immune and circulatory systems.[10]

One way to explore the interaction of the mind/body connection is by measuring the effects of stress, something the medical community has the ability to do. Indicator levels for the hormone cortisol, blood pressure, heart rate, and even our ability to heal injuries are all used as benchmarks for how we handle stress.[11] If any one of these indicators is abnormal, we may find ourselves dealing with serious emotional or physical problems.

Studies have actually shown that long-term caregivers have significantly decreased immune function. Research has also shown that widows and widowers can take up to a year to restore immunity after the death of a spouse. Victims of sexual abuse and those with posttraumatic stress disorder show increased negative cardiovascular activity along with cortisol function abnormalities.[12]

All this indicates that some of life's biggest sources of stress, such as bereavement, long-term caregiving, loneliness, anger, trauma, and marital difficulties can negatively affect the balance of the mind/body connections. It behooves us to do what we can to keep this delicate balance on an even keel.

So just how do we maintain that balance?

Keeping the Balance

*Through balance man conserves nervous energy and thus
directly benefits all his activities, mental as well as physical.*
—Mabel E. Todd

Did you know that hearty laughter can enhance your immunity for up to twelve hours?[13] Or that getting a massage or listening to music decreases your levels of the stress hormone cortisol?[14]

Research now shows that we can positively affect our health by using any of the following tools: love, friendship, laughter, spirituality, maintaining a positive outlook, meditation, yoga, exercise, massage, participating in the creative arts, journaling, being in nature, having a pet.[15]

What other helpful activities can you think of to add to this list?

In other words, what we do or don't do to manage both stress and our moods can certainly have long-term effects on our body. This is what mind/body medicine is really all about. It treats the whole person, examining not just our physical side but also the mental, emotional, and spiritual sides. In this way, balance between them all is maintained.

The usual medicine for restoring mind/body balance includes such things as relaxation training, meditation, hypnosis, biofeedback, psychotherapy, guided imagery, and prayer. Each of these is a field unto itself. The basic philosophies are the same, however: that the mind and body have the power to heal themselves.

But there is one tool, not yet on this list, that people are starting to recognize as equally valuable in helping keep the mind/body balance. That tool is lifelong learning.

How Does Lifelong Learning Fit with the Mind/Body Concept?

Lifelong learning fits beautifully with the mind/body way of thinking. As you read through this book, the strength of the mind/body connection to lifelong learning will become very apparent. In the meantime, here's a short synopsis of some of the ways they are connected.

Epidemiological studies that were mentioned in a previous chapter have shown that people with few social ties are significantly more likely to become ill than those who have more social connections. In the study, men who reported more social relationships—movies, church, classes, or trips with friends or relatives—were significantly less likely to die during the study period.

> We have a fantastic program for personal discovery. We base everything on the belief that our capacity to learn and grow does not decrease as our years increase. In fact, through learning and the adventures we embark on, we actually embrace self-fulfillment.
>
> —David Dudgeon, Herkimer, New York

Lifelong learning programs promote that needed social interaction; they offer a wealth of social activities. In fact, as discussed earlier, people join lifelong learning programs as much for the social aspects as for the learning. We'll talk more about this in Part 3.

Lifelong learners enjoy another valuable mind/body tool: laughter. He who laughs, lasts![16] Did you know that most adults laugh only about forty times a day, whereas children laugh four hundred to five hundred times in that same time period?[17] Walk down a hall past lifelong learning classes or gatherings, however, and you'll hear laughter and lots of it. Lifelong learners have a positive outlook on life; they are funny, gregarious, and not afraid to laugh—with others and at themselves.

Being engaged in lifelong learning activities is also a wonderful de-stressor. Recent studies at the National Institute on Aging show that individuals who keep their minds actively engaged in new learning report themselves as happier and more fulfilled than older adults who are less active.[18] If you are happy, you are not being overly stressed. It's that simple.

We all have stress in our lives. The secret is using tools to bring that stress level into balance. The sheer joy of learning something new and interesting, of interacting with others equally interested, and of being able to share life's ups and downs with like-minded folks, is today's medicine for decreasing stress.

And then there is love. Not only have people who are involved in life-long learning made new, lasting, and deep friendships, some have even found romance. There have been many marriages between lifelong learners.

Lifelong learning programs also offer a vast array of courses, many that make it easy to incorporate the mind/body balancing tools into your daily life. For instance, classes on spirituality, meditation, yoga, exercise of all types, the creative arts, journaling, and nature are all part of these programs. There are even courses on the mind/body connection itself.

Finally, it can be said that lifelong learners embrace three distinct mind/body attributes:

- They have pledged to make their third age the best it can be by experiencing lifelong learning.
- They are responsible for their own destinies and make the decisions and choices that will ensure an enriched third age.
- They enjoy the demands of learning and the subsequent stimulation.

Recent neuroscience and behavioral studies indicate that the mental, physical, and emotional habits of older adults play a significant role in cognitive functioning and a sense of general well-being. The coming years will bring even more new and exciting discoveries in these fields as more and more researchers delve into the complexities of this connection.

For now, there's no doubt that lifelong learning makes it convenient and easy to use any of the mind/body tools to help maintain your body's delicate balance. And in so doing, lifelong learning becomes perhaps the most valuable tool of all.

In the words of John Dewey,

The very problem of mind and body suggests division. I do not know of anything so disastrously affected by the habit of division as this particular theme. In its discussion are reflected the splitting off from each other of religion, morals, and science; the divorce of philosophy from science and of both from the arts of conduct. The evils which we suffer in education, in religion, in the materialism of business and the aloofness of intellectuals from life—in the whole separation of knowledge and practice—all testify to the necessity of seeing mind-body as an integral whole.

A Search for Meaning in Life in Retirement

Bob Baum

Bob Baum is a member of the Institute for Learning and Retirement, Boca Raton, Florida.

The essence of our lives prior to retirement consisted of a core represented by our chosen vocation or profession, family, and in some instances religion. These things were enhanced by peripheral recreational activities; i.e., travel, theatre, concerts, sports, etc. The core nourished us with the significant and essential meaning of life, while the recreational activities served as a respite and diversion from the routine and the anxieties of the travails necessary for our essential existence.

A dilemma arises when retirement separates us from the core, which gave meaning, and we continue to participate in the peripheral activities. Those who attempt to substitute the peripheral activities associated with leisure for the core activities which furnished us with meaning soon conclude that in most instances this substitution does not work.

Rabbi Abraham Herschel in his essays on human existence said in discussing the elderly:

> What is the role of recreation in the life of the aged? Is it merely to serve as a Substitute for work one has done in earlier years?...that an overindulgence in recreational activities aggravates rather than ameliorates a condition it is trying to deal with, namely, the trivialization of existence.

The evanescing of our physical strength in our advancing years need not lead to an intellectual vacuum, devoid of challenge. It would appear to me that to a great many, lifelong learning has effectively served in some measure as a suitable substitute for the core activities. To many of this superannuated generation, the attempt to substitute peripheral activities for the core fell far short of a satisfying experience. Lifelong learning furnishes us with the stimulation that gives us essence, and we better enjoy the leisure activities that served the same function in our earlier lives.

The intellectual exercise of study is as essential to us in advanced age as is our physical well-being. Last, but certainly not least, it affords all of us the opportunity to associate with people who have learned this lesson and made the same choice.

LEARNING LATER, LIVING GREATER
MY WAY!

Jim O'Brien

Jim O'Brien is a member of the PLATO program, sponsored by the University of Wisconsin–Madison.

The phone rang at 1:15 a.m. Groaning, I answered.

"We have a perfect match kidney. Do you want it?" The speaker was my transplant coordinator; the call was out of the blue; I was completely unprepared for major surgery.

"I'll have to think about it," I stalled. Then, seconds later, "Yes."

"Be at the hospital tomorrow at eleven." The coordinator hung up.

Two years from retirement, I was sickening with kidney failure. We had made plans to move to Madison, Wisconsin, where I expected to receive a marginally acceptable kidney from my brave and generous wife. But as I came out from under the anesthetic, I knew already that the transplant was working. And, as I continued to ponder my incredible good fortune, I sensed that a new stage in life was beginning and a new sense of purpose would be needed.

The move to Madison brought an abundance of possibilities. I joined a newly forming church choir; I registered for a jazz improv class; and I discovered PLATO (Participatory Learning and Teaching Organization), which offered a wide range of classes for the retired.

As a college teacher for thirty years, I had always enjoyed both teaching and learning, and I sat in on other courses when my schedule permitted. But PLATO looked like hog heaven to me—Greek plays, current events, American history, literature, Japanese film, jazz explorations, on and on. The fifty-dollar yearly membership entitled the bearer to take up to six classes every fall, spring, and summer. I was determined to be reasonable. I settled for jazz, Greek plays, and reminiscence writing.

When the instructor for Japanese film died suddenly shortly before the semester was to begin, I offered to fill in. The course was well received, and a colleague and I have continued to teach the course to steadily enlarging audiences for going on five years now.

The jazz was going well, too. A casual clarinetist for most of my life, I wondered if I could cut it by going to a class and actually practicing. And, by golly, practicing helps. In my first jazz improv class, the average age of the students was twenty-one, including my sixty-six years. When I took a solo, the students listened as if it were history, maybe J.S. Bach sitting in. I moved to a more age-appropriate class; we formed a band and have been playing at rest homes, retirement homes, and other age-appropriate venues for four years.

After a recent gig at the local library, a neighbor told me that an older couple they knew had gone to the engagement and reported that it was "the best night out they had had in months." The gentleman had early-stage Alzheimer's, but the old songs that we play had brought back vivid memories. That kind of feedback makes it all worthwhile. And that hasn't been the only one.

In other words, I'm enjoying myself; I'm contributing to my community; I'm finding my bonus life rich with meaning and value. I'm busy and sometimes pressed, but I remind myself that everything that I do is something that I want to do, and it makes it all quite easy.

Charting My Journey

• • • •

Charting My Journey

• • • •

Chapter Five

Lifelong Learning in the After-Fifty Years

To resist the frigidity of old age one must combine the body, the mind and the heart—and to keep them in parallel vigor one must exercise, study and love.
—Karl von Bonstetten

So we've taken a look at the new brain research showing that lifelong learning is key to keeping your brain cells thriving. And we've explored the mind/body connection and the role lifelong learning plays in that delicate balance. Now let's take a few minutes to talk about the special aspects of lifelong learning in the after-fifty years.

Who Are the After-Fifty Lifelong Learners and What Are Their Characteristics?

Everyone is, to some extent, a lifelong learner. The neighbor next door and the person down the street are lifelong learners. After all, lifelong learning is much more than the acquisition of knowledge. It really is the daily absorption of all that goes on around us.

Informal lifelong learning begins at birth and continues throughout life. It's all about learning to live within society and learning how to navigate our way through the intricacies of life. Informal learning happens as we pass through different stages in our lives, such as starting a career or business, becoming a parent, or dealing with a death in the family. Informal lifelong learning can be planned or unplanned, based on needs that arise out of our everyday life and experiences. However, for the purposes of this book, which is focused on more formal ways of lifelong learning for older adults, we can say the following: After-fifty lifelong learners are enthusiastic, ready, willing, able, and empowered when it comes to their own learning. They are inquisitive about anything new or puzzling; they ask questions, ponder, and discuss it with friends and family; and they often read and write about it.

They also are not afraid to make mistakes. Lifelong learners are willing to step outside their comfort zone, taking calculated risks in their quest for knowledge. They deliberately seek out new opportunities for learning in any setting. They view everything that happens—both the good and the bad—as chances for learning.

Lifelong learners take full responsibility for their learning, doing whatever is necessary to create an atmosphere that is conducive to it. They are not content to sit back and wait for the learning to come to them. They go out and do what has to be done to make it happen. They are self-starters.

Lifelong learners understand that there is no one right way to learn, and they want to expose themselves to every variance and nuance of learning. They often encourage others to join them. They are always spreading the word about their programs. They see lifelong learning not only as an altruistic act, but also as a way to engage in reciprocal learning by developing a learning community of like-minded individuals.

It's been said that people who are lifelong learners are more tolerant, more stimulated in their lives, and more upbeat. Along with that, having special interests really stretches a person. Their life takes on an added dimension and often brings a different perspective to a particular viewpoint. For some, lifelong learning has saved their lives. The stories throughout this book tell how people have been able to get on with their lives after life-changing events because they are involved in lifelong learning.

As I peer out the kitchen window at 6:30 a.m., I notice a new bird at the feeder. What is that creature with the yellow and red feathers? I quickly write a description to take to my bird-watching class today. I tuck it into the book *Lincoln*, which I am reading for the other course I am taking on the life of the Civil War president. Although I am not pressured to be prepared, because there are no grades, tests, or transcripts, the incentive to learn comes from within each of the learners who gather at the campus with me to take classes. It's a fascinating and deeply rewarding addition to my life in retirement.

—David Dudgeon, Herkimer, New York

They understand that learning is a process that can always be improved, and they are continually striving to raise the bar. They know that anything worthwhile takes time and effort. The end result, however—one they fully understand—is that learning is a critically important undertaking. It will lead to a fulfilled life.

Lifelong learning helps a person set goals and can also open doors to new thoughts and social interactions. It can increase your sense of self-worth and fulfill the human desire to discover and understand.

Validating After-Fifty Lifelong Learning

Validation for lifelong learning programs has grown dramatically, especially in the last twenty years. Here are just a few of the many ways these programs are being supported, both in this country and abroad.

In 1997, the Minnesota Humanities Commission organized the Minnesota Learning in Retirement Network (LIRN), a statewide association of university- and community-based senior learning organizations. The aim of the Minnesota LIRN is to promote older adult learning in the humanities. Through studying the humanities, LIRN members become familiar with enduring ideas, reflect on experience, analyze important issues, and contribute to the educational well-being of the communities. These organizations are all receiving LIRN grants from the commission.

Since 1997, the Minnesota Humanities Commission's work with retired adults has expanded to include a variety of other programs, including National Issues Forums, the Evergreen Read and Elder Reading Circles, and intergenerational humanities programming.[1]

The Bernard Osher Foundation is a charitable foundation established in 1977 by Bernard Osher, a businessman and community leader. His philanthropy has benefited a wide range of educational, cultural, and other nonprofit organizations primarily in the San Francisco Bay Area and his native Maine. In the 1990s, the foundation funded a series of Osher Scholar programs, extending scholarship assistance for post-secondary education to nearly thirty colleges and universities as well as to professional and technical schools in California and Maine.

Then in early 2001, the foundation provided a large, multimillion-dollar grant to the University of Southern Maine, which operated a successful Senior College. This endowment provided multiple opportunities for the university to enlarge and improve the excellent program it was already offering. With the gift, the Senior College at USM changed its name to the Osher Lifelong Learning Institute, becoming the first of what would eventually grow to a network of one hundred Osher Lifelong Learning Institutes nationwide.

Along with this funding, the State of Maine legislature puts money into the budget of the University of Southern Maine each year to support a Senior College initiative for older adults all across the state. There are now fifteen Senior Colleges (the Maine name for lifelong learning institutes) throughout the state.

In California, in the spring of 1992, the state legislature passed a resolution to support learning in retirement. Its purpose was to give status to groups wishing to establish lifelong learning programs on campuses of state-supported institutions, and to provide impetus to the movement.

The United Kingdom sponsors an annual Learning in Later Life Campaign and gives awards for events that celebrate learning in older citizens.

Lifelong learning has also become an important social goal of the European Union (EU), as defined at the Lisbon summit in March 2000: "to make the European Union the world's most dynamic and competitive area, based on innovation and knowledge, able to boost economic growth levels with more and better jobs and greater social cohesion." To this end, AGE, the European Older People's Platform, was recently established to voice the interests of older and retired people with EU institutions. Lifelong learning is one of the topics AGE will be addressing.

How Lifelong Learning After Fifty Can Help

The benefits of lifelong learning are almost too numerous to list, but here are a few. Lifelong Learning:

- helps us fully exploit our natural abilities while striving to lessen our faults.
- enables us to immerse ourselves in the wonders of life.
- provides us a measure of how our lives should be lived to the best of our ability.
- points out the pitfalls of life so we can avoid them in our pursuit of

happiness.

- teaches us to look beyond the surface and see the truth as it really is.

- simulates our natural curiosity about the world around us.

- helps us increase our wisdom during our third age and use our experiences to make the world a better place.

- enables us to face the inevitable changes of society

In the words of Harvey Mackay, author of four *New York Times* bestsellers, "You don't go to school once for a lifetime; you are in school all of your life. That's why they call graduation 'commencement'—it's just the beginning."

He goes on to say,

You can grow as much as you want to. Your mind has plenty of room to hold information. We typically use only 10 percent of our brains. Would you be satisfied to get that little service out of any other part of your body? …We live in the information age, the space age, the early years of the new Millennium. Technology has given us access to facts and figures and people and places at the touch of a button. We have every opportunity to learn and grow at any hour of the day. Today is the right time to start expanding your mind.[2]

And, if the 1990s were the mandated Decade of the Brain, then it has been suggested by Sandra Timmermann, director of the MetLife Mature

There is no doubt that the benefits of lifelong learning are amazing. Hundreds of thousands of us already know the joy we experience being involved with such adventure. I moved to a retirement community three years ago and promptly got involved in helping find new study leaders and lecturers. I helped start an education advisory committee and a lifelong learning lecture series. Never give up; the happiness you'll find being involved with lifelong learning is without limits!

—Gretchen Lankford, Pittsburgh, Pennsylvania

Market Institute in Westport, Connecticut, that the 2000s will be the decade known as the Mainstream Era for older adult lifelong learning. She cites several reasons for this:

- Research on the brain and how the mind works has revolutionized the way we think about learning as we age.

- More nontraditional organizations and institutions want to know about older adults—what they are experiencing physically, socially, and emotionally—and how to provide information to them most effectively.

- The boomers will take lifelong learning for granted and incorporate education in their lives well into old age.

- Continual learning is increasingly viewed as helping older adults unleash their creativity and find meaning in their lives.

- There will always be committed, creative individuals who will have ideas for adult-learning programs that will capture our imaginations and take off.[3]

As further proof of the validity of creative lifelong learning, in 1999, the largest documented study on aging in the United States, Successful Aging, concluded that involvement in social, recreational, and creative activities is a key factor in successful aging.[4] Furthermore, another research study involving aging has released the following preliminary results, again demonstrating benefits to persons involved in programs where creativity is an ingredient. Older adults involved in these programs showed the following characteristics:

- Better overall health
- Significantly fewer doctor visits
- Diminished use of medications
- Significantly less depression and loneliness
- Increased involvement in activities[5]

These are certainly goals worth striving for, starting today.

And today, as Harvey Mackay said, is the right time to start expanding your mind. You have taken that first step just by reading this book. At no other time in history has our society been so poised to accept the value of later-life learning.

Lifelong learning, as the research shows, makes our lives better. Since each of us has to live our entire life with ourselves, doesn't it make sense for us to want to be informed, reasoning, and interesting beings? By engaging in lifelong learning, we will be those people. And by doing so, we will have happier, more fulfilled lives.

Interview with an Expert

Mark D. Levine, Ph.D.

Mark D. Levine, Ph.D., was the director of community service at the University of Massachusetts, Lowell, where, in 1988, he established the Learning in Retirement Association (LIRA). The authors were going to interview Mark during the summer of 2005, but before we were able to do that, he passed away.

In honor of Mark's contribution to the field of lifelong learning, we are printing instead, with permissions, an article he wrote for the 2003 *Senior Citizens Guide*, published by Spindle Publishing Company, Pittsburgh, Pennsylvania. This article eloquently speaks to what has been discussed in the previous chapters.

Learning as a Later Life Passion

For many of us, the automatic nirvana of retirement is illusory. A short time passes and the anticipated delights—sleeping late, traveling, romping with grandchildren—often prove insufficient. Those retirees who have been single, or have become divorced or widowed, soon feel quite isolated. The worker misses colleagues and mental activity, sometimes without identifying these yearnings consciously.

In part to fill this void, an academic enterprise for seniors has burgeoned over recent years, offering opportunities for educational commitment and connection, for collectively and supportively unearthing within the participants old, and finding new, learning challenges.

Such programs or associations, located in the hundreds bi-coastally as well as in the national heartland, typically feature the peer-learning and peer-managing of an educational program. They are often based at or near a University or College and are characteristically available at low or moderate cost (although there are a few ivyish exceptions). In institutes (as they are sometimes known generically), retirees select, deliver and administer their own college-level learnings, accompanied by glowing reports. Literally, life has been enriched, if not extended, in the process.

Members I interviewed at one institute waxed eloquent about the benefits:

- I found a passion, the joy of learning
- a community of help
- keeps me in the mainstream
- it helps me be not just protoplasm, but provides me an opportunity to make choices
- stimulating, I meet people of like interests
- keeps me involved in learning new things
- provides an occasion to get dressed up in the morning
- fills up my time, my mind is always working on ideas from the program
- keeps me alive!

I heard paradox as well as exuberance. A retired manager from the business sector spoke bluntly: "Later life learning can open up people's eyes to things they've put down for years; for me, the subjects were classical music and Shakespeare."

The institute member (a retired teacher of Latin) who coordinated the Shakespeare study group commented: "How wonderful to find people who are interested in Shakespeare." There was the paradox and the exuberance: stumbling into delight, and finding a community of the delighted, something for everyone.

At the lunch table at the institute, a retired elementary school teacher quite calmly attributes "keeps me alive" to her peer-learning activity. She notes the growing monotony of her and her husband's lives (he was the high school Latin teacher) just after retirement: "We had two cups of coffee, read the whole paper, then what?"

Excitement is now in her voice. "The program gives you a reason to get up in the morning. You meet new people, you have new learning—so much more fun, so many new ways of looking at things, a chance to try something never before attempted, a reawakening of things from your past." She and fellow members who enjoy watching over their learning regularly sit on one of the program's various committees, spend hours designing the curriculum of an art and music study group. Making lifelong learning happen seems as critical for her as the actual education.

Here, one finds colleagues, fellow workers, people with whom to regularly share life's joys and challenges, to work collectively on presentations. To counter the sameness of one's retirement life horizon, the learning environment provides novelty: new friends, new interests; one discovers freedom and mastery; after years of being buffeted by life and institutional constraints, by children's developmental demands and workplace structure, members experience a special delight grappling with an endeavor controlled by themselves and their peers.

Power to the learner! I regularly marvel at this application of an academic ideal from the 1960s: the learners' control over the substance and process of their education. Here, lifelong learners engage subject matter uncontrolled by strict academic demands, while they are at the same time guided (through affiliation with the university or college) by traditional as well as by contemporary events and interests.

The range of the curricula of the self-selected, participatory study groups (in form, like graduate seminars) is great: a few hands-on classes, some requiring homework, some not, occasionally the teaching of skills, mostly featuring exposure to liberal arts areas new to the group, from drama to memoir writing, from the arts to the sciences. Members of the program I interviewed learned from an experienced member quilter to create a wall hanging quilt for the program office, in the process activating skills buried in previous generations; debated current events and foreign policy (study groups especially popular in the post 9/11 period). Some groups play a role in intergenerational campus or community programs, increasing their sense of being valued and effective.

While my informants spoke much less of physical than of mental benefits, there's a growing body of scientific literature that proclaims the healthfulness of intellectual activity: "Aging brains need fresh challenges to stay agile" proclaims an online article in *US News*, 2000. A neurologist suggests that education directly affects brain structure throughout our lives, in fact helps prevent disease by building up reserve capacity. A Harvard University and Massachusetts General Hospital gerontology researcher found education among the factors promoting retention of elders' intellect. The others were strenuous activity, lung function and the feeling that what people do makes a difference in their lives.

That there are benefits seems of little doubt!

Learning Later, Living Greater
My Way!

Steve Kates

Steve Kates is a member of the Institute for Learning in Retirement in Boca Raton, Florida.

After my retirement in 2000, at age sixty-four, I actively investigated activities which either time constraints or lack of knowledge had prevented me from pursuing earlier in my life.

I have always liked to write—mainly lyrics and factual articles—but I never stuck with it on any consistent or intense level.

I came to the Institute for Learning in Retirement (ILR), in Boca Raton, in 2001, attracted primarily by two courses being offered": "The History of Hollywood and the Movie Moguls" and "Memoir Writing." I was hooked!

Those courses, plus others, provided me with new insights, simple pleasures, and a confirmation and honing of my writing skills. Since then, I have taken whatever writing and film courses have been offered, along with studies in history, politics, psychology, music, literature, drawing, and film criticism.

For the past two years, I have been a contributing writer to the ILR newsletter, SENIORSPEAK, and was named its editor this past year. I have also been hired as the film reviewer for the Boca Raton *Observer*, a monthly publication that gives me great leeway in venting my often contrary evaluations of today's movie fare, plus a nice stipend for each review. (I have also been doing some features for the magazine.)

The final (thus far) achievement that was spawned from my after-fifty involvement in learning is the course "Writing the Short Story," which I will be co-teaching at ILR this fall with one of my writing instructors. How sweet is that?

I have learned a great deal; I have grown in ways I didn't anticipate; I have made some wonderful acquaintances and friends; and I have established, in a tiny way, a new career that I love. It just doesn't get any better than that!

Charting My Journey

• • • •

Charting My Journey

. . . .

PART THREE

Health Clubs
for the
Brain

Chapter Six

Lifelong Learning
in the Classroom

*It has been too much the custom to think of education as an affair of
youth...but it really should be the work of the whole of life.*
—Charles W. Eliot

As we have previously discussed, current studies have indicated that the
brain is a vital organ that responds to new stimuli. It needs to be challenged and thrives in enriched environments.[1] Just like the physical body
needs to be taken care of, the brain's health too depends on the care it is
given—and the perfect environment for that care is a Lifelong Learning
Institute, a health club for the brain!

Education is the perfect food for the brain. In fact, education plays a
big role in the psychological and physical wellness of older adults.[2]
Continuing our education in some form beyond the traditional model is
becoming very common. According to the National Center for Education
Statistics, the number of adult learners is both large and growing.

Look at the numbers. In 1999, ninety million Americans participated
in some form of adult learning. That's up from the fifty-eight million registered in 1991. And of those ninety million adult learners, twenty-three
million were over the age of fifty.[3] Clearly, people are beginning to realize
that continuing learning is essential to their longevity. Lifelong learning is
becoming a way of life for many people who are entering their middle and
later years, and a segment of these people are taking part in a special type
of program called Lifelong Learning Institutes, or LLIs.

A best guess is that approximately 250,000 older adults are now taking
part in between 500 and 750 organized classroom-type Lifelong Learning
Institutes across North America. That number is sure to grow as our population ages, especially as people become more aware of the value and

opportunities LLIs afford them.

This section *of Learning Later–Living Greater* is all about Lifelong Learning Institutes. Along with keeping our brain healthy, participation in these programs challenges our personal standards for excellence. We reach for new levels of growth and health. Participation in LLIs stretches our minds and provides us with opportunities to expand our knowledge. If you join a Lifelong Learning Institute, your sense of personal empowerment, self-esteem, and feelings of contribution will take a big leap. Participants in LLIs also gain insight on how to make their personal lives more efficient, effective, and enjoyable. They develop new interests by simply trying something new. Lifelong Learning Institutes keep us motivated when life gets a little overwhelming. Finally, these programs help us fulfill personal aspirations and ensure continued growth and intellectual stimulation.

Lifelong Learning Institutes can be a valuable tool for those of us facing thirty or more years of postwork life, if we want those years to be rich and fulfilling.

History

How did these programs come into existence? For years, colleges and universities have offered continuing education programs for the local community. Along with these programs, adult education is offered in most communities at local schools. Adults of all ages take advantage of these low-cost opportunities, and they continue to be a wonderful resource for

Extrinsic rewards pale in significance when measured against the benefits members have realized. The founders envisioned an organization run by and for the members. We strangers came together and built an organization that met our needs and wishes for meaningful intellectual interchange among peers with mutual interest. Our close affiliation with each other in decision making, development, and implementation of our programs resulted in a sense of ownership and pride of accomplishment to add to the personal enrichment and camaraderie the program provides each of us. It continues to be an exciting and rewarding activity for all involved.

—Gretchen Lankford, Pittsburgh, Pennsylvania

many. The types of programs we are talking about in this book, however, are different from these well-known programs.

Back in 1962, a group of retired educators came together to discuss ways to stay intellectually challenged beyond what continuing education courses offered. They gathered at the New School for Social Research (now called the New School University) in New York City and conceived of a program run by and for older adults, offering a college-level curriculum. The New School enthusiastically welcomed the older adults onto their Greenwich Village campus under the name of the Institute for Retired Professionals (IRP). From the outset, the IRP program thrived, and it is still going strong today. In the words of its current director, Michael Markowitz,

> Being part of a university with a historic mission of inclusiveness helped make the IRP so successful. Today, the program is viewed as a vital member of the diverse campus population. IRP students take part in most university events open to degree students.
>
> After almost forty-five years, our efforts are not directed toward growth and recruiting but are focused on the critical issues of maintaining standards and on ensuring participation and students' investment in supporting the academic community and in developing a curriculum and student body as diverse as the city and university that is our home.
>
> More than 90 percent of the members contribute to the fundraising drives of the IRP and the university. In the past, IRP has cosponsored events with the New York City Department for the Aging and other metropolitan area groups. These have included the first national conference on elder abuse and a pre–White House conference on aging event.

Between the start of this program in 1962 and the mid-1980s, the learning in retirement, or LIR, movement, as it came to be known, grew slowly, with approximately fifty more institutes being formed at institutions such as Harvard, Syracuse University, Duke, and the University of California, Los Angeles (UCLA), among others. These early programs often relied on the founders at the IRP to help get them started. IRP directors Hy Hirsch and Henry Lipman personally hosted and visited many of these developing programs.

In fact, so strong was their contribution to the learning in retirement movement that it's safe to say we all owe a large debt of gratitude to both these men. The movement is successful today because of their vision and perseverance in laying the groundwork during the 1960s and '70s.

Elderhostel Institute Network

By the mid-1980s, however, word was starting to spread about this wonderful opportunity for older adults. The early visionaries of the movement were becoming overwhelmed with requests for help to start new programs. Clearly, some kind of national mechanism to coordinate the start-up of new programs needed to be established.

Growing somewhat in tandem with the expansion of the learning in retirement movement was Elderhostel, Inc. Established in 1975 as the country's first, biggest, and best educational travel provider for older adults, their mission was the same as that of the LIR movement: providing outstanding educational opportunities for older adults. (We will talk much more about Elderhostel in the next section.)

Consequently, it was only natural that Elderhostel and the early lifelong learners should come together. By the mid-1980s, Elderhostel was running a very successful, large, decentralized operation, and their expertise was just what the founders of the LIR movement were looking for to help them develop new institutes.

So in 1988, after informal discussions between the leaders of both groups, the Elderhostel Institute Network opened its doors at Elderhostel headquarters in New Hampshire. The mission of the EIN is to strengthen and support the effectiveness of Lifelong Learning Institutes, to encourage the establishment of new institutes, and to disseminate information about the institutes and the movement in general.

Between 1988 and 1999, a staff of five Elderhostel/EIN employees traveled all across the country, leading workshops and giving advice on how to start new Lifelong Learning Institutes, then called Institutes for Learning in Retirement.

According to Jim Verschueren, EIN's first director:

It was not an easy start. Among the perhaps seventy-five ILRs at the time the network was launched, several were skeptical of

Elderhostel's involvement. Would the well-established international organization attempt to take over? As one member asked in a large public meeting, "Is this like the federal government— bringing good things to us with all kinds of strings attached?" Over time, as all associated with the network worked hard to support, but never to direct, the exponential growth of ILRs, much of the resistance subsided. To the network's credit, promotion of the ILR concept immediately bore fruit. As new ILRs were launched at an ever-increasing pace, affiliations grew annually, from fewer than one hundred the first year to almost three hundred by year six.

Credit for the success of this initiative goes to many. Elderhostel president Bill Berkeley and the board of directors were unflinchingly supportive. Leaders of established ILRs, such as Henry Lipman (ILR, New School, New York), Ken Young (ILR, American University, Washington, D.C.), Sara Craven (Duke University ILR, North Carolina), and Nancy Sack (ILR, Harvard University, Massachusetts), were all early, influential, and long-term activists. Perhaps most of all, Francis Myers brought the network concept to fruition. A prominent member of the Plato Society, UCLA, and president of a California association of ILRs that preexisted the network, Francis's determination to grow the national movement was profound.

More than two hundred new programs were started during these years. Today, the Elderhostel Institute Network is North America's largest and most respected educational network for older adults, with more than 350 affiliated Lifelong Learning Institute members.

Elderhostel, now headquartered in Boston, still provides support and guidance, at no charge, to all the institutes through its sponsorship of the Elderhostel Institute Network. In turn, EIN, through its website and by email, continues to offer a wide variety of resources to established LLIs and to support new start-up programs.

ALIROW

Another, smaller network exists to promote connection between Lifelong Learning Institutes. That network is the Association for Learning in

Retirement Organizations of the West, or ALIROW. ALIROW is an active association of independent learning in retirement associations. Their member-directed activities are generally located on campuses of sponsoring universities and colleges in the western United States.

ALIROW council members meet periodically to exchange information and to learn the skills and requirements needed to ensure the successful operation of the individual campus organizations. All officers and delegates serve as volunteers; there is no paid staff. ALIROW is supported through nominal dues.

Formally organized in 1984, this is the first umbrella organization to support university-level, self-directed learning institutes for retirement-age learners. ALIROW supports the educational objectives of all national associations related to learning in retirement. Their goal is to cooperate with everyone in the academic community who supports this rapidly growing movement.[4]

Many of the LLIs that belong to ALIROW also belong to the Elderhostel Institute Network, increasing their resources even further. Thirty-six programs in Arizona, California, Oregon, Nevada, Washington, and British Columbia belong to the ALIROW network.

What Is a Lifelong Learning Institute?

Now that we know a little about the origins of the learning in retirement movement, let's take a look at the specifics of a Lifelong Learning Institute.

Lifelong Learning Institutes are programs run by and for older adults. Most of the programs that belong to the Elderhostel Institute Network are housed under the auspices of a college or university. But not all.

Today, more and more programs are being started independent of colleges and universities. Many are being developed at active adult retirement communities and others at continuing care communities. Some are stand-alone programs formed by local residents within a community.

Whether they are formed with the help of a local college or university or by committed older adults, all but a very few programs are open to *anyone*, regardless of previous academic history. These programs offer a mix of college-level, noncredit courses and social events.

So what makes them different from community or adult education programs? They are different because they are run *by and for* older adults, usually those over the age of fifty. People join these programs and pay fairly low membership dues, sometimes as little as twenty-five dollars a year. This sense of belonging fosters a feeling of ownership and commitment among members. A strong volunteer aspect and a real feeling of community are also hallmarks of such programs.

LLIs are organized, governed, and attended by local people who commute to the program from nearby communities. They participate regularly, year after year, and get to know one another as friends, co-volunteers, and classmates.

Each Lifelong Learning Institute (the umbrella term for all these programs) is unique, with its own individual name. There are, of course, variables within each program, depending on how they are set up. Academic study, travel/study, membership activities, financial accountability, community outreach, public relations—all are developed and expanded by direct member input and decision making.

About Lifelong Learning Institutes

Here are some factoids about Lifelong Learning Institutes that will help give you a good overview of the programs.

- Each LLI is a unique, self-sufficient entity with its own set of guidelines, courses, and activities.
- Each LLI goes by its own name, but all are Lifelong Learning Institutes.
- Programs provide well-run learning environments full of wisdom, diversity, and intellectual and cultural stimulation.
- Each LLI has a strong sense of community among its members.
- All institutes are very reasonably priced. Most have a small membership fee and course fees.
- A typical LLI has between two hundred and four hundred members, but some have several thousand members.
- Classes are held during the day.
- During any one term, more than five thousand courses are available at LLIs across the country.

- A typical program offers between twenty and forty courses per term, and has two or three terms each year.
- Most members take two or three courses per term.
- Classes can be held on college campuses or in local community facilities.
- Classes can be peer-led, facilitated by current or retired faculty, or led by outside experts.
- An atmosphere of shared experiences, not a lecture format, is prevalent in most classrooms.
- There is never any homework or tests. Grades are not given.
- LLIs are open to anyone regardless of previous academic experiences.
- The only requirement to join is a desire to keep your mind active and stimulated.
- Social activities can include field trips, all types of social outings, and group travel.
- Volunteers usually staff LLIs, although some have paid office staff.
- Members make up all the necessary committees, such as curriculum, special events, and long-range planning.
- Members staff the governing boards and make all decisions about the LLI.
- Members can and usually are active in service to their communities.

LLI Participants

The camaraderie at an LLI fills the classrooms and spills into the halls, the cafeteria, and even the parking lot. Stimulating discussions fill the air. Laughter, intensity, and a real *joie de vie* envelop everyone involved. To an outsider at first glance, it might seem like a group of young people intent on comparing the latest rock bands. But a second look would show these students are special: they've experienced life and all it has to offer. They are truly living!

Closer study shows that LLI participants are self-motivated learners, intent on making their later years the very best they can be. They come from all walks of life. Some have college degrees; others do not. In an LLI, it's a level playing field.

LLI members are dedicated students of retirement age, whose common bonds are intellectual curiosity and generational experiences. They share opinions, knowledge, and expertise with humor, creativity, mutual respect, and an intense vitality. The volunteer work each member does at an LLI helps create a well-run learning environment full of diversity, insight, wisdom, and intellectual and cultural stimulation. At the same time, they get to share in the joys of learning and friendship while being challenged to broaden their horizons.[5]

In other words, everyone is there to keep their brains active and alert. Everyone is there for the sheer joy of learning. Everyone has something to contribute because all members have life experiences that have shaped and formed them. Life experience is experiential learning at its very best. All members bring their experiences to the classroom. Give and take between the members and the course facilitators is a hallmark of lifelong learning programs. The facilitator learns as much from the participants as the participants do from the facilitator.

Unless it's a special lecture, most of the time you will not find talking heads in LLI classes. Rather, you will find facilitators anxious to guide participants on a journey of self-discovery, finding a new way to look at an old topic, listening to both sides of an issue, and exploring something new and exciting in a relaxed and stimulating environment. In other words, the perfect learning venue.

Curriculum

At the very heart of every Lifelong Learning Institute is the curriculum. Committees composed of LLI members decide what courses are to be offered, based on input from other members. A curriculum committee puts in long hours planning and organizing. That hard work shows in the quality of the courses offered by each LLI.

Here is a brief sampling of some of the courses offered at Lifelong Learning Institutes:

- Music in French Civilization
- Four from J.S. Bach
- The Elements of Music
- Memorable Musicals
- Art & Ideas: Romantic America
- Beginning Watercolor

- Pen & Ink
- Basic Drawing
- American Mystery Writers
- Modern Short Fiction of the American South
- James Fenimore Cooper's Greatest Novels
- Louisa May Alcott: Her Life & Work
- Creative Writing
- Everywoman's Story Project
- Life Writing
- A Playwright's Theatre
- Theatre & the Public Good
- Play Reading for Culture
- Plays in Production
- Reading & Understanding Poetry
- The Epic
- Schoolroom Poets
- Understanding Shakespeare's Sonnets
- Nutrition & Food Issues
- Biology of Aging
- Medical Test Results
- The Mind/Body Connection
- Civil War
- Celts: A History of Ireland, Scotland, Wales
- Lewis & Clark

- Early American History
- Local Ecosystems
- Local Island Ecology
- Municipal Government
- Aquaculture Research
- Current Affairs/Events
- Foreign Policy
- Great Political Decisions
- Tax Law Changes
- Astronomy
- Celestial Navigation
- Introduction to Forestry
- Geology
- Basic & Advanced Computer Courses
- Natural Golf
- Basic & Advanced Internet Courses
- Beginning Piano
- The Philosophy of Religion
- Christianity
- World Religions
- Philosophy: Beginning & Advanced
- Financial Planning
- Wills & Estates
- Retirement Planning & Investing
- The Stock Market
- Scandinavia
- Poland: Its Art, History &

Culture
- The Seminoles
- Judaism
- Chivalry

- Period Furniture
- Fly on the Cheap
- Mysteries of the Food Industry

The Social Aspect

The social nature of lifelong learning also helps us live longer. As we have said, people join Lifelong Learning Institutes as much for the socializing as for the education. Social activities are a strong component of Lifelong Learning Institutes. There, people make lifelong friends.

Statewide and regional conferences are also another way LLI members interact on both professional and social levels. Conferences are a great way of bringing LLIs together to discuss the nature of their programs and their missions, policies, and procedures, and to share concerns, find solutions, and celebrate their many victories.

LLI members and staff meet and mingle with their counterparts from other LLIs. A conference may be composed of LLIs from just one state or perhaps from several different states. It may even be made up of LLIs from many states who want to meet because they are similar in structure or have the same concerns. LLI members from all across North America are always welcome to attend any of these conferences.

Benefits for an Academic Host

If an LLI is hosted by a college or university, the benefits for that institution and their faculty and students, and indeed the entire community are numerous. Here are a few:

- Having people of vast experience and great intellectual curiosity on campus provides fresh inspiration and focus to both the faculty and the students.

- An institute on campus means faculty will have the opportunity to try out creative and innovative methods of teaching. At the same time, they broaden their knowledge of the subject, since the viewpoints of older students may provide many different perspectives.

- Providing support for an institute enhances the quality of education for traditional students.

- LLI programs provide the institution with an opportunity to offer a wide variety of intergenerational opportunities to younger students.
- An institute adds age diversity to the campus.
- Sponsoring an LLI helps fulfill the school's responsibility to act as an educational resource for the whole community.
- Hosting an institute ties the needs of the community to the expertise of the school.
- An LLI serves as an ambassador for the institution.
- An institute located on campus may influence where people decide to retire—it brings active, intelligent people into a community.
- LLI members attend cultural events at the school.
- LLI members give money to fund scholarships and special events.
- LLI members will "market" the institution to their grandchildren and others.
- LLI members are often leaders in the community and can help the school build support for legislative appropriations.
- LLI members become "friends" of the school, which expands fund-raising opportunities.
- LLI members volunteer their time and expertise, which enhances the institution's abilities to be the best educational facility possible.

Benefits for LLI Members

As participants, we reap a host of benefits by belonging to a Lifelong Learning Institute. Here are a few of them:

- Enlarges the scope of our interests.
- Enriches established friendships.
- Provides opportunities to meet new people.
- Keeps us current, active, and young.
- Enables us to make new contacts, relationships, and connections.
- Expands our horizons.
- Allows us to have fun, gain respect, and exchange ideas.

- Provides opportunities to develop new ideas and handle change.
- Opens our minds to what is new…instead of us dwelling on the past and rejecting the new out of hand.
- Gets us involved in the give and take of lively discussions.
- Provides a chance to learn more about current events.
- Allows us to gain a better understanding of the world and ourselves.
- Gives us a chance to engage in camaraderie with our peers.
- Makes us a seeker and sharer of knowledge.
- Gives us a chance to try out new ideas and insights.
- Allows us to participate in domestic and international study/travel.
- Provides us opportunities for volunteer work on the local and national levels.

Validating Later-Life Learning

In Chapter 5, we mentioned several ways that lifelong learning was being validated by large organizations. Here are more.

The state of Mississippi, in recognizing the value and importance of lifelong learning for older adults, has a developed a program called Certified Retirement Cities. In order to receive this designation, a city must meet certain requirements, chief among them the availability of high-quality educational and cultural opportunities for older adults.

I am going to the Beth Israel Medical Center for two or three days to have a pacemaker inserted…I suppose the two or three days are to check on how it is working. I'm so attached to the world of lifelong learning, I'd like to take a volume of Shelby Foote's *Civil War*, which I'm currently studying, but it's too heavy to hold in a hospital. Instead, I am taking Grant's memoirs, which some critics say is the best of war memoirs. Lifelong learning is such a large part of my life that I can't bear to be away from it, even for something as important as this trip!

—Ena Morris, ninety-two years old, New York City

Therefore, the LLIs found in these Certified Retirement Cities are prominently featured in all the state's retirement and relocation literature. Texas has just begun a similar initiative.

Also in Chapter 5, we mentioned how The Bernard Osher Foundation was giving $100,000 grants to Lifelong Learning Institutes. This money has made a huge difference in the state of Maine. In the words of Kali Lightfoot, coordinator of the Maine Senior College Network and executive director of the National Resource Center (NRC) for the Osher Lifelong Learning Institutes,

> We have done research here in Maine that shows that Senior College members feel that they have become more knowledgeable and interesting as a result of their continued learning, "We don't just feel more interesting, we are more interesting."[6] This seems to have been particularly true for women who participate in Senior College courses. Maine is now the "oldest" state in the union, so anything that helps the overall physical and mental well-being of its older residents is a good thing for the whole state, economically and culturally.
>
> Because of its success at coordinating a statewide network of lifelong learning programs, USM has been named to host the National Resource Center for all of the Osher Lifelong Learning Institutes nationwide. The NRC will provide many services to help Osher Institutes to communicate and share information, with the aim of constantly improving the educational opportunities available to people over fifty in the United States.

This is irrefutable evidence that lifelong learning certainly has arrived and is getting stronger every single day.

Lifelong Learning Institutes are a life-enriching, life-enhancing, and life-prolonging concept. They provide a stimulating educational atmosphere of self-governance that enables mature adults, no matter what their previous academic history, to come together and take college-level, non-credit courses for fun and discovery.

If you have already left the full-time workforce, pick up the phone today and call one of the LLIs near you. If you are still working, tuck this information away until you are ready to leave the world of work and embark on your own lifelong learning adventure.

And if there isn't a Lifelong Learning Institute near you, think about starting one. Many other people have done so already, and so can you. Established LLIs are always willing to lend their expertise and help to get you started. You will also find an entire section on the Elderhostel Institute Network website designed to help you start a new program.

Lifelong Learning Institutes are where you can begin making the most of your after-fifty years. To find a Lifelong Learning Institute near you, visit the Elderhostel Institute Network website at *elderhostel.org/ein/intro.asp*.

Thoughts on Belonging to a Lifelong Learning Institute

Betty Bennett

Betty Bennett is a member of the Institute for Learning in Retirement sponsored by the University of Wisconsin-Green Bay.

What at its beginning might have been considered a pleasant alternative to boredom has elicited a much more surprising and significant response. Many of us see this reaction to the opportunity for lifelong learning together as an unexpected and extremely important part of our lives. It is as if pleasure has grown into need.

The experiences of learning together, sitting in a full classroom, arriving early to get a good seat, sensing the group excitement of being challenged to learn and accept ideas and theories, reexamining facts, perhaps reading a play together and finding something there we had not glimpsed before—all of this comes close to healthy addiction.

In a play-reading group, some of us spoke the words of Anne Frank and her family, and history became truth. And in a course on Lewis and Clark, we came to understand the sacrifice of a journey that lasted years. The diaries became reality; the hazards and hardships touched us; the suffering necessary to open up our country turned into reality.

I think this kind of participatory learning, gulped at an age when crafts, sports, and card games were all that had been offered, makes us not only grateful but hungry for more.

Some of us have always gone off on our own when retirement came—to complete college degrees, audit classes, or to study a beloved pleasure in depth—for no other reason than to satisfy a thirst for more knowledge and to get a sense of completion. But now we are flocking to share these needs together. What was an isolated and solitary phenomenon has become a movement to fulfillment.

We could not have been more surprised. Since the formalization of the lifelong learning movement, we feel gratitude; like for the women's movement for equality, this surprise will obviously become a firm expectation.

Our generation has proved its viability and its permanence as a still-important entity in society. I see this as something to be reckoned with. The old fuddy-duddy image of aging has proved false, and older persons (*not* senior citizens) can be seen as a segment of the population that is worthy of respect. The myth of our later years as being a time to relax and enjoy idle pleasures is far from our only pastime. We want much more than entertainment and a way to keep busy.

One of the great rewards of participating in this addiction to lifelong learning is the sweetness of finding life in retirement a great joy.

I am convinced that we only live once, and this business of learning together—this glorious sharing—is a form of rejuvenation. Our growing numbers prove this. It's not only about togetherness and laughter and recognition of facts seen in a new light; it's about a life thrust we have found together.

I will take this one step further, to the personal. To me, lifelong learning is often a haven from humdrum life. It is a place for me to be with people of like mind (not in opinion but in purpose). Together we want to explore, walk roads not yet traveled, examine old facts, and find new conclusions.

The myth of old age has vanished. It is possible to live longer and dream more.

A Glimpse at one Lifelong Learning Institute

Ruth Flexman

Ruth Flexman has been the director of the Academy of Lifelong Learning for ten years.

The Academy of Lifelong Learning at the Wilmington campus of the University of Delaware offers mental stimulation and enrichment, plus opportunities for intellectual and social exchange. Our success is demonstrated by program growth, primarily resulting from members inviting friends. Since its founding in 1980, the academy has added about one hundred members annually, up to the current membership of two thousand.

The two hundred courses we offer vary broadly in content and teaching methodology. Liberal arts courses involve lectures or videos and discussion. Music and dance courses offer group participation and individual expression. Guided listening helps students learn about a variety of musical genres. Health issues are addressed through medical lectures, yoga, tai chi, and a walking club. Our popular classes include offerings in both the natural and social sciences. Computer courses also are popular.

Members are our most important resource. Some teach; others serve on committees; all learn. Instructors are volunteers. Out of their interest and expertise, courses develop. Without degrees or promotions as rewards, motivation comes from course quality and the instructors' enthusiasm. The joy of learning is evident; applause breaks out at the end of some classes. What instructors give is amazing. What they receive would rank at the top of the avenues for meeting social, self-esteem, and self-actualization needs.

Courses are offered within a structure combining the university's focus on learning with the energy of a volunteer-led program. The Academy of Lifelong Learning Council governs the program. Committees implement the academy's operations, including the curriculum, a newsletter, reception, travel, equipment, and member relations. Paid staff members—three full-time and three part-time—provide continuity and coordination with university services. Membership fees cover costs for space, services, staff, and equipment.

Support for the program comes from multiple sources. Arsht Hall, named after generous benefactors, provides beautiful classroom, lounge, and lunch space. The location at a branch campus adjacent to a conference center and golf course provides six hundred parking spaces. Support also comes from guest speakers from the university and the community.

Members are supportive of one another. One participant said, "The program saved my life. I was depressed and my wife nagged me into coming. I am surprised at how much I enjoy life now." A daughter gladly drives her father to school: "With the courses and people he enjoys, he has a whole new identify." As one of the oldest and largest lifelong learning programs, the academy has served as a model and inspiration. Find us on the web at *www.udel.edu/ce/allhome.html*.

INTERVIEW WITH AN EXPERT

Ronald J. Manheimer, Ph.D.

Ronald J. Manheimer, Ph.D., is executive director of the North Carolina Center for Creative Retirement, an award-winning lifelong learning, leadership, research, and community service program of The University of North Carolina at Asheville, where he also holds an appointment as a research associate professor of philosophy. In 1999, Manheimer was elected a fellow of The University of North Carolina Institute on Aging, headquartered at Chapel Hill. Before becoming the NCCCR's first director in 1988, Manheimer was director of older adult education for The National Council on the Aging (NCOA) in Washington, D.C. He is also the author of numerous studies and books on issues of later life, including his newest: *A Map to the End of Time.*

You have been very active for many years in promoting lifelong learning for older adults. How are things different now than back in 1988 when you became the first director of NCCCR?

In 1988, when I first took the helm of the North Carolina Center for Creative Retirement [NCCCR], most of our participants were fully retired and few had expected either the boon of a longer and healthier life or the opportunity to reenter the classroom, whether as a student or a teacher. The idea of a Lifelong Learning Institute was new, and people felt like they were making history as they tried out all sorts of courses and tried their hand at teaching—especially if that hadn't been part of their earlier career.

Now, with 10 to 15 percent of our membership under age sixty—with some semiretired and some fully retired, there's a much higher set of expectations. The younger crowd is already familiar with the idea of lifelong learning. Their interests are fairly specific: what's new in science?, technology and social issues, comparative religion, Excel software applications.

Fortunately, so far, the level of commitment to volunteering to serve on committees, to teach, and to help govern is still strong. As the center has grown in numbers, in complexity with added programs, and with having our own building, the volunteer tasks are more demanding. We're struggling to see where the line comes between what we could expect only from a paid staff person and what we could expect from a volunteer.

And then we've added programs that generate funds which help underwrite other functions, such as added staff time, additional equipment, and funds to underwrite new start-up programs that haven't yet produced income. Sometimes the center feels more like a small business than an educational or public service, which is how the university classifies us— as a line item category. We have to think about marketing, about competition, about our niche, and long-range goals. All those things.

What impact do you see the baby boomers having on older-adult lifelong learning?

We've just finished a yearlong study of how members of the boomer generation might impact our program—how to get ready. And we've already heeded some of the guidelines. We're just launching the first of what we call *self-qualifying certificate programs.* The first is an environment education program focusing on helping people get to know their home in the Blue Ridge region. It involves classes, field studies— a kind of paraprofessional approach that is more systematic than most of what we've done in the past. Yet we are not trying to compete with the regular university curriculum in environmental studies. The first component, a yearlong program called "A Sense of Place," is already filled, mainly with folks in their fifties and one in her late twenties (we dropped age restrictions several years ago).

Are you changing or revamping any of your programs to appeal more to the coming wave of baby boomers?

We think topics like the ones above that have an activist or advocacy angle and that are well focused and still fun with some hands-on elements, that this will appeal to the new generation of retirement-age people. We recognize that most are either not retired, are semiretired, or maybe are just taking a break before they decide what they'll do next. Still, we have to be sure that those participants feel some ownership of the program, lest we turn into a continuing education program, not a learning community.

What are your thoughts about the value of lifelong learning for older adults as it relates to brain health?

There seems to be pretty good evidence that continuing to use your mind, challenging yourself, and having good, supportive relationships all contribute to both physical and mental flourishing. But whether the *use it or lose it* slogan is universally true, I'm not sure. I'm concerned that we're replacing one stereotype, the disengaged, frail older person, with another, the robust, productive person in his or her fifties, sixties, seventies—whatever—who's made a success of aging.

This stereotype easily leads to blaming people who fall prey to dementia. A friend of mine, cultural historian Tom Cole, calls this the morality of the *good versus bad aging*. I know too many bright, engaged people who have nevertheless succumbed to some type of dementia or neurological disorder related to a disease process. So all the talk about brain health leaves me cold. It's fine for the professionals to justify some of what we do by pointing to mental health benefits. But it's not how I want people to think about participation in our programs. Thriving, yes. Brain health, no.

What do you feel are the most important benefits people get out of belonging to an LLI?

The studies done on motivation to join an LLI all point to the same list of benefits: intellectual stimulation; staying in touch; socialization; the pleasure of learning for its own sake as well as to learn some particular skill, such as a computer application, a language, how to write a novel, or how to be a more effective grandparent. For some, joining a learning community is important. They want that sense of belonging. For others, the social part is secondary. A small minority love sharing classroom time with undergraduates in our intergenerational courses. I'd say that about a third of our members like the idea of having a say in how the program is run and helping to run it. They take some ownership and are proud of what they, and we, have accomplished.

Can you tell us a short story—something memorable or life-changing that happened to one of your members as a direct result of belonging to NCCCR*?*

Raising four and a half million dollars and building our own facility, Reuter Center, was a huge accomplishment shared by hundreds of people who helped in different ways. The fact that we could do it still amazes us all and shows what we're capable of. So there's the giving factor—not just money but commitment, doing for and with one's peers. This comes out in the very high rate of community service practiced by our members.

Participation in a lifelong learning program can be transformational. I think of Alice Green, who told me that when she and her husband, Art, started attending the center, she saw herself as a rather shy, retreating person. Art was the extrovert. But she took a class in improvisational drama, just for fun, and the instructor told her she had great talent for getting up in front of people and projecting herself—that she was a natural leader. She was amazed. "Me?" she exclaimed. That emboldened her, and so when she was asked to chair a center committee, instead of demurring, she said yes. Eventually, she became chair of the biggest center program. Later, she cochaired the fund-raising campaign even though she'd never done anything like this. She still laughs, "If my friends from years back could see me now, they wouldn't believe it. 'Alice Green did that?' No way."

Learning Later, Living Greater My Way!

Betty Smith

Betty Smith is a member of the Osher Lifelong Learning Institute sponsored by the University of Southern Maine, Portland.

Many years ago, a small announcement in our local paper caught my attention. The University of Southern Maine, through a program called SAGE, was offering a series of lectures, on Tuesday mornings for nine weeks. Each lecture examined a different topic. Some were subjects about which I had a bit of knowledge, some about which I knew little or nothing. Some sounded fascinating; others…umm…I wasn't so sure.

I gave it a try, however, and not only did I attend the lectures, but I was also drawn into the work needed to make the program run. The circle of interesting people I met through that process continually widened, and my knowledge of things happening in our community also increased. 'Twas a gift for a curious mind!

Then an even brighter and more stimulating world opened for me when I chose to enroll in the initial classes of a novel offering—an exciting new idea for our area—Senior College at USM.

I must admit to having approached that adventure with both excitement and a bit of caution. I was unsure if I'd jumped into a situation for which I was unprepared. The reason: I had never gone to college. I had heard that this new program held great appeal for retirees in the area, most of whom had attended college in their younger years. My history included no college degree, let alone advanced degrees as many of those retirees had earned. Most of my knowledge had been gained from life experience, not in towers of higher learning. A few years of employment in an office were followed by running a household, raising our children, and taking care of elderly family members and a longtime friend. Through those years, the emotional and social needs of my family, as well as the special medical challenges of the later stages of life, were my learning focus. It was quite an education, albeit an unconventional one.

Then, as I neared my sixtieth birthday, another educational opportunity came into my life. This time it was oncology. My "professors" were surgeons, radiologists, pathologists, and the gentle nurses specializing in this field. It was in that haven where the subjects of new trials, personal solutions to daily challenges, and the value of our treasured loved ones would mix with renewed awe of this cherished world and pit-of-the-stomach terror.

In time, I supported the needs of new members, learned even more, and eventually became the group's facilitator. My education again was through personal experience—not in a structured classroom. Would it matter in this new senior college?

It turns out it mattered not a bit! With great joy, my experience tells me there's a common denominator that blankets the majority of those attending our classes. We all seem to share the fulfilling satisfaction of learning.

As I read, listen to daily news reports, or reflect on a creative idea, I'm aware of a direct connection to some classroom discussion. We have knowledgeable instructors who are invigorated by the give and take of questions and answers from all sides.

In the long run, what a perfect place to come together and learn from each other here at USM. We enjoy the opportunity to explore new issues and to share different points of view, thereby helping us to better understand our world and those who exist on this planet with us.

Today, I'm even more involved than ever in what was SAGE/Senior College. Both have become a new program—the Osher Lifelong Learning Institute—and their class offerings continue to expand my knowledge, energize me, and keep my world growing.

Charting My Journey

• • • •

Charting My Journey

• • • •

Chapter Seven

Other Types of Community-Based Learning Programs

Learning is ever in the freshness of its youth, even for the old.
—Aeschylus

In the previous chapter, we looked at what is perhaps the most well-known of all later-life learning organizations—Lifelong Learning Institutes. In this chapter, we will look at two other equally life-enhancing organizations: OASIS programs and the Shepherd's Centers of America.

We'll also take a brief glimpse at programs and learning opportunities that can be found in most communities. Although these resources are not primarily focused on just older-adult learning, they should be listed so you better understand the scope of lifelong learning in your community.

There's a wealth of opportunities out there once you begin focusing on lifelong learning and all it has to offer. With so much variety, you're sure to find a program that suits you. After all, the goal of this book is to inspire you to include lifelong learning as part of your after-fifty life. How you do that is something only you can determine.

OASIS

OASIS is a national nonprofit educational organization designed to enrich the lives of mature adults and strengthen communities. Offering challenging programs in the arts, humanities, wellness, technology, and volunteer service, OASIS creates opportunities for older adults to pursue vibrant, healthy, productive, and meaningful lives.[1]

OASIS is a public-private partnership that serves more than 350,000 members age fifty plus through a national network of centers in twenty-five cities. The OASIS Institute in St. Louis is the national headquarters.

Primary centers are in department stores. Each center is a specially designed space with offices, a lounge, and classrooms, providing a comfortable setting where members can relax and meet people with similar interests. Additional programs are offered in other community locations.

Local sponsors, such as health care institutions, nonprofit agencies, department stores, banks, businesses, foundations, and individuals, provide financial support. An OASIS director manages each center with assistance from staff and member volunteers. OASIS is nationally sponsored by The May Department Stores Company Foundation.[2]

Background

OASIS was founded in 1982 by Marylen Mann as a resource for older adults who wanted to continue to be active, productive members of the community. An initial grant from the U.S. Administration on Aging funded a two-year project to demonstrate the feasibility of a public-private partnership. From an initial start in four cities, OASIS today has programs in twenty-five different cities across the United States.

In the last several years, OASIS has received grants from several well-known foundations, including nearly one million dollars from the Robert Wood Johnson Foundation for the Active for Life Program, $500,000 from the SBC Foundation for computer training, and $250,000 from the National Endowment for the Humanities for a Lewis and Clark project. OASIS also partnered with the SPRY Foundation to develop Science Across the Generations with funding from the National Science Foundation. The program brings together OASIS volunteers and children to explore math, science, and technology concepts. Grants such as these certainly lend validity to the outstanding programs of OASIS.[3]

Programs

OASIS offers a unique approach that integrates educational, health, and service opportunities to address the needs of the whole person: intellectual, physical, and social. Each center offers a broad scope of classes, special events, and volunteer opportunities.

Course offerings vary widely from city to city but usually include art, computer, consumer information, intergenerational opportunities, literature, music, science and nature, exercise and dance, health and aging, history, personal development and enrichment, philosophy, religion and spirituality, politics and world affairs, sports, and a myriad of volunteer opportunities.

The most far-reaching community service opportunity is the OASIS Intergenerational Tutoring Program, which promotes literacy with a proven approach designed to build children's self-esteem and positive attitudes toward learning. Working with elementary schools, OASIS pairs older adults with young children having underdeveloped reading and language skills. The adults work one-on-one with the students each week as their tutors, mentors, and friends. Since 1989, volunteers have helped over 211,000 children learn to read and be more successful in school. The program has proved to be beneficial to both the students and the tutors and consistently receives high marks from educators.

OASIS Today

Today, OASIS is widely recognized as a successful model for productive aging. Its members share a desire to remain active and involved, to develop new talents, and to enjoy the companionship of others. Most important, OASIS members represent a valuable resource who can actively participate in and contribute to society.[4]

The OASIS website at *www.oasisnet.org* offers a wealth of information, including all program locations, and is well worth exploring.

Shepherd's Centers of America

Shepherd's Centers of America (SCA) is a network of interfaith community-based organizations that provide meaning and purpose for adults throughout their mature years. The role of SCA is to build and support this nationwide network of over seventy-five member organizations in twenty-one states.

All Shepherd's Centers have a commonly understood mission to empower older adults to use their wisdom and skills for the good of their communities. Lifelong learning opportunities and social services are provided through partnerships with organizations of many faiths and the community at large. Volunteers are the leaders in providing in-home and community-based services for their neighbors. The vision is that individuals will experience meaningful lives through all phases of their mature years.

History

Since 1972, older adults have contributed to and benefited from the Shepherd's Center movement. It originated in Kansas City, Missouri, when the senior minister of a large mid-city church recognized the need to redefine and restructure the way Americans approach aging.

The minister, Rev. Elbert C. Cole, understood the postretirement time in life as spiritually meaningful and potentially healthy and enjoyable, full of new possibilities for learning and for staying current with the rapid changes in this modern world. He also saw the mature years as an opportune time for older adults to share their talents and wisdom to make their communities a better place for everyone. The first center was founded with twenty-five Catholic, Jewish, and Protestant congregations in one section of Kansas City, Missouri, to nurture a new image of aging and to respond to the increased longevity of contemporary adults. Shepherd's Centers of America, a not-for-profit, interfaith, umbrella organization, was founded in 1975 to oversee Shepherd's Centers in twenty-one states and seventy-five communities.

A combination of in-home and destination programs are selected from more than thirty-five types of programs and services on SCA's menu of options to address the unique needs of each community. Such programs as Partners in Health, Meals on Wheels, Adventures in Learning, Home Health Aide, and Handy Hands help people remain in their own homes with improved quality of life.[5]

Shepherd's Centers are funded by congregations, participants, friends, businesses, civic organizations and clubs, United Way, public funds, and foundations.

Adventures in Learning

One of the most popular of all the Shepherd's Center programs is its Adventures in Learning program. Offering programs on a variety of subjects, Adventures in Learning enables older adults to continue their lifelong learning and keep their brains active and alert. Most classes are taught by older adults themselves. The purpose of Adventures in Learning is to provide an arena for older adults to share their knowledge, talents, skills, and new interests with peers in a mutual quest for lifelong learning and personal growth.

Classes are generally held during the day and are organized on an academic semester or quarterly basis. Some centers offer alternative programs, such as fairs, picnics, trips, or short-term classes with different teachers during the long breaks—the center recognizes that many participants count on the friendship and stimulation of Shepherd's Center activities.

Many centers enjoy a noontime fellowship, often called the Noon Forum, as a highlight of the Adventures in Learning program. Students, teachers, and volunteers come together at this time to share a meal and friendship. The coordinator of the program makes brief announcements, recognizes teachers, celebrates accomplishments, and welcomes and introduces those attending for the first time. Usually a program follows, such as musical entertainment, a short theatre presentation, or an address by a community leader or a guest speaker on a topic of particular interest to participants.[6]

Adventures in Learning classes are taught by retired and active educators, health professionals, hobbyists, and other persons knowledgeable in various subjects. The "yearning for learning" is a powerful attraction to older adults, and word has spread about these programs.

The Shepherd's Center founder, Dr. Elbert Cole, says that the classes generally fall into five categories that he dubbed "the five Hs." They are:

- Head—Classes with an intellectual theme
- Hands—Classes requiring skills using the hands
- Heart—Classes emphasizing giving to others and caring about yourself.

It was a beginner's class in painting, and I was struggling. I had never, *never,* tried painting, drawing, or any artistic rendition, but isn't that what lifelong learning is about—trying new things? I finally managed an old-fashioned blue pitcher holding sunflowers that somewhat resembled a pitcher holding sunflowers that belonged to my grandmother and that I keep in my kitchen. The pride I felt at finishing what was a tough challenge for me empowered me to try other new things I'd never attempted before. Now, I search out challenges and enjoy opening myself up to new experiences.

—Ann Daggett, Harrisonburg, Virginia

- Health—Classes that enhance the active health and health awareness of older adults
- Hind end—Classes for relaxation[7]

At each center, which is planned and developed by the people who use it, you will see people taking a wide variety of courses. Here is just a sampling of those courses: foreign languages, local history, tai chi, computer skills, social studies, arts, religion, literature, health awareness, life enrichment, performing arts, writing, travelogues, movies, crafts, book reviews, beginning watercolor, speechcraft, astronomy, world events, and money management.

Shepherd's Centers Today

A Shepherd's Center is a new social model informed by a healthy view of life after retirement, providing new benchmarks, vital involvement, and significant and meaningful living in the later years. Today, their Adventures in Learning program is serving the lifelong learning needs and enriching the later years of more than fifty thousand adults across the country.

Shepherd's Centers of America maintains an active website full of useful resources, including program locations, at *www.shepherdcenters.org*.

Other Lifelong Learning Venues

If joining a formal program like a Lifelong Learning Institute, OASIS, or Shepherd's Center program is not your cup of tea, don't despair. There are a host of other venues within your community where you can dip your toe in the lifelong learning waters. A little sleuthing will yield great rewards.

The diversity of many community-based organizations means they are perfectly poised to offer a wide variety of lifelong learning opportunities to the residents. They have established locations and programs, and they are willing to share their knowledge. Let's look at a few of those organizations now.

Libraries

If you prefer a less structured form of lifelong learning, then libraries are the perfect setting. Within your community, the library serves as a central resource and brings together local residents, organizations, programs, and materials. A library is committed to serving everyone, and programs for older adults are among their most popular events.

What's nice about libraries is that you get to choose the style and type of learning that best fits you. Those who want to learn independently can do so. Those who prefer to learn within a group can also be accommodated. You can take part in programs that include people of all ages or just your contemporaries.

Some libraries even have staff designated as older-adult specialists, while others handle all age groups. In either case, they help organize programming and events for everyone. Programs cover a wide range of topics and formats. Book discussion groups are very popular, as are travelogues and current events, but the gamut of what is offered at libraries is far more extensive.

Libraries are also ideally suited to call on a wide variety of experts from the local community to lead workshops, lectures, and courses. And they can even provide meeting rooms for local groups.

Check out the opportunities for lifelong learning at your local library. You'll be glad you did.

Museums

Make a list of all the museums within twenty-five miles of your home. What did you come up with? History? Art? Cultural? Technical? Horticultural? Science? Which of them interest you the most? Now give them a call and ask what kind of classes they are offering to the general public. You'll be amazed at the wealth of lifelong learning opportunities found at museums—almost all of them have education departments. Museums are, after all, primarily educational institutions. In fact, the U.S. government classifies them with schools and libraries so they qualify for federal programs.

Museums offer innovative programming that enlarges the scope of learning for people of all ages, not just older adults. And studies have proved that museum education—because it is experiential, visual, and "hands-on"—increases retention of information and understanding of the subject materials.[8]

Museums large and small offer common opportunities for wider learning. Since they are public spaces and cultural centers where learning and leisure combine, they can encourage adults (who may find more formal education intimidating) to take a first step toward self-directed learning. Moreover, the special circumstances of engaging with real objects, which offer so many pathways into the past, can inspire creativity, curiosity, and further study.[9]

Museum education department staff pride themselves on offering a wide range of courses dealing with the subject matter of their museum. Drawing, creative writing, archaeology, the Bible, ancient Egyptian art, and paleontology are just the tip of the iceberg when it comes to course selection.

You can even take museum learning one step further by becoming a docent—someone who leads tours for the general public. In order to become a docent, you have to be extremely knowledgeable about a particular museum and what it offers. Docent learning, and museum classes in general, are just about guaranteed to keep your brain active and alert.

Adult/Community Education Centers

Adult/Community Education programs are designed to empower learners so they become self-sufficient as they enhance their personal growth, increase their personal development, and pursue self-actualization. This then helps them evolve and become universally literate in body, mind, and spirit. Students then are able to pass their knowledge on to others, demonstrating ways to reach their full potential as productive citizens in today's world.

We all have untapped veins of creativity and mental acuity. We can always strive for more, to go further than we did yesterday. For some of us, Adult/Community Education Centers can be a better fit than the more traditional learning venues. Adult/Community Education Centers offer a wide spectrum of courses and workshops for anyone interested in expanding their personal consciousness.

And if you don't see something at an Adult/Community Education Center that you want to study, let them know. They welcome requests for courses that are not currently being offered and will do their best to find the necessary teachers whenever possible.

SeniorNet

SeniorNet is a national organization made up of adults aged fifty and older who are interested either in learning about computers or in teaching other older adults how to use them. SeniorNet is dedicated to enhancing the lives of older adults everywhere through technology.

Since its beginning in 1986, SeniorNet has helped millions of older adults become computer proficient. With over 240 learning centers throughout the United States and abroad—along with a quarterly newsletter, a wide variety of other teaching materials, regional conferences, and a very extensive website—SeniorNet, at *www.seniornet.org*, ensures that its goals are met. Thanks to their extensive connections, they are also able to offer discounts on computer-related products and services to their members.[10]

Houses of Worship

Churches, synagogues, and mosques as lifelong learning venues? Absolutely. To some this may be surprising, but the venue makes perfect sense. After all, people attend religious services to learn. Most houses of worship already sponsor theological classes for children, so it's not much of a stretch to delve into adult classes as well. Some members of a congregation will undoubtedly be educators who may have an interest in leading adult classes. And most houses of worship have additional space that makes perfect classrooms.

Not all the classes need have a religious bent. At one Unitarian Universalist church, they offer classes ranging from church history and philosophy to personal theological exploration, health and wellness, politics, and arts and music.

If you already belong to a local house of worship, you might want to investigate any lifelong learning opportunities they offer. You may be pleasantly surprised.

College Auditing, Lectures, and Forums

One of the most obvious sites for lifelong learning is your local college or university. That institution likely provides a wealth of lifelong learning opportunities for the general public. For instance, older adults can take advantage of the auditing option offered by most institutions. This is a long-established tradition, but the number of older adults who now take advantage of this benefit is growing every day. Some private universities charge a few hundred dollars or less for a course, although most state colleges and universities admit older adults (usually over age sixty) for free or for a very nominal cost.

In fact, property developers are building retirement communities near college campuses because they know that the atmosphere of a college town and all it has to offer can be a big attraction for empty-nesters. They use the proximity of a college as a marketing tool, and this approach has been very successful.

Local colleges and universities also offer lectures, seminars, colloquiums, speakers' series, and forums on all manner of topics. Most of these are open to the public and provide a wonderful venue for independent lifelong learning.

Societies and Other Organizations

Open up any newspaper that lists local events and happenings and you're sure to see all types of classes and courses offered by nearby societies and other organizations. For instance, historical societies are always offering lectures; the horticultural society may offer classes for gardeners; and the photography club may teach picture taking. The list goes on. Once you begin looking for lifelong learning opportunities, you will be amazed at what can be found in your community.

Online Courses

The Internet is the newest way to pursue lifelong learning. Many national organizations are already firmly entrenched in cyberspace. For instance, the AARP has dedicated an entire section on its vast website to online courses in such topic areas as computers and technology, history and memory, health and well-being, personal finance, and family caregiving. And then there's the lifelong learning section. A quick glance shows such areas as book reviews, adventures in activism, arts, travel, and music.[11]

The Public Broadcasting Service (*www.pbs.org*) devotes an entire section to lifelong learning. The PBS campus offers more than 120 courses through TV and the Internet for pleasure or for a degree. *P.O.V.*, the award-winning PBS series, offers unique online ways to interact with their programming. Community Engagement campaigns are designed to build audiences, inspire civic dialogue, and, when possible, foster ongoing community involvement in issues raised in selected programs. Check them out at *www.pbs.org/pov*.

Almost all colleges now offer online, noncredit courses through their continuing education departments. A quick Google search, using terms such as "online noncredit courses," will open the door to an incredible array of offerings.

Another excellent online resource is the Great Lecture Library. This site comprises lectures and sermons that have taken place at the Chautauqua Institution. Internationally renowned as a center for education, the arts, religion, and recreation, Chautauqua was founded on the belief that everyone "has a right to be all that he can be—to know all that he can know." In accordance with that belief, it offers a comprehensive online library in order to allow everyone access to over 1,200 lectures and sermons. The library encompasses forty-five major categories of interest, including though not limited to art, business, history, religion, government, health care, the environment, family, and ethics. Perhaps the most exciting aspect of the library is that it has only begun to grow. New speakers and topics are being added to their immense catalogue on an ongoing basis. So be sure to visit their website at *www.greatlecturelibrary.com*.

Thanks to the Internet, learning is truly global and the options are limitless. In the next chapter, you will learn how lifelong learning in other countries has taken on the Internet in a big way.

The best part of online learning? If you can't get out due to weather, illness, or other obstacles, you can learn in the privacy of your own home, at your convenience.

Book Groups

Book groups are not a new phenomenon, but today they are more popular than ever. You will have plenty to choose from—in bookstores, the public library, and even in private homes. They are a wonderful way to keep your brain active and alert.

If the thought of joining a book club appeals to you, ask yourself the following questions:

- What kind of books do I really enjoy reading?
- Do I want a gender-specific or a mixed group?
- What's on the reading list?
- How do members choose the titles?

These questions are important in order to identify the correct book group for you. Try to get a feel for how you would fit into a particular group. If the group isn't right, you won't enjoy yourself and you certainly won't learn. A good group will have members who get along and have the same reading tastes.

Many online book clubs also exist if you can't find one in your area that suits your needs. Search for reading groups under Yahoo Clubs at *www.clubs.yahoo.com*.

Another good source is Book-Clubs-Resource.com at *www.book-clubs-resource.com*. This site hosts a complete guide to book clubs and reading groups. Included on its many informative pages are a huge collection of links, information about using coupon codes with discount book clubs, reader information, and much more. If you have questions about how to start your own reading group or even participate in one online, you'll find plenty of material here to answer all your questions.

Finally, a Google search for book clubs will yield millions of hits. Somewhere, there's a book group that's perfect for you.

Book Group Resources

If you want a group that does more than read the latest best seller, then joining a club that uses one of the following resources might be for you.

Great Decisions. Great Decisions sponsors discussion groups across the United States with the goal of educating people about global affairs. Although not limited to just older adults, Great Decisions discussion groups are sure to educate and inform. Great Decisions celebrated its fiftieth anniversary in 2004; it offers a wide range of other programs, including publishing an annual Briefing Book, Great Decisions TV, a National Opinion Ballot Report, and the *Great Decisions Online* newsletter. Find it at *www.greatdecisions.org*.

Great Books. The Great Books Foundation (GBF) offers busy, engaged adults intellectual stimulation to complement other activities they enjoy. The foundation was established in 1947 by Mortimer Adler, a prolific author and advocate of intellectual pleasure for adults who are not in academia. The foundation grew, spreading a vision of discussion groups in which ardent readers meet and talk about enduring issues and ideas. Today, it comprises some eight hundred groups meeting in homes, libraries, etc., across the country. Thousands of participants help each other reveal the wealth of great written works, using their Shared Inquiry study method. In Shared Inquiry, group members help one another seek answers to questions raised by a text they have read. Participants develop their own unique views of a text, then they try to build on these views by exchanging ideas.

Shared Inquiry discussion leaders act as co-learners. They direct the group by asking interpretive questions that have more than one possible answer based on the text, as well as follow-up questions that encourage participants to clarify comments, support ideas with evidence from the reading, and consider other proposed interpretations.

The foundation also produces anthologies of great, brief writings by authors from all times and places, specifically chosen to be suitable for fruitful discussion. The anthologies provide supporting notes about the author of each text and its important elements, as well as sample questions to initiate discussions.

To learn more about the foundation and its mission, method, anthologies, and so on, please visit their website at *www.greatbooks.org*. To find a group near you, simply call their toll free number: 1-800-222-5870 (8 a.m.–4:30 p.m. CST, Monday through Friday). Callers can follow the prompts or press "0" as directed to reach the operator and ask about the adult programs.

The Teaching Company. The Teaching Company uses DVDs and CDs to bring the best courses directly to you. It seeks out the work of talented professors from top universities and colleges who then develop programs for lifelong learners of all ages. So if you prefer to learn independently, then check out what they have to offer at *www.teach12.com*.

Senior Theatre

Does the smell of greasepaint, the roar of the crowd appeal to you? If

Taking summer mini-courses through the University of Wisconsin helped me learn some basic concepts of good writing. I improved on my knowledge of the basics. I became a biographer in a desire to learn about my ancestors. I began to write family histories and hope to someday see much of my work published. But I never would have tried any of it if it hadn't been for the courses I took.

—Judy Larkin, Madison, Wisconsin

so, a whole new genre of learning has appeared on the scene: senior theatre. All around the world, this new phenomenon is thriving. Whether senior theatres are part of lifelong learning programs, as many are, or stand-alone endeavors, they are hugely popular with older adults who love being onstage.

According to Bonnie L. Vorenberg, president of ArtAge Publications, "What was once a trend is now a movement. New books, plays, research, academic programs, funding, and some healthy media coverage help expand the field. It's challenging, rewarding, and fun. With all this vibrancy, it's a great time to be in senior theatre."

She goes on to say, "The strongest development in senior theatre is the incredible growth in the number of performing groups. In 1999, only seventy-nine senior theatre companies existed. In 2001 there were 291; in 2002 there were 378; and in 2003 there were 419 groups. You can imagine my excitement when last month the number of senior theatre companies in the United States topped 530. The growth is astonishing."

Bonnie also says, "Senior theatre companies range from amateur to professional and are sponsored by such diverse groups as educational institutions, retirement communities, senior centers, and community theatre groups."

Senior theatre is the perfect way to let the wisdom and insight of older adults shine. Works include reminiscence, life review, dance, and exploration of family and social topics. The stage is the perfect venue for a discussion of topics of concern to audience members, such as health and wellness, volunteerism, women's rights, and the environment, to name just a few.

Senior theatre—it might be just what you've been looking for! Find out more at *www.seniortheatre.com.*

Study Circles

Want to start your own lifelong learning group? Study circles may be your answer. Study circles are a simple yet powerful method for learning; they rely on the skills, knowledge, and experience of their members. They expand horizons by ensuring that the differing viewpoints of all members are heard. A study circles is small-group democracy in action, and as such, it requires a leader who can help give the group focus, while at the same time encouraging group ownership of the discussion.[12]

Although leaders do not have to be experts in the topics under discussion, they need to have enough familiarity with the subjects to be able to raise viewpoints that have not been considered by the group. Leaders come from all walks of life, and most have not had formal training in group leadership.

Manuals and other resources are available to help get a study circle started, to train leaders, and to develop a curriculum. One source for these materials is the Study Circles Resource Center at *www.studycircles.org*. The Study Circles Resource Center is dedicated to finding ways for all kinds of people to engage in dialogue and problem solving on critical social and political issues. SCRC helps communities by giving them the tools to organize productive dialogue, recruit diverse participants, find solutions, and work for action and change.[13]

In Pursuit of Lifelong Learning

For those of you who are committed to lifelong learning, the following list from Autodidactic Press—*www.autodidactic.com*—is an excellent compendium of ways to keep lifelong learning in your everyday life. Autodidactic Press is dedicated to two propositions:

- That lifelong learning is fundamental to living a full and interesting life
- That the learning necessary to gain competence in a job or career is far, far more important than how or where it was acquired

According to the site,

Self-education is the essence of genuine learning. Self-education provides the vitality that enables us to turn information into knowledge and to use it in such a way that it adds meaning to life. Indeed, without the dynamism of self-education, we fail to develop our own interests to the degree that they become driving forces in their own right. When our motivation arises from internal sources the value of lifelong learning becomes readily apparent to us.

Adult learning is more than alternative education, self-help, self-study or training. Self-directed inquiry can free you from the cultural traps of today's postmodern world. When you think for yourself, you take control of your life. Intellectual ability and critical thinking soon become substitutes for paper credentials. You'll enjoy a higher quality of life, make smarter career choices, and begin to see ways to better our society.[14]

52 Ways to Pursue Lifelong Learning

1. Look up a new word every morning and figure out three ways to use it during the day.

2. Read that book you picked up months ago and haven't opened yet.

3. Listen to audio books or language tapes while you drive.

4. Watch only informative TV shows.

5. Write a letter to the editor of the newspaper or magazine of your choice expressing your opinion on the issue.

6. Find out how to send email to the president or another lawmaker of your choice. See if you can get a dialogue going.

7. Investigate one or more newsgroups on the Internet and check in at least once a day.

8. Attend an open meeting or public forum each noon hour or evening for a week.

9. Sign up for a night course, workshop, or seminar.

10. If you work in a large company or organization, pay a visit each day to someone you barely know—in another department, for instance. Get better acquainted with these people; find out more about their work and how it relates to your own.

11. Take photos of ten things (places, objects, people) that best symbolize who you are. Then take ten more of things that represent your dreams. (Twelve each would fill a twenty-four-exposure roll.) Put the photos together in an album or a montage.

12. Pick two prominent figures—one from history and one now living. Find out as much as you can about their roles in society, their family lives, and their accomplishments. Then make a side-by-side list comparing the two.

13. Visit a library or bookstore every day and spend some time looking through sections you've never explored before. Make a list of the

titles or subjects you find to be most interesting.

14. Attend a lecture.

15. Go to a foreign movie—or to a foreign country.

16. Compile a reading list of books you intend to read during the next year, and pick one to start off with.

17. Plan or start your own personal library of the books that mean the most to you.

18. Share with others a list of the most inspiring books you have ever read.

19. Reread a book you thought was difficult or over your head the first time you tried it.

20. Form a roundtable discussion group to discuss books and ideas.

21. Join or start a friends of the public library group.

22. Join a book club.

23. Choose a prominent figure in history, science, politics, or the arts. Resolve to see how much you can find out about that person in books, movies, newspapers, and conversation with friends and associates over the next year. Study the person's original work, and compare your opinions with the commentary of others.

24. Write an article for your company, institution, hobby, club, or community organization newsletter or magazine.

25. Write a letter to the editor of your local paper. See how clearly and succinctly you can make your point.

26. Visit a museum or gallery.

27. Sign up for a class on a subject that's new to you but highly interesting.

28. Offer to teach a class for a community education enterprise. (A sure way to learn a subject is to teach it.)

29. Listen to literary classics or foreign language instruction tapes in your car every day for a week, instead of music.

30. Watch an hour of public television each night instead of cable.

31. Practice the tutorials for a new piece of computer software.

32. Write a brief summary of your life so far, or depict your life graphically on a large sheet of paper.

33. Spend a week reading material with which you strongly disagree.

34. Create (or update) your resume.

35. Search a large computer database using your favorite subjects as key words.

36. Write your own obituary. What goals do you hope to meet in your lifetime? What do you want most people to remember about you?

37. Spend some time asking the oldest (and hopefully the wisest) people you know what were the major lessons that they have learned from life.

38. Read the *Declaration of Independence* and the *Constitution of the United States*.

39. Volunteer eight hours of your time to a nonprofit organization.

40. Spend a day or a week "media-free"—no radio, TV, books, or magazines—and entertain nothing but your own thoughts.

41. Peruse introductory books to philosophy with the goal of discovering your favorite philosopher.

42. Sign up for music lessons.

43. Learn enough of a computer programming language to write a simple program.

44. Set aside a half-hour each day to examine some of your fundamental beliefs about the world. Contrast them with opposing views. For example, why do you belong to one political party instead of another? And are your reasons for believing as you do your own, or did you borrow them from friends and family in the process of growing up?

45. Outline the major events in your life as if it were a play. How many acts would there be and how would they be named? What would be the name of the play?

46. Study the nature of your career, occupation, or the means with which you earn a living, and make some predictions about the future of that enterprise. If you are retired, examine the career field of a friend or relative.

47. Write an essay (or make a list) describing what you think were the greatest errors and accomplishments of the twentieth century. How can these lessons make life better in the twenty-first century?

48. If you are a worker, read a book about management; if you are a manager, read a book written from the perspective of workers.

49. Take the time to master that piece of hi-tech equipment that you dread the most. Read the instruction manual; call the engineers who designed it.

50. Memorize a poem.

51. Take an art class.

52. Subscribe to the *Self-University Newsletter* (Autodidactic Press).

The above ideas are just a few of the lifelong learning opportunities that can be found both in your community and online. They are meant to be a starting point for you to begin your journey of self-discovery and learning. If you keep your eyes and ears open, and read notices on bulletin boards, the small print in newspapers, and local flyers in stores, libraries, and other places, you will begin to realize just how many choices and selections there are right in your own backyard to keep your mind active and alert. Searching them out is half the fun.

INTERVIEW WITH AN EXPERT

Carol Greenfield

Carol Greenfield is the founder and president of Discovering What's Next: ReVitalizing Retirement, a volunteer-led, community-based organization in Newton, Massachusetts, that seeks to provide midlife and older adults with information, interaction, inspiration, and opportunities for community involvement. Greenfield is also principal at What's Next Lifestage Consulting, where she works with businesses and organizations to prepare them for the aging of the baby boomer generation. After receiving her master's degree from the Harvard School of Public Health, Greenfield pursued a career in public health and aging.

Give us an example of one type of programming the Newton Free Library in Massachusetts offers for older adults.

Discovering What's Next: ReVitalizing Retirement (DWN) is being offered as quarterly Library Forums on a range of topics. Forum topics include Exploring Your Options for the Future, Can I Really Afford to Retire, Work in Retirement: Opportunities and Realities, Resiliency in the Face of Life Changes, Prime Time: How Baby Boomers Will Revolutionize Retirement, Exploring Your Options for Lifelong Learning, My Time: Growth, Love, and Relationships in the Bonus Years, Looking (after) Yourself after Fifty: Our Quest for Rejuvenation, Exploring Your Creative Side, and Being Your Own Boss after Fifty: Self-Employment.

In addition, we opened a Discovering What's Next Hub at the library in the fall of 2005. This is a one-stop shopping center for midlife and older adults who are transitioning to and within retirement; it is staffed by Transition Navigators—trained volunteers who can assist visitors in navigating to community and other resources as they journey through this life stage.

What makes a library so valuable for this type of programming?

The library is the focal point of community collaboration. We have developed a unique way for community organizations to collaborate to connect midlife and older adults with the resources they need and to each other.

What do you see in the future for the use of libraries as a resource for older adults?

The library has tremendous potential as a resource for midlife and older adults. The baby boom generation in particular has a view of senior services that is equated with being served. They still feel like they want to continue to be the servers going forward. Libraries are age-neutral and intergenerational and thereby have the potential to attract midlife and older adults in new ways that serve this population and the community at large.

The one limiting factor is that programs at libraries must be free of charge. Therefore, the development of effective programs like Discovering What's Next will require funding from foundations and sponsorships from the private sector. Fee for service is not an option.

As for the future, I hope that libraries will look toward having a new kind of collection—a collection of people assets—that can be tapped to serve community needs. Discovering What's Next is working on developing such a collection—a so-called asset database—that can be deployed in new ways to provide meaningful service opportunities as well as meet community needs.

LEARNING LATER, LIVING GREATER
MY WAY!

Nancy Green

Nancy Green is a member of the Oak Hammock Lifelong Learning Institute in Gainesville, Florida.

My husband and I moved to Oak Hammock, in Gainesville, Florida, several years ago. Oak Hammock is a retirement community devoted to lifelong learning and complete health care to the end of one's life. Here, I am free to pick and choose my activities in the independent living stage of my life, but should health problems arise, I can move to assisted living, rehabilitation, or skilled nursing, whichever I need.

Oak Hammock has an active interaction with the University of Florida. We may attend lectures, take classes, go to sports events and concerts, even participate in research projects. Our on-site lifelong learning program offers lectures, concerts, and classes on our campus as well. In addition to all of this, the residents of Oak Hammock have also organized their own painting classes; gardening club; woodworking, bridge, poker, and book clubs; and music groups.

When I retired from teaching in 1999, I found myself at home alone doing not much more than playing solitaire on the computer, reading, and watching TV. I was becoming very aware that I was growing *old!* I couldn't move without my bones and joints aching. My ankles would not support my weight. I had lost contact with my still-working colleagues. I felt that I had no friends, and I was growing depressed.

Now, after moving here, I work out in the fitness center every day, alternating between weights and a Pilates class. I facilitate a book club, I have organized a chorus, I take classes that interest me, and I attend concerts and art shows at the university. My calendar is so full of things I love to do that I have to consult it every day or I miss something! And the difference in my attitude and sense of well-being is something you would not believe. Occasionally, my hip joints get stiff, but my ankles no longer hurt and I can walk briskly. There is a smile on my face every morning when I wake up. I feel younger and brighter. I know from this experience how much stimulating activities can increase the joy of living.

Charting My Journey

• • • •

Charting My Journey

• • • •

Chapter Eight

The International Perspective

All men, by nature, desire to know.
—Aristotle

Since the development in New York City of the Institute for Retired Professionals in 1962, the concept of lifelong learning for older adults has spread around the world. Programs may differ slightly from one country to the next, but the mission of all the programs is the same: providing stimulating educational opportunities for older adults so they can continue learning and interacting.

Whatever the country, in the words of Swindell and Thompson,[1] today everyone realizes that:

- Education can foster older adults' self-reliance and independence, thereby reducing the increasing demands being made on public and private resources.

- Education is a major factor in enabling older people to cope with innumerable practical and psychological problems in a complex, changing, and fractured world.

- Education for and by older adults strengthens their actual or potential contribution to society.

- Older adults' self-awareness, self-interpretations, and communication of their experiences to other generations foster balance, perspective, and understanding—qualities that are valuable in a rapidly changing world.

- Education is crucial for many older adults who strive for expression and learning.

> U3A Online courses offer so much for so little cost.
>
> —U3A Online course participant

With these precepts in mind, let's take a look at the international perspective on lifelong learning for older adults.

History

In Europe, the concept of a place of learning for older citizens was launched in France in 1972. A highly rated gerontology course, run by the University of Social Sciences, Toulouse, exclusively for local retired people, led to the formation of the first University of the Third Age (UTA). Although called universities, these organizations have no educational qualifications for membership. Those who teach are also those who learn, and all are members of the University of the Third Age.[2]

By 1975, the idea had spread to other French universities, as well as universities in Belgium, Switzerland, Poland, Italy, Spain, and even across the Atlantic to a university in Quebec.

When the movement reached the United Kingdom in 1981, however, the French model underwent a significant change. Rather then relying on university goodwill, the founders of the British model adopted an approach in which there was to be no distinction between the teachers and the taught. Members would be the teachers as well as the learners.

In other words, the British model was and is more autonomous, community-based, and member-taught, while the French model is directly affiliated with a university and is extremely academic- and research-oriented.

The self-help approach adopted by the British has been very successful there, as well as in Canada, Australia, and New Zealand. Some of the strengths of the British approach include:

- minimal membership fees
- accessible classes offered in community halls, libraries, private homes, schools, and so on, with flexible timetables
- negotiable curricula and teaching styles
- wide course variety, ranging from the highly academic to arts, crafts, and physical activity
- no academic constraints such as entranced requirements or exami-

nations

- the opportunity to mix with alert, like-minded people who enjoy doing new things

Since the early years, the lifelong learning movement has spread far and wide to countries all around the world. These programs vary in their concept and design. Some are modeled on the French version, others on the British, and still others are a mix of both. To see the global impact of lifelong learning, check out the U3A website at *www.worldu3a.org*. This site does an excellent job of bringing U3As around the world together.

Today, most continental programs call their programs UTAs instead of U3As, which is the more popular form in English-speaking countries such as the United Kingdom, Australia, New Zealand, and Canada.

International Networks

International networks exist to provide important services and help to individual programs. Here are the main ones:

The International Association of Universities of the Third Age (AIUTA) was formed in 1976. This organization and programs in many countries have joined, primarily to take part in conferences and ongoing research.

The Third Age Trust is the national representative body for the U3A movement in the United Kingdom and includes all the programs in that country. The Third Age Trust provides a wide range of services, including a magazine, *Third Age News*, an annual national conference, insurance for local U3As, sponsorship of research projects, a national travel club, material for curriculum networks, study resources (including the magazine *Sources*), and other relevant services.

Third Age Learning International Studies (TALIS) was created in 1990 as an international forum for older adult learners, teachers, programmers, and researchers. Different countries host annual seminars, and members generally represent third age educational grassroots organizations. Membership is composed of a core of continuing members. Members generally communicate at the annual conferences, where they share program information, deliver their research, and build international bridges of understanding.[3]

> When I eventually retired, I discovered U3A Online, which seemed an excellent way of keeping the mind active. I have found it is a lot more.
>
> —U3A Online course participant

In 2000, Canada developed its own national organization, the Canadian Network for Third Age Learning (CATALIST). The purpose of this bilingual network is to promote and support older-adult learning organizations by sharing information and resources, including federal and provincial government assistance programs. Approximately fifty programs belong to CATALIST, many of which also belong to the Elderhostel Institute Network. Most of the Canadian programs are university-affiliated and are a mix of the British and French models. Visit the CATALIST website, which can be found at *dev.www.uregina.ca/catalist*.

U3As Around the World

Each U3A in the United Kingdom is independent and is run by a democratically elected management committee of members. Today, there is a very strong network of more than 550 U3As with more than 150,000 members. These U3As are all members of the Third Age Trust, the national umbrella organization. For more information, visit their website at *www.u3a.org.uk*.

Most of the UTAs in continental Europe—and there are programs in every country—are linked in varying ways to universities, more like the French model than the British one. All programs have very high academic standards and strong research components. Most are members of the international organization, AIUTA. To see a list of international programs in Europe, be sure to visit the AIUTA website at *www.aiuta.assoc.fr* or the international U3A website at *www.worldu3a.org*.

The British model of U3A was introduced in Melbourne, Australia, in 1984. Within ten years, the movement was providing a wide variety of intellectually demanding courses, crafts workshops, and social activities to more than one hundred groups. Today, the Australian lifelong learning movement is thriving. Not only do they have more than 160 programs, with over fifty thousand members throughout the country, they have also developed the first website that enables their far-flung citizens, many in very remote areas, to take online courses. To get an idea of what courses are being offered, check out *www.u3aonline.org*.

U3A programs did not come to New Zealand until 1989, when the first program was developed in Auckland. Since then, the movement has been spreading throughout the country; today, there are more than fifty programs with close to ten thousand members. Each group is independent and modeled on the British example. Although many of the programs take place in private homes, the educational content remains high. U3As in New Zealand share many resources with Australia, such as the online courses and a main website. Like Australia, they do not have a national coordinating organization. To find programs in New Zealand, check out the Australian site at *www.3.griffith.edu.au/03/u3a*.

In China, the U3A movement entered the country in the 1980s, and today China has the largest number of U3As—more than nineteen thousand, with almost two million members. Universities for the Aged (UAs), another movement in China, has almost three million citizens taking classes at special schools or universities throughout the country. Since the end of the Cultural Revolution, Chinese governments have regarded education as important for helping the more than one hundred million older Chinese people to adapt to social change. This emphasis on education has led to a strong lifelong learning movement for older adults.

The lifelong learning movement in Japan is rather new, but thanks to lifelong learning legislation, large numbers of older Japanese adults now take classes in *elderly colleges*. More specialized programming is being planned, and programs similar to Lifelong Learning Institutes are also being developed.

Curriculum

Like Lifelong Learning Institutes in the United States, U3As abroad study popular subjects such as literature, music, science, government, artistic hobbies, drama, play reading, poetry, art, computing, news and debate, exercise, current events, creative writing, and personal history. Courses offered at the U3As vary widely in content, style of presentation, and format. In general, they include open lectures, negotiated access to established university courses, contracted courses, discussion study groups, workshops, excursions, and physical health programs.

Language is high on the curriculum want list in other countries, but lower on the list of priorities for U.S. members. U3A members pride themselves on their ability to grasp a foreign language and then use it by traveling to that country and, it is hoped, perfecting it. Although lifelong learners in the United States also do a lot of traveling, they usually speak English no matter where they are.

Online Courses

Yet another way that U3As differ from LLIs in the United States is through their use of the Internet to bring courses to isolated older adult learners. In Australia, they have developed an extensive website to help distribute courses to U3A members throughout the world who cannot attend regular courses.

U3A Online, the first U3A in cyberspace, was started in 1998. Its main aim was to provide interesting, intellectually challenging activities via the Internet for seniors who become isolated from mainstream activities in their community. Isolation is common in later life, caused by many circumstances, such as bereavement, illness, disability, caring for others, inadequate transport, and so on. The project has also proved popular with many other seniors who have been attracted by the wide variety of high-quality courses, which have been written by retired volunteers.[4]

The site is full of information on programs, curriculum, and other topics of interest. Find them at *www.3.griffith.edu.au/03/u3a*. It will give you an excellent feel for the very impressive scope of their online lifelong learning courses for older adults.

According to a 1996 "UNESCO Task Force on Education for the Twenty-First Century" report, education is at the heart of both "personal and community," development; its mission is to enable us, without exception, to develop all our talents. Lifelong learning for older adults certainly fits that mandate, as it is a powerful tool for developing one's self to the fullest.

Lifelong learning for older adults is thriving in other countries. The European Parliament declared 1996 the Year of Lifelong Learning, and thirteen countries have developed lifelong learning policy initiatives. The need for social capital, along with rapidly advancing technology, has brought lifelong learning to the attention of just about everyone.

AGE, the European Older People's Platform, was recently established to voice the interests of older and retired people with EU institutions. Lifelong learning is one of the topics AGE will be addressing; it has become an important part of the new social goal of the EU. The aim is to launch a European debate on a comprehensive strategy for implementing lifelong learning at individual and institutional levels and in all spheres of public and private life.

In Far Eastern countries, lifelong learning programs aimed at enhancing computer skills and personal enrichment, among other things, are now in the start-up phase. In Japan, the Cabinet Office's 2001 white paper on the aging of society cites "a high interest in lifelong learning" and "a strong ability to adapt to IT" as features of the baby boomer generation.

According to an opinion poll on lifelong learning conducted by the Japanese government in 1999, only 10 percent of those in their fifties cited standing out at work as a goal of lifelong learning, compared with 25 percent who cited the aim of improving their family or daily life in the community.

Universities of the Third Age, like Lifelong Learning Institutes in the United States, offer older adults a chance to meet new friends and a variety of opportunities to use their knowledge, skills, and experience—and to acquire new ones—in an informal, friendly atmosphere.

Older adult lifelong learners around the world may, as the Third Age Trust says, "be retired, but they are not retiring!"

Interview with an Expert

Jean Thompson

Jean Thompson has been active in the U3A movement since 1987. She served six years on the National Executive Council and was national chairman from 1992 to 1995. Jean now coordinates two networks: Internetwork, which encourages the use of computer technology and resources, and International U3A, which links internationally minded members from around the world. She was elected to the Association Internationale des Universites du Troisieme Age (AIUTA) Governing Board in 1994 and was the U3A International representative for six years. Jean encouraged the growth of U3A Online courses and is a writer/tutor for three of them.

How do you think belonging to U3As has changed the lives of the members?

U3As provide an active social life with many opportunities for discovering new interests and continuing to learn.

Do U3As have any plans to make changes to appeal to the coming wave of baby boomer retirees?

Yes, indeed. This is one of the main subjects for discussion at our August national conference.

Are any special plans in the works for new and innovative programming?

Local U3As (550 of them) are thinking hard. Their ideas will be discussed at the national conference. In the meantime, our members are very active in our online courses and in communicating with other older adult learners all over the world. The International U3A Network works through its website at *www.worldu3a.org*. Your readers are welcome to join its discussion list "cooperation" and to take part in its projects. The URL for this section is *www.worldu3a.org/cooperation/myu3a.htm*.

Have U3As received any special recognition from official government or academic sources?

Yes. In the past, we have talked with government ministers and those involved in adult learning programs. One of our ex-chairmen has been awarded an OBE for services to U3A. (Several of our Australian colleagues have received official recognition for their U3A work with the award of an AM.) In the United Kingdom, we have an active joint research program with museums, the Royal Institute, theatres, and universities.

What do you know about similar programs in other European countries?

Lots. I have visited many of them and collected personal accounts of UTAS from twelve countries so far in the ongoing project on *www.worldu3a.org* under "My U3A." Also see the French website: *www.aiuta.asso.fr.*

What do you see as the future of U3As in Great Britain?

I expect U3As to go from strength to strength from our present membership of 150,000 in more than 550 local U3As. Each group is self-supporting and runs its own program from its own resources, which makes it a dynamic and democratic setup. The U3A model has already been adopted in Australia and New Zealand, and it has recently spread to South Africa, Cyprus, and Spain.

Thoughts on Older Adults
and the Internet

Tom Holloway

Tom Holloway describes himself as "a community webmonger."
He set up the first UK email network for Lloyds and the insurance industry in 1973. His reminiscence website, *www.timewitnesses.org*, grew out of his work for his charity for
speech-impaired children, and he is still very active in The
International Network for Universities of the Third Age,
www.worldu3a.org.

One of the most exciting things about the Internet is that people in
every community and every age group believe it belongs to them. Just
occasionally, I get the chance to remind younger audiences of teachers and
professionals that, in fact, it was the Elderhostel and U3A generations that
invented and developed it all.

Naturally, I thank them for joining us in this great adventure, but I
sometimes wonder what sort of Internet our current crop of young people
are going to inherit. I suspect it won't be anything like the one we have
now.

I reckon we made a good start, however. As far as I know, the
Memories project we started in the late 1980s was the first major attempt
at an international schools project—now absorbed into *www.timewitnesses.org* and still popular; and the intergenerational email projects we run
at *www.WorldU3A.org* are still pointing the way for schools around the
world.

But anyone who has sat behind a group of these brilliant kids as they
play their interactive online games or twitter endlessly to each other via
messenger or ICQ over vast distances, like flocks of virtual starlings, will be
aware that the Web is already changing beyond our comprehension; it is
being shaped by forces, good and bad, that we barely understand and certainly cannot control.

But that doesn't mean we don't matter anymore—far from it—and it's my belief that precisely *because* of the pace of change, they need us more than ever. They have patted us on the head and made us comfortable for our sunset years, but without our presence and the perspective and experience that we bring, they will be deprived of a worldview, an understanding, that they will certainly need to guide them as they travel through their own second age and eventually become the third agers of the future.

To avoid that, I believe we must be prepared to approach PTAs, schools, and school boards with suggestions for curriculum-based email projects involving elders. Yes, there *are* issues of safety and security, but they can be overcome; they have been overcome by personal contacts and diplomacy. Two websites that will give you excellent examples of what has worked in the past are *www.timewitnesses.org* and *www.worldu3a.org/cooperation/-breakfast.htm*. It isn't true that we don't matter anymore and that we can now relax into an exciting and active retirement—far from it. It's my belief that precisely *because* of the pace of change, our children and grandchildren need us more than ever, and they need us available and online.

Up Close and Personal

Harriet Joachim Leckich

Harriet Joachim Leckich is director of the Mississippi Gulf Coast Community College Lifelong Learning Institute.

A few months ago, I answered my office telephone and there was a quiet pause before the voice on the other end said, "This isn't the Jackson, Mississippi zoo, is it?" I replied the usual, "Yes, this is the zoo, but not the one you want."

The voice on the other end was Dorothy Magruder, a charter member of our Gulfport, Mississippi, Community College Lifelong Learning Institute, founded in 1996. Our Lifelong Learning Institute is a participant-driven program. Committees composed of members make all the "who, what, when, where" decisions that determine the courses and activities.

By joining MGCCC-LLI each year, you can travel to interesting places, take classes, attend monthly luncheon lectures, or learn the most recent computer and mixed-media technology. Although members are retired from a wide range of backgrounds and experiences, all MGCCC-LLI participants share in common a belief in lifelong learning and friendship.

Dorothy Magruder, one of our most witty, active lifelong learners, died suddenly of a heart attack on Monday, May 9, 2005. This story is a tribute to her.

Laughter is a great release when we get ultra-absorbed in life's expected and unexpected experiences, or when we are overcome by the ambivalent and frequently paradoxical dimensions of life and sudden death. When we suddenly lose a special friend, we straddle that awkward place between our faith and our feelings. Our linear mind cannot filter our human feelings of pain, grief, and sorrow or our unwillingness to let go. Aware of hope, filled with teachings of resurrection and eternal life, we find ourselves suspended in a fog of paradox. Laughter helps us navigate through that fog.

Lightening up was an effective and essential dimension of Dorothy's daily life of service. She frequently expressed how humor helped lighten heavy loads. "Without humor," she once stated, "we lose the spark and passion that is needed to serve others well. Without laughter, I doubt even Jesus could have kept Himself sane in the midst of so many daily challenges to His enthusiasm."

Dorothy's experiences at our lifelong learning program were many and varied.

Dorothy's legacy of loyalty and laughter creates an added dimension that lifelong learners experience as narrative medicine. Her twenty-five years of volunteer service at the Biloxi, Mississippi Armed Forces-Kessler Family Clinic provide an excellent example of what constitutes good lifelong learners' narrative medicine:

- Weekly experiences far outside of the ordinary
- Temporal evolution
- Character development
- Plenty of dramatic tension
- Trillions of laughs

In her experience as a patient activist, Dorothy compassionately listened to and helped many to transform their confusion and fear into a structured story line with a sharper focus. People who crossed Dorothy's path knew they were being heard and respected beyond their clinical and biological data.

Dorothy once told me, "There is no such thing as an 'uninteresting person.' These patients—strangers, like all of us lifelong learners—are in need of listening hearts and hands, people who can lead and intercede with good reflection-action-evolution. The end result of compassionate connection is the same as being involved in an LLI—maturation."

Dorothy's life and service reminds us to synthesize wisdom from our long life experience and to treat strangers with reverence and kindness. She often reminded her peers that "God came to earth as a stranger!"

One day, an elderly, frail woman appeared in the clinic while Dorothy was on duty. Dorothy quietly asked, "Ever been in a hospital?"

"Once," replied the woman.

"When?" Dorothy inquired.

"In 1912," came the answer, "because of a broken arm."

"How did you break your arm?"

"A trunk fell on it!" replied the woman.

"What kind of trunk?"

"A steamer trunk from the boat I was traveling on."

"How did a steamer trunk fall on your arm?"

"Well, the boat I was traveling on lurched."

"What boat?"

"Oh, the R.M.S. *Titanic!*"

The woman had been a passenger in steerage when the doomed ship hit the iceberg. Despite the broken arm, she made it to a lifeboat and was taken to safety, eventually making her way to California and Mississippi—where she and her husband retired.

Serving and compassionately loving others by helping, holding, listening, healing, teaching, learning, and laughing in life are, in part, narrative acts—the human capacity to understand their meaning, significance, and gift is in every life story. To recount the insights and gifts gained in the roundabout way we humans travel—to recognize, to reconsider, to retrace, to revisit questions, and consequently to learn and relearn the truth we have mined in the deep discovery and continual adventure of maturing in lifelong learning IS life's ever unfolding path.

Dorothy Magruder's legacy is that she created something altogether new in every moment, while at the same time pointed to what was to come. She discovered new life as a consequence of the maturation process because she saw and acted upon what was beyond the physical level of life.

The purpose of being engaged in lifelong learning is this maturation process; not simply to continue or elongate what was about life, but a process that creates something altogether new in this very moment, while at the same time pointing to what's to come.

The Dorothy Magruders of the world strengthen and extend our lifelong learning roots, and they expand our lifelong learning reach. We are profoundly grateful that Dorothy and her legacy were part of our lifelong learning institute here in Mississippi.

Our ageless friend has spread her wings in an eternal flight. Dorothy, who opened her hands to serve, and her heart to intercede with gladness, unconditional love, acceptance, forgiveness, and humor, has now become an ageless angel who will always be the wind beneath our wings.

Learning Later, Living Greater
My Way!

By H. Peter Sinclair

H. Peter Sinclair is a life president of Harrow U3A, London, England.

Several good friends had told me about U3A following my retirement. I joined a local U3A group in central London (England), some fifteen miles from my home, and began attending their outstanding weekly Monday morning lecture meetings.

A few months later, after hearing that a new U3A group, nearer my home, was about to be launched, I attended the initial gathering. Approximately fifty retired men and women had gathered in a church hall to discuss the group's formation, and many enthusiastically volunteered to serve on a local management team. Given my existing involvement with the U3A in London, I was asked to become chairman, and Harrow U3A began. From a founding member, I became founding chairman, a position I held for more than four years.

Much has been written about the necessity for older adults to keep mind and body active by joining dedicated organizations like U3A or their equivalent in other countries. Their importance, diversity, scope, common purpose, and necessity are universally acknowledged.

My particular interest also involved making use of a then relatively novel medium—the Internet. At the beginning of 1996, local U3A groups in the United Kingdom did not have their own websites. Harrow U3A's website, at *www.harrowu3a.co.uk*, launched in the fall of that year, was the first.

I was also determined to include a webpage with links to other similar institutions anywhere in the world, which I named www Links. I felt there was increasing interest in creating greater international understanding and cooperation to cater to the continued mental and physical welfare of an exponentially growing elderly population

Initially, progress was slow. Google was not in existence at that time, and Internet search engines were in their early stages of development. One of my first links abroad was in Australia, followed by others in the United States. Little by little, my collection of links to local U3A groups in the United Kingdom and equivalent organizations abroad grew.

The Elderhostel Institute Network—*www.elderhostel.org/ein/intro.asp*—in the United States, was particularly helpful in providing me with up-to-date information and links in their country as well as in Canada and Bermuda. In Germany, I had the invaluable assistance of "Learning in Later Life" (*www.lill-online.net*). Within two years, we had a substantial list of valuable links, and now there are several hundred links to websites in the United Kingdom and abroad in no fewer than twenty-eight countries. And there are now more than 150 U3A websites in the United Kingdom alone. I was very fortunate in receiving wholehearted support from many hundreds of my webmaster contacts, in the United Kingdom and abroad, who gladly established reciprocal links to our Harrow U3A website WWW Links at *www.harrowu3a.co.uk/u3a_sites.html*.

This cross-fertilization has proved to be enormously beneficial and useful to Internet users in the global village, and it also has led to the establishment of new groups and new websites. Most important, it has enabled those looking on the Web for a local group of like-minded people to locate contacts for further information.

I am confident that the international aspect of lifelong learning programs for older adults, which provide the mental and physical stimulation we all need, will assume an ever-growing dimension in all our societies.

Charting My Journey

....

Charting My Journey

• • • •

PART FOUR

Up, Up,
and
Away!

Chapter Nine

Lifelong Learning through Educational Travel

The real meaning of travel, like that of a conversation by the fireside,
is the discovery of oneself through contact with other people.
And its condition is self-commitment in the dialogues.
—Paul Tournier

Educational travel—where the world, as Elderhostel says, really is your classroom. What an exciting thought for those of us planning for our after-fifty years. What a wonderful vehicle for our continued exploration of ourselves and all we have to offer to society.

Educational travel is tremendously helpful in this self-exploration. It helps us understand and appreciate different cultures. It also changes us by broadening our perspectives and teaching us about new ways to measure our quality of life.

While we are still part of the workforce, however, we usually cannot take the time off that is necessary for truly in-depth educational travel. Despite our dedication to free enterprise and the American way, it is said that people in the United States actually work more hours than people in any other country. We simply do not have enough time to really explore what the world has to offer.

All that changes, however, once we leave the workforce and embark on the journey of our after-fifty years.

About Educational Travel

Today, people tend to think the words *travel* and *vacation* are synonymous. They think of them as ways to avoid work, seek out leisure, and avoid anything serious. But please don't confuse the two. There is a real difference.

Vacations are just that—vacations—and they certainly have a valuable place in our lives. But in this book, we are talking about travel—educational travel. Yes, educational travel is fun, but at the same time, you are also learning about the history, culture, and politics of your destinations, and you are absorbing the essence of the places you are visiting. You are not soaking up the sun on a beach or heading toward the eighteenth hole. Those things belong in another part of your life.

As technology shrinks our world and brings us all closer together, the opportunity to learn about our neighbors grows. Don't we owe it to ourselves to delve into this landscape and explore the cultures of different people? By doing so, we learn all about their history, the rise of their civilization, and perhaps even its downfall. By viewing both the highs and the lows, we come away with a much better view of not just them, but also of ourselves. Educational travel gives us the ability to do this in ways nothing else can. It gives us the opportunity to immerse ourselves in the exotic spectrum of life on Earth.

Educational travel leaves us with much more than a typical vacation. We gain a deeper knowledge of the world. We get to experience life—to truly live it. It can be a life-changing experience.

Benefits of Educational Travel

Here are just a few of the many benefits you will derive from educational travel:

- View beautiful and historic sites

My wife and I started Elderhosteling in 1982, and we finished our thirtieth trip early in 2005, with another scheduled for mid-August of that year in West Virginia. Our studies have taken us to almost twenty of the contiguous United States. My wife's sister and her husband have taken more than 130 Elderhostel excursions. My brother and sister-in-law are both staunch Elderhostelers. The adventures we've all had are enough for many books. I guess you could say we're an Elderhostel family.

—George Hartman, Bridgewater, Virginia

- Learn about the culture and history of faraway places
- Discover, learn, and grow
- Challenge inhibitions while gaining new perspectives
- Gain a global viewpoint
- Satisfy your curiosity about places of special interest
- Develop lasting memories and friendships
- Step outside your comfort zone

History of Educational Travel

Explorers since the time of the Arabs in AD 800, Marco Polo in AD 1200, and more recently from the Middle Ages on have written memoirs about their travels. Those writings opened the world up for the rest of us to experience. This was the first real incarnation of educational travel.

From the Middle Ages on, northern Europeans traveled to great centers of learning and to the ruins of the classical civilizations of Italy and Greece. These travels were chronicled in letters and other writings sent back to their homelands. These chronicles in turn formed the basis for further exploration and learning. As is evidenced by these works, while they were covering the ground outwardly, they were also advancing inwardly.

In the mid-nineteenth century, thanks to social change and the new technologies of the Industrial Revolution, intrepid men and women traveled throughout the world in organized pursuit of knowledge.[1] And it was during the 1830s that Baedeker wrote the first modern guidebooks.

It has been said that the writings of the men who traveled during this time tended to cover the *what* and *where*, while the women travelers, especially those who traveled during the Victorian Era, the golden age of women travelers, tended toward the *how* and *why*. Even today, their writings fuel the desire in many of us to learn more.

Judith Adler, writing about the history of sightseeing (1989), says, "Most travel was not for sightseeing, but to encounter important people and civilizations and to visit sacred places."[2]

In the nineteenth and early twentieth centuries, independent travel by those who could afford it was just about the only way to learn about other cultures. The Chautauqua movement (see Chapter 2) brought education to the common man, but it was education limited by the boundaries of one's own home and community.

Today, things have changed. People are living longer, and they have more free time and more money. Thanks to technology, they can travel wherever and whenever they want. But the emphasis of most of this travel has not been on education. It's been on having fun, relaxing, and de-stressing.

Colleges and universities have tried over the years to shift that emphasis toward educational travel by offering opportunities to their students and graduates through student exchange, study abroad, and alumni travel programs. Many other people, however, were missing out on the opportunity of learning and traveling at the same time. And of those, most were older adults. There was nothing out there geared specifically to their needs and wants in the way of educational travel.

The lack of educational travel opportunities for older adults came to an end in 1975 when Elderhostel, Inc., came into existence. These modern-day explorers have opened the door to the worldwide opportunities of lifelong learning for older adults. They have brought educational travel into the twenty-first century.

Today, thanks to Elderhostel, the field of educational travel is booming—not just for older adults, but for people of all ages. We will take a look at both the history of Elderhostel and the current state of educational travel in the next chapter.

For now, however, think of travel as an educational, spiritual, and even a creative activity, an activity that broadens our self-understanding.[3] And self-understanding is what the journey of our after-fifty years can be all about.

Format of an Educational Travel Program

Most educational travel programs offer the participant a combination of lectures, field trips, and free time. Here's a quick overview of a typical international program:

In the morning, you might listen to a lecture by a well-known expert in a particular field (for example, on the building of the castles of Germany.) Then you might view a slide show while you're listening to a presentation on the history of the castle inhabitants. After lunch, you might visit one of those castles with your group, armed with what you had learned in the morning and escorted by a competent and knowledgeable guide. Later, you might eat dinner with a local family whose ancestors were directly affected by the daily activities at the castle. At day's end, you drift off to sleep aware that you have experienced a day full of learning, exploring, and personal growth.

Each day's format would roughly follow this outline of lectures, field trips, cultural interaction, and reflection. Each day would be full of activities guaranteed to stimulate the brain cells and keep you challenged while you're still having fun.

Miscellaneous Thoughts about Educational Travel

- Traveling by yourself is easier on an educational travel program because you'll be in the company of like-minded adults, a nice mix of both couples and singles.

- If you prefer, there are organizations that will match you with a traveling companion.

- Regardless of physical capability, special interest, or budgetary challenge, there are a host of exciting travel options for you to consider.

- The travel industry is aware of the growing interest in travel for enrichment, and more and more tour operators are gearing their offerings in this direction.

- Service/educational travel programs are available that offer the opportunity to give of your skills and experience by volunteering in a new location.

When I retired, I realized that for the first time in my life, I truly owned my life. Each day was one of choice for me. No one else owned my time. How was I going to choose to spend it? I wanted to grow, to enlarge myself. What did I want to be? One of the greatest surprises for me upon retirement was to realize that a large slate of educational opportunities was open to me. I began a new adventure in my life, and it's one that continues to provide me with fresh challenges, exciting opportunities, and a wealth of interaction I simply couldn't get anywhere else.

—Patricia Edie, Playa del Rey, California

Cultural Heritage Travel

A close cousin to educational travel, and one that definitely bears mentioning, is a fairly new phenomenon that the U.S. Department of Commerce (USDOC) is calling *cultural heritage tourism*. Cultural heritage tours emphasize authenticity and hands-on participation, with richly orchestrated itineraries, including historic homes, buildings, and locations; art galleries, theatres, and museums; cultural events, festivals, and fairs; ethnic and regional foods and music; ethnic communities; architectural and archeological treasures; and national and state parks. Demand for this type of travel is growing, and according to the USDOC, older Americans are leading the charge. They go on to say that museums have now eclipsed theme parks in popularity among U.S. travelers.[4]

Baby boomers will be seeking a new level of enrichment from leisure activities, and the USDOC's Office of Tourism has partnered with the private sector to create American Pathways tours. American Pathways also helps boost local economic development and pride by harvesting existing assets under the management of those who live the cultural connections, including indigenous peoples.

"The popularity of these tours points to a changing paradigm in our maturing society—the ownership of cultural assets," says Leslie R. Doggett, deputy assistant secretary, Tourism Industries, USDOC, which initiated the program.[5]

To learn more about cultural heritage travel, visit *americanpathways.com*.

If you have already left the workforce, begin to investigate the educational travel options available for mature adults. You'll find many that will make you want to start packing. If you are still working, and free time is at a premium, tuck this away until you are ready to leave the world of work and embark on your own after-fifty voyage. Educational travel is a life-enriching, life-enhancing, and life-prolonging concept that gives you the opportunity to:

- fill your after-fifty years with joy and stimulation
- help change the stereotypical views of older adults
- leave a lasting legacy for the next generation

Educational travel is too important and life changing to miss!

Learning Later, Living Greater My Way!

Jan Schiager

Jan Schiager lives in Salt Lake City, Utah

In 2002, my husband and I embarked on our greatest Elderhostel adventure: a trip to French Polynesia. It began in Tahiti at a somewhat typical resort hotel. The weather was deliciously warm, and since we had left a cold Salt Lake City in March, we were happy. Things really began to get interesting as we boarded our freighter in Papeete.

The Elderhostel group was scheduled to spend more than two weeks aboard a freighter delivering supplies to the Marquesas Islands in the South Pacific. I expected to be thrilled with the sights and experiences on the various islands, but I did not expect to be blown away by the tattooed sailors aboard the freighter. Now, realize that I am your average 64-year-old American female. We see tattoos here in America and are very repulsed. Well, tattooing in French Polynesia is a different story. It is a show of wealth and status for these men. The tattoos portray beautiful designs that are very pleasing to the eye and that show their ancient history. No "I Love Mom" here.

Besides the visual effect of seeing these sailors in tattoos, we began to admire their work skills and organization. They were responsible for delivering supplies (and tourists) to remote islands. For the residents of these islands, these visits were their only contact with the outside world, and it happened only once every three weeks. They needed and received food, beer, cement, horses, refrigerators, automobiles, gasoline—you name it. These beautifully tattooed men organized and sorted all these supplies and delivered them from the freighter to a whale boat or barge and then onto the shore. They also picked up items from the islands to be delivered to other islands or back to Tahiti.

Once when I was swimming off a beach, I suddenly realized that some of the sailors were close by loading several horses into whaleboats. What a surprising sight!

When the sailors weren't lifting freight, they were lifting us, so that we could experience what life was like on the beautiful islands. They would alert us to whether it would be a dry or wet landing as the freighter got close to an island. Often there were no docks; the terrain was too rugged for that. If the sea was rough, the sailors simply picked up passengers to put them in or out of the whaleboats. It became an exciting event and usually happened more than once a day. We were dependent on their skills.

Most of the sailors had tattoos over their arms and chests, but one lead sailor had his entire bald head tattooed. The weather was such that little clothing was necessary for sailors or Elderhostelers alike. These men earned our respect in a very short time. It was absolutely fascinating to watch them work.

Observing the culture of French Polynesia was fascinating. We learned a great deal about their history. It was a wonderful experience, but the highlight for me was meeting these tattooed men. They were beautiful to behold! They lived a life very different from my own, and they taught me the beauty of tattoos.

Life lesson: different isn't always bad!

Charting My Journey

• • • •

Charting My Journey

• • • •

Chapter Ten

Educational Travel Organizations

The world is a book, and those who
do not travel read only a page.
—Saint Augustine

Over the last thirty years, due to the unparalleled success of Elderhostel, Inc., educational travel has grown exponentially. In this chapter, we'll take a look at some of the best programs available to older adults.

Today, travel providers are very aware that educational travel is here to stay. As the baby boomers—the most educated generation in history—move into their later years, travel organizations are scrambling to offer programs with educational content. Not all of them, however, are doing a good job. The less reputable firms simply toss in a lecture or two and call it an educational travel program—a thinly veiled attempt to lure the unsuspecting. So, as with everything else, it's imperative that you do your homework. Look over the itinerary, study the curriculum offerings, and decide for yourself if the program you are interested in will stimulate your intellect and suit your needs.

Since we will be looking at some of the best programs, we therefore begin this chapter with the story of Elderhostel, Inc. As the pioneers and founders of the educational travel industry for older adults, their history sets the tone for this section, and their programs are the "gold standard" by which all other educational travel programs are measured.

The Story of Elderhostel

Take one aging nonconformist, add a college educator, mix in concern for the plight of older adults in the climate of the 1970s, stir well, and serve up a brand-new opportunity for enrichment and fulfillment in your later years—Elderhostel, Inc.

In the late 1960s, Elderhostel cofounders Martin (Marty) P. Knowlton, a social and educational innovator, and David Bianco, a graduate student at Boston University (BU), met while they both worked at the residential student program at BU. They were drawn to each other by the unconventionality of their thinking. Both were impatient with the status quo and wanted to explore ways to make education more meaningful. While they were at BU, they collaborated on an article published in the *Journal of Education* in 1969. In this article, "A Proposal: An Institute of International Life at Boston University," the roots of what would later become Elderhostel were very evident.

Now jump ahead to 1974. Marty Knowlton had just returned from a four-year backpacking trip across Europe. While he was there, he participated in archeological digs in England and Germany and became familiar with youth hostel programs and the folk schools of Scandinavia. He was "impressed by the way in which the availability of a network of modest accommodations encouraged and nurtured an adventuresome hostelling spirit in European youth." He also observed "the very positive impact a residential setting had on adult education programs offered by the folk high schools."[1]

In the meantime, David Bianco, after serving three years as the dean of freshmen at Brandeis University, was now working as director of residential life at the University of New Hampshire (UNH). The university had called for a major effort to look at ways the campus could be utilized during the summer. This led to the development of UNH's American Youth Hostel program, and thanks to their earlier collaboration, Marty was invited to become director of that program.

Reunited, Marty and David once again began to look at innovative ways education could be improved. Marty, just back from his European travels, was talking with David about what he had witnessed. In Marty's words,

> I was talking with David, and I was telling him some of the experiences I'd had in Europe with older people, some of which David found rather exciting. And in a burst of enthusiasm, he said to me, "This campus ought not to be having a youth hostel, it ought to be

having an elder hostel." And there was the day. It was one of those occasions, a serendipitous occasion. The name came first, and we put the program under it."[2]

After that epiphany, it was all hard work on Marty's and David's part. They spent long hours discussing the program concept, what this nontraditional initiative should and should not be, program details, and the cost. Early on, they agreed that the format of the program should mirror that of the European youth hostels—a residential program with simple, affordable accommodations.

Both men strongly believed that "when you're older, you learn every bit as well as you ever learned, and probably better."[3] Therefore, the program would have a strong educational component, but the courses would be not-for-credit. They also agreed that the program would be strictly for older adults, and they set the minimum age at sixty.

From these early brainstorming sessions, other university faculty and administrators became involved. They sent letters to people who would likely be interested in this new and innovative concept of elderlearning.

It was decided that older adults would go to college campuses to attend weeklong educational programs for the joint purposes of "self-enhancement" and the "development of an elderly cadre for community integration."[4] More field study took place. Colleges and older adults were polled about how they saw this kind of program developing and what they wanted offered. After months of hard work writing grant proposals, developing curriculum and marketing materials, and rounding up support, in the summer of 1975, Elderhostel, Inc., opened its doors.

About that first summer, Marty Knowlton says,

We worked like slaves trying to generate an audience for our courses. And the first Elderhostel met and there were only six people. But we held it—we lasted through the week. We were delighted with the experience and so were the hostelers. And the next week, there were seven. And the next week, because the first week group had gone home and begun to talk about it, we had thirteen in the class. And after the fourth week of Elderhostel, for the rest of the summer season, we were filled right up and were beginning to turn people away.[5]

By the end of that first summer, 220 hostelers had stayed in campus dorms while they were attending courses. That number swelled to over three hundred when commuters were added to the mix. When Elderhostel asked the participants if they would like to return the next year, every single participant said "yes." This was the beginning of a pattern of multiple program attendance, of Elderhostelism, as it became known.[6] The hostelers had also shown great enthusiasm and vigor for the educational programs, proving that the idea of older adults as used-up, useless, and incapable of learning was very wrong.

The growth of Elderhostel was phenomenal. In 1975, five New Hampshire colleges offered fifteen weeks of programs to 220 participants. In 1976, twenty-one colleges in six states offered sixty-nine program weeks to two thousand enrollees, and another two thousand applicants were turned away. By the third summer, sixty-one colleges in twelve states offered 156 program weeks, and there were almost six thousand applicants for 4,800 enrollment openings.[7]

The rest, as they say, is history. Within ten years, Elderhostel was offering programs in all fifty states and had begun an international expansion.

Elderhostel Today

Today, Elderhostel is not only the nation's first not-for-profit, educational travel organization for adults age fifty-five and over, it is the largest. From their offices in Boston and their state-of-the-art call center, they offer over ten thousand domestic and international programs of the highest educational quality in over ninety countries, to over two hundred thousand older adults every year.

Elderhostel is proud of its all-inclusive, affordable pricing and strives to keep program costs as low as possible. Elderhostel programs are a superior value because, unlike for tourist travel or commercial tours, with Elderhostel programs there are no hidden expenses. In addition to accommodations, they include all meals, lectures, field trips, cultural excursions, gratuities, and insurance coverage. Elderhostel provides high-quality experiences with an outstanding level of service at an extraordinary value.

Elderhostel takes care of all the details so you don't have to. Whether it's simplifying registration; offering comfortable accommodations in hotels, inns, retreat centers, and select campuses (nearly all with private baths); offering single rooms on almost 90 percent of U.S. and Canada programs; preparing meals infused with local flavor; and having caring staff, everything is taken care of so you can enjoy your program.

The Elderhostel website, at *www.elderhostel.org*, gets over eighty thousand visitors a month, all looking for innovative educational programming. Every one of the more than ten thousand programs is described on their easy-to-use website. The site enables you to register online, contact them by email, and get all the information you need to make an informed decision about your educational travel.

For those without computer access, U.S./Canada, International, and Adventures Afloat catalogs can be obtained by asking to be put on their mailing list. See the Resources section for more information on this.

Elderhostel believes learning is a lifelong pursuit that opens minds and enriches lives. They believe sharing new ideas, challenges, and experiences is rewarding in every season of life. Their participants come from every walk of life to learn together, to exchange ideas, and to explore the world.

Examples of Elderhostel Educational Travel Programs

At the Art Institute: Focus on Impressionism and Post-Impressionism (Reprinted with permission, 2004 Elderhostel, Inc.)

Be introduced to the museum's 19th-Century Impressionist and Post-Impressionist collection through gallery walks, slide lectures and discussions led by staff members from the Department of Museum Education. Courses examine ideas, techniques and achievements in the work of artists such as Monet, Renoir, Cassatt, van Gogh, Gauguin, Toulouse-Lautrec and many others. In addition to outstanding art courses, be instructed in the art of Tai Chi, an ancient exercise that teaches self discipline and body/mind coordination. Gain awareness of physical and mental expression using sustained motions. Tai Chi classes at the club from 8:30–9:30 a.m., no special clothing needed.

Chicago/The Art Institute of Chicago—View a wide range of world art at this remarkable resource: 19th-century paintings, modern and contemporary art, American paintings, sculpture, and decorative arts from the Colonial period to 1900. Textiles, Japanese prints, architectural drawings, and photography are also on view. Located in downtown Chicago's Loop on the Magnificent Mile. Visit the new Millennium Park, a 24-acre public space of sculptures, fountains, and pavilions. Program in association with The Art Institute of Chicago.

Stay at a downtown club with pool and athletic facilities, a 5-minute walk to the museum. Breakfast and dinner at the club, cafeteria lunch at the School of the Art Institute.

Pathways Through Culture—Spain

Your journey through Spain follows the cultural pathways that led this nation from cave to palace, and into the new millennium. Madrid's monuments and museums show you how the Spanish define themselves. Granada, the last Moorish stronghold in Spain, shines with the grandeur of the Muslim civilization that once ruled here. Long after the end of the Muslim Empire, traces of that culture remain today. In Seville, layers of civilization are unearthed, from the biblical Tarshish to the Castilian Golden Age and beyond.

In Madrid, your journey begins in the nation's capital. Worldly, yet highly traditional, Madrid is Spain's vibrant hub. You study the birth and continual rebirth of Spain from the time of the Iberians, Romans, Visigoths and Moors; the epic struggle to unify a fragmented people; ill-fated imperialism; and 20th-century tragedies and triumphs. Field trips take you to the Archeological and Prado Museums; the Royal Tapestry Factory; the massive Escorial; Segovia's Roman aqueduct and enchanting castle, and medieval Toledo, a center of cultural exchange among Jews, Muslims and Christians. There are also excursions to Old Madrid and the Plaza Mayor. Activities include a tapas night and concerts from available offerings.

The jewel of Granada is the Alhambra rising above the city, triumph of the great Hispano-Arab civilization that thrived for more than seven centuries. Granada grew as Muslims sought refuge from an expanding Christian presence, falling in 1492 as Isabella united fragmented kingdoms into one nation. Lectures focus on the Moorish legacy in Spain, the decline of Muslim rule, Isabella's unification of her nation, and the North African heritage which lives on in Andalucía. You take field trips to the Alhambra, the Generalife summer palace and gardens, and the Moorish refuge Alpujarras. You also explore Albaicín, the earliest Muslim neighborhood; Cartuja monastery; Lorca's home, and walk to plazas, the Alcaicería market, and Arab souk (market).

Seville is a city of flamenco, flower-draped balconies, Moorish tile, and a rich, colorful past. She has welcomed the great civilizations that shaped both Spain and Western Europe. Spain's gateway to the west on the Guadalquivir River, Seville received New World treasure and exported Spanish culture. You study the unique art of the South: flamenco music and dance, and ancient and modern architecture. Field trips in Seville include the Reales Alcázares and Plaza de España. In Córdoba, we see a monument to the Jewish philosopher Maimónides and the Mezquita, the largest mosque outside the Arab world. You explore the Cathedral, the Jewish quarter, the Jerez wineries, Itálica, birthplace of two Roman emperors, and enjoy a tapas night, a flamenco tablao, and a horse show. Accommodations are in comfortable hotels; double occupancy bedrooms with private bathrooms.

Adventures Afloat Study Cruise—Essential Greece: Athens and the Cyclades

Azure waters, crisp white hilltop buildings, and remnants of an ancient civilization are the exquisite backdrop for your exploration of the Greek Aegean Sea. Examine ancient history and contemporary culture—the early glories of Athens, the mysteries of Delphi and its famed Oracle—and local heritage and culture on this cruise of the Cycladic Islands. Delve into the rhythms of modern life in enchanting Santorini, historic Delos, and cosmopolitan Mykonos while studying traditions, food, and music in a region that has inspired and challenged humankind for millennia.

The capital city of Athens is a magnificent showcase for Greek history. Named for the goddess Athena, it is the nation's economic, political, and cultural center. Lectures introduce history, ancient religions, and the city's

Lifelong learning has brought so much joy to life and learning for me; it has opened my mind to areas I never dreamed I would have the opportunity to study earlier in my life. And I have gained an extraordinary amount of close friends I never would have known otherwise.

—Marilee Martin, St. Louis, Missouri

famed monuments. Field trips and excursions take you to Acropolis, the city's crowning landmark and the setting of the famed Parthenon; the Agora, the marketplace and political heart of ancient Athens, and on an illuminated drive through the capital. A daylong field trip outside the city explores Delphi, one of the most important religious sites in ancient Greece, and home of the priestess Pythia, the legendary Oracle. A special dinner introduces foods of ancient Greece. Comfortable hotel in Athens; limited singles are available. Registering for single occupancy includes single accommodations in hotel and aboard ship.

On board, immerse yourself in the most historically and culturally important Greek islands. Lectures examine ancient civilizations, gods and goddesses, art and culture, and modern Greek life. Field trips and excursions explore Kea; Santorini, believed by some to be ancient Atlantis; Naoussa, with its traditional chapels and whitewashed houses; enchanting and vibrant Mykonos, and the ruins on Delos, an archaeological site on what was the most important religious center in the region.

Your cruise ship is an intimate, four-deck Greek yacht built in 1995. At 153' long by 30' wide and cruising at 12–14 knots she can carry 32 passengers, all of whom may be Elderhostelers. Public areas, linked by stairs include a restaurant with lounge, and sundeck. Outside double-occupancy cabins have lower beds and air conditioning, private bathroom with shower. Limited singles available.

Interview with an Expert—James Moses

James Moses, president and CEO of Elderhostel, Inc., since October 2001, joined the organization in 1979. He has served in a variety of management roles, from managing the registration efforts of the organization to overseeing development of its international programs.

To what do you attribute Elderhostel's amazing success over the last thirty years?

For thirty years, Elderhostel has provided high-quality learning adventures at superior value and, with more than four million enrollments in our programs over the years, the word has spread that we are an organization on which you can rely. In many ways, we're a reflection of our participants—we have strong values and a clear identity and mission. We focus on providing the most stimulating academic content, a warm social environment, and, while we provide fine accommodations and meals, they aren't the heart of an Elderhostel experience—learning and exploration are. We've earned the trust of our participants and we believe in them as much as they believe in us. They are our greatest assets.

What's different about Elderhostel programs now than when the organization first started in 1975?

The one overriding constant in Elderhostel over the past thirty years has been that the essence of the program is its simplicity: learning for its own sake. That has not changed. What has changed is accommodations. The early Elderhostel pioneers were excited about sleeping in college dormitories and going down the hall to use the bathrooms and showers. But that didn't hold, and by the early 1990s and today, almost all Elderhostel accommodations provide private bathrooms.

What benefits do older adults get from taking part in Elderhostel educational travel programs?

The people who choose Elderhostel decide that learning is a more exciting way to spend their time than shopping or lying on a beach. They are people who care more about what is on the inside than what is on the outside. Warm and spirited camaraderie seems to develop naturally among people who come together to think and learn about subjects in which they share an interest. Or maybe it's just that they share an interest in learning in general, and discussing new ideas happens naturally in a welcoming and stimulating environment. Learning is fun, especially when it is shared with good people. You don't have to worry about dressing in fancy clothes on an Elderhostel program, and you don't just look at a place or culture through a bus window—you have the chance to experience a place or subject from the inside. I think that combination of a warm social environment and a stimulating learning adventure away from home is enormously enriching and changes the way people feel about and experience themselves. A learning adventure in many ways provides a great opportunity for self-exploration that enhances the person you are when you return to your daily life.

What are the differences between the new Road Scholar program recently developed by Elderhostel and regular Elderhostel programming?

We developed Road Scholar specifically because a new generation of learning adventurers has arrived. These folks in their forties, fifties, and sixties may never think of themselves as old, and for them, *elder* is a word they associate with their parents or grandparents. We wanted to provide them with access to educational opportunities that take advantage of Elderhostel's vast educational network, but speak more to the needs of their generation.

Road Scholar has been quite successful since its modest launch in February 2004. More than two thousand people have participated already, and the average age of a Road Scholar is sixty-four, almost ten years younger than the average age of an Elderhosteler. The most popular aspects of Road Scholar do appeal to boomers. Groups are no larger than twenty-three, while Elderhostel programs can have more than forty people. While Elderhostelers enjoy socializing with their peers and learning in a group, Road Scholar programs provide more opportunities for independent exploration, as well as more free time. Elderhostelers love the classroom components of the program and are some of the most inquisitive and enthusiastic students ever to grace a lecture hall. Road Scholars, while just as enthusiastic, prefer the hands-on components of our programs, and experiential learning is an important part of the Road Scholar experience.

Elderhostel celebrated its thirtieth anniversary in 2005. How do you see the organization changing in the coming years?

As a nonprofit, nothing is more important at Elderhostel than fulfilling our mission of promoting lifelong learning among older adults. Our participants are our shareholders and are the people we work most to please. In the coming years, as people continue to live longer, a program like Elderhostel will take on an even more significant role in society. Research shows that intellectually active and engaged individuals are more likely to remain vital later in life. Experts urge us to continue learning and taking on new challenges in our later years to ensure our mental health as we grow even older. Elderhostel programming will continue to evolve to challenge the interests of these future generations of lifelong learners.

Other Educational Travel Organizations

Elderhostel has led the way and set the standards for educational travel programs for the last thirty years. Because of their success, other educational travel providers have also come into existence. Here are five of the best.

Close Up Foundation

The Close Up Foundation is the nation's largest nonprofit, 501(c)(3), nonpartisan citizenship education organization. Since its founding in 1970, Close Up has worked to promote responsible and informed participation in the democratic process through a variety of educational programs. Each year, more than twenty thousand students, teachers, and other adults take part in Close Up's programs in Washington, D.C. Since the inception of its Washington-based programs in 1971, the Close Up Foundation has welcomed nearly 650,000 students, educators, and other adults to the nation's capital.

Close Up's mission is built on the belief that textbooks and lectures alone are not enough to help students of all ages understand the democratic process and make it work. Citizens need a close up experience in government. Close Up's national, state, and local experiential government studies programs strengthen participants' knowledge of how the political process works, increase their awareness of major national and international issues, and motivate them to become actively involved in the world around them.

All individuals deserve the opportunity to become fully engaged citizens of our democracy. The Close Up Foundation strives to make its programs accessible for all citizens, regardless of age, race, or ability. The support it receives from foundations, corporations, individuals, and Congress allows Close Up to provide tuition fellowships for economically disadvantaged students. This assistance ensures that they, too, will understand the true meaning behind a democracy—that each citizen has a voice and that each citizen's actions can make a difference.

Working with Elderhostel, Close Up offers older Americans an opportunity to visit Washington, D.C., to obtain an insider's view of the government at work. For more information, visit the Close Up website at *www.closeup.org* or the Elderhostel website at *www.elderhostel.org*.

Examples of Close Up Educational Programs

The Close Up Foundation's Elderhostel programs offer the comfort and convenience of the perfect vacation paired with the stimulating aspects of a learning experience. Since 1984, more than ten thousand participants from across the country have come to Washington on Close Up's adult education programs.

Offered in cooperation with Elderhostel, the Close Up Foundation's adult programs offer one-of-a-kind travel/learning experiences in the nation's capital. Programs combine all the pleasures of vacationing with the fulfillment of learning. Participants gain firsthand knowledge of our nation and the democratic process.

Your week in Washington includes:

- Face-to-face meetings with Washington insiders—such as members of Congress or their staffs, policy experts, government officials, and journalists

- An in-depth look at Capitol Hill, including the Senate or House of Representatives, the Supreme Court, and the Library of Congress.

- An extensive study tour of the nation's capital city as a cultural and historical center.

- An insider's visit to a foreign embassy or international organization.

- Seminars on current national and international issues.

- Independent time for exploring Washington's many cultural and historical sites such as the Smithsonian Institutions, the National Archives, Arlington National Cemetery, the National Gallery of Art, Georgetown, the Franklin Delano Roosevelt Memorial or the new World War II Memorial.

Eclectic dining, quality accommodations, and professional program leaders are all included in this civic education experience.

Close Up Washington, D.C.—Your Nation's Capital

Become part of the invigorating political and cultural scene by traveling to Washington, D.C., with Close Up! Experience a D.C. not often seen by visitors through Close Up's experiential learning program. This educational travel opportunity includes onsite discussions of the historic and political significance of major memorials; study visits to the diverse neighborhoods of the city; Close-Up-arranged meetings with members of Congress or their staff; seminars with Washington insiders; current public policy or historical discussions led by professional and knowledgeable Close Up instructors.

In addition you will be introduced to D.C.'s cultural life, eclectic eateries, renowned museums and an evening at the theatre. From the sophisticated ambiance of Georgetown to the bohemian rush of Adams Morgan, D.C. is a world-class city offering visitors an unparalleled blend of history, politics, and culture. One of our nation's magnificent metropolitan creations, it is home to both grand monuments and humbling memorials.

Other programs include:

- Monumental DC: Experience Washington, D.C., through its monuments, memorials and remembrances with Close Up! Examine how your nation's sons and daughters are remembered. Learn what monuments tell about the people who created them, the time they were created, and the people and events memorialized by them through seminars with memorial founders and policy experts, daily discussions on historic and current issues, and in-depth study tours led by professional instructors. Close Up's experiential learning program will introduce you to memorials, monuments, museums and historic sites both on and off the National Mall.

- World in Transition: Examining World War II and its Legacy: Examine our country's role in the community of nations. Explore defense and foreign policy issues while probing the impact of World War II. Study historic figures and watershed events through on-site briefings at D.C.'s monuments and memorials. Visit the National Museum of American History, the newest Smithsonian Air and Space facility, the FDR Memorial and the International Spy Museum. Honor those who served our country as you visit Arlington National Cemetery and the newly dedicated World War II Memorial. Examine the effects of the Cold

War on the current administration's foreign policy. Gain an understanding of history's role in international relations and the challenges our nation currently faces.

In addition to these programs, Close Up has partnered with the Smithsonian Institution to provide an in-depth exploration of the Smithsonian's famed collections. Discover the Smithsonian Institution's hidden treasures. Enjoy a visit that combines expert-led tours with opportunities to view collections not open to the public. Experience private tours and professional Smithsonian staff presentations of world-renowned collections such as those at the National Museum of Natural History and the National American History Museum. Enjoy the museums at your own pace with time for independent exploration. Spend time at one of the many great museums away from the National Mall museum, such as the National Air and Space Museum Udvar-Hazy Center. Professional Close Up Foundation instructors will also provide topical seminars and a fascinating historical exploration of the city.

The partnership between the Close Up Foundation and Close Up has also yielded an intergenerational program that grandparents can share with their grandchildren:

Grandparents and Grandchildren Explore Washington, D.C. Together

Share the history of the capital city and the legacy of the "nation's attic" with your grandchild during this exciting educational experience.

Discover historic artifacts and primary sources through behind the scenes visits at the National Museum of American History and National Museum of Natural History, and the National Air and Space Museum. Discuss your observations at the National Zoo. Explore the memorials, monuments, and neighborhoods of D.C. through staff-led briefings. Share your ideas and impressions during interactive group activities designed for all ages.

Smithsonian Journeys

Although Smithsonian Journeys are not exclusively designed for just older adults, but rather for adults of all ages, we are including them here because of the high quality of their programs. The following information taken from their web site *www.smithsonianjourneys.org* is reprinted here with reprinted with permission.

Smithsonian Journey programs are filled with discovery, quality, and the fun of learning. Smithsonian Study Leaders are ranking (often world-renowned) experts in their fields. But more than that, they're highly personable, and they share informal moments with you along with the talks they give. They care that you get the most out of your experience, and truly make the difference between being a tourist and an informed traveler.

One-of-a-kind journeys are researched and custom-crafted by creative, dedicated staff, with lots of suggestions from Study Leaders. They go to some of the most compelling places in the world. Journeys are designed to maximize the time you spend in the places of greatest interest, to avoid "tourist traps" and to minimize the hassles of travel.

Smithsonian Journeys itineraries are designed with special "behind the scenes" visits made possible by the Smithsonian's unparalleled network of resources. Wherever they go, local experts are eager to meet with groups, knowing that guests are both interesting and interested in what they see.

Examples of Smithsonian Journeys Educational Travel Programs

Gibraltar to Patagonia: A Cruise to West Africa, the Atlantic Islands and South America

Join Smithsonian Journeys on a unique once-in-a-lifetime adventure cruising aboard a small ship of luxurious comfort, the Corinthian II, from the southern tip of Europe, along the northwestern coast of Africa, to the southern tip of South America, traversing over 7,200 nautical miles, 70 degrees of latitude and seven nations. Enjoy the spirited interest of like-minded travelers and exclusive excursions that will provide you with a taste of many exotic cultures.

Your first ports of call are enchanting - Marrakech and Tenerife. Meet traditional Berber villagers and experience life at the edge of the Sahara Desert before visiting the rarely visited Cape Verde Islands. At the conclusion of the Atlantic crossing, discover Brazil's multicultural northeastern coast. In the 16th and 17th century colonial cities of Recife, Olinda, Salvador, and Porto Seguro, you will find Dutch, Portuguese, Native American and West African influences blended together in a wonderful assemblage of old town squares, pastel mansions, and musical street life. Accompanying you will be a Smithsonian Study Leader, and we will be joined by travelers from the Explorers Club and the American Geographical Society.

Rail Journey through Southern India Featuring the Deccan Odyssey Train

India's lush southern states offer a fascinating and colorful tapestry of landscapes, culture, and history—languages and poetry more than 2,000 years old, an amazing diversity of wildlife and some of the country's most remarkable temple architecture. This tour focuses on the on the treasures of southern India.

Of particular interest in this program are the four nights spent on the new Deccan Odyssey train, traveling in the utmost comfort to the World Heritage sites of Ellora and Ajnta to see the famous rock-cut cave shrines.

In early 2004, the Deccan Odyssey train brought the luxury rail experience to southern India. Offering 48 staterooms with modern features in richly appointed settings, the train is a welcome alternative to bus travel on busy roads. Two restaurant cars, a spacious lounge coach, a conference/library coach, beauty shop, and on-train spa are some of the amenities available on board the train. Each of the accommodation coaches house four plush staterooms, a lounge area for breakfast and refreshments, and an attentive English-speaking saloon captain.

Papua New Guinea Expedition

Papua New Guinea is a tapestry of towering mountains, enormous jungle rivers, lush rainforests, and an incredibly diverse population speaking more than 200 languages. Here, each village has a spirit house, hereditary chiefs still rule with the aid of powerful sorcerers, and magic and ritual are part of everyday life. Papua New Guinea' daunting mountainous interior has kept isolated and intact age-old ways of life.

Follow in the footsteps of renowned cultural anthropologist Margaret Mead. At a traditional sing-sing in the Southern Highlands, home to the Huli Wigmen, observe their fantastic decorated headdresses of human hair adorned with flowers, feathers, leaves, and cuscus fur. Search for the brilliant bird of paradise at Tari Gap, where forests are filled with psychedelically colorful birds and butterflies. Explore the remote Sepik River aboard the *MTS Discoverer,* a seagoing catamaran. Stop at village spirit houses, meet with the artisans who create artifacts used in ritual ceremonies, and experience firsthand a traditional face-painting ceremony. End your exploration in Madang, considered by many to be the prettiest town in the Pacific.

Classical Pursuits

While not geared specifically toward older adults, Classical Pursuits offers a variety of learning vacations for adults of all ages from all over North America.

Want to share your love of art, literature, music, and more in a laid-back and informal setting? Then Classical Pursuits, Adventure for the Mind, Travel for the Soul, may be just what you're looking for. Classical Pursuits works hand-in-hand with the Great Books Foundation in Chicago, providing many of the program's discussion leaders in Toronto, Canada, and abroad. This partnership provides a high level of how to meaningfully interpret literature, art, and music.

Classical Pursuits layers its travel adventures with in-depth discussions, informal talks, active social participation between fellow travelers and group leaders, guided walks and tours that immerse participants in the local history of trip locations, and plenty of free time for participants to explore by themselves. The result is a unique learning adventure that opens the mind and expands the learning palette. Visit them at *www.classicalpursuits.com.*

Examples of Classical Pursuits Educational Travel Programs

They Came to Paris

(Reprinted with permission, 2004 Classical Pursuits)

Lifelong learning filled a void in my life when I needed it the most—just after I retired. I have taken over thirty courses across an incredible spectrum of interests. I'm proud to say I'm getting ready to sign up again this fall and look forward to continuing my quest.

—Bill Johnstone, Harrisonburg, Virginia

Rediscover the writers and artists who made the Twenties the century's greatest decade and Paris their creative center. Discussions will be held in their own cafes, and you will walk the streets where they lived and worked.

Classical Pursuits in the Summer

Each July, Classical Pursuits hold a weeklong program offering a dozen different seminar options on the serene and shady campus of the University of Toronto's St. Michael's College in the heart of one of North America's most cosmopolitan cities. Seminar examples include Charles Dickens: *Bleak House*, Northrop Frye: *Words with Power*, Homer: *The Iliad*, Ovid: *The Metamorphoses*, the Book of Job, Russian short stories, *The Decalogue* by Krzysztof Kieslowski, The Play's the Thing, *Gotterdammerung* by Richard Wagner, J.S. Bach: *Mass in B Minor*, Gabriel Garcia Marquez: *A Hundred Years of Solitude*, and The Poetics of Space in Art.

Interview with an Expert—Ann Kirkland

Ann Kirkland, founder of Classical Pursuits, was born in Philadelphia. She studied art history and then city planning. Ann worked for many years in health policy and administration in the area of geriatrics and has lived in Toronto for over thirty years. Ann started Classical Pursuits in 1999. Her greatest pride is two imaginative, inquisitive, and compassionate daughters; her greatest delight is her two small grandchildren, who remind her of what is important.

How long has Classical Pursuits been offering programs?

The summer program in Toronto began in 1999, with forty participants and four offerings—Dostoyevsky's *Crime and Punishment*, Plato's *Republic*, Dante's *Inferno*, and Wagner's *Tristan und Isolde* (opera). Since then, we have grown in the summer to twelve offerings and over 150 participants from across Canada and wide U.S. representation (about fifteen states). I began offering programs in other locations in 2002 with a two-week trip, Classical Pursuits Goes to Medieval Italy, to discuss Umberto Eco's *The Name of the Rose*. This year, I will be offering six trips—three abroad and three in North/Central America. In 2006, the number of trips will increase to about ten.

I have now distinguished the two parts of Classical Pursuits by calling the summer program Toronto Pursuits and the single book or theme programs in other destinations Travel Pursuits.

The distinction between the two programs is that in Toronto, we have small concurrent seminars going on, with a large group congregating for lunch and afternoon and evening talks, walks, and excursions -but *without* any direct connection between the texts (or music, film, or art) to Toronto. With Travel Pursuits, we use the literature as a lens to help us walk in the shoes of the protagonists portrayed, in both place and time. For instance, *The Name of the Rose* and *To Hell and Back with Dante* trips to Italy looked exclusively at medieval Italy—the thought, customs, food, politics, culture, etc.,—to put our discussions in context. At the same time, great literature is great because it continues to speak to us in our place and time. So we take away ideas that are universal and helpful to us in our present lives.

How did you first get interested in offering such programs?

My daughter was an undergraduate at St. John's College in Santa Fe, New Mexico. She went there at my strong encouragement to give her some appreciation for the rich traditions of Western civilization (those dead white men she was so inclined to dismiss). It was at a parents' weekend, where we got to experience firsthand their seminar style of learning, that I became so excited about Shared Inquiry as far superior to the passive regurgitation of secondary sources that had been my own Ivy League experience. I went to the St. John's Summer Classics program for three years. When I decided I did not wish to finish my working life in the health sector, it was the coupling of reading great (albeit difficult) literature and then exploring it with a small group to discover the treasures to be found there that turned me into a kind of missionary—wanting to share this wonderful experience with others.

Approximately how many older adults participate in your programs?

At Toronto Pursuits, we have about 150 adults participating. On any given trip, the number ranges from a low of twelve to a high of forty-five. In the case of the large number, I bring three discussion leaders, so the groups remain small and participants get to experience a variety of leaders.

What are the most popular subjects studied?

This is difficult to say. But some of the highly popular programs in Toronto have been:

- The Play's the Thing—several plays plus a trip to Stratford
- *Death in Venice*—a comparative analysis of Thomas Mann's novella, Benjamin Britten's opera, and Luchino Visconti's film
- The Idea of Renaissance—with representative works from music, art, and literature
- C.G. Jung and Joseph Campbell: Myth and Modernity
- *The Metamorphoses* by Ovid
- Also the standard big works like *The Aeneid, Anna Karenina, Bleak House, Don Quixote, Democracy in America,* books from the Bible, and Shakespeare. We also offer sessions in art (The Object Stares Back: On the Nature of Seeing), opera, and music (Wagner's *Götterdämmerung,* Conductivity—Musical Maestros, Martinets or Metro-Gnomes), and film (*The Decalogue* - the ten-part film series by Krzysztof Kieslowski and Federico Fellini's *La Dolce Vita*).

The Travel Pursuits programs that have been most popular have been:

- Classical Pursuits Goes to Medieval Italy (*The Name of the Rose*)
- To Hell and Back with Dante (*The Divine Comedy*)
- They Came to Paris (the "Lost Generation" of the Twenties)
- Vive le Quebec!
- Po' Boys and Naughty Girls in N'Awlins (this November's sold-out trip was naturally cancelled)

This summer I had three wonderful trips:

- Irish Literary Genius (James Joyce in Dublin and Irish playwrights dealing with the idea of "The West" on the Aran Islands)
- The *Other* Poland (Postwar poetry in Kraków)
- On Persephone's Island (Lampedusa's *The Leopard* and two collec-

tions of short stories in Sicily)

Is there any difference between your program now and when it first started?

At the heart of the program, I have stuck to the key principles of choosing works that are both rich with ideas and highly discussable and sticking to the Shared Inquiry method of conducting the sessions. Beyond that, for Toronto Pursuits I have added peripherals both on and off campus, such as after-lunch speakers, guided walks, tastings, concerts, yoga, and excursions.

The formula for the trips is a combination of text-based discussions, guided walks, informal talks, great food, and unscheduled time. The only change here is to drop the third meal, as we were spending too many hours at the table and eating more than anyone cared to.

What benefits do you feel older adults get from attending your programs?

From what they tell me, they get what I get—a sense of feeling fully alive. We experience the joy and pleasure of being immersed in a masterpiece. We get a chance to explore the big questions of meaning that we ask as children and then tend to set aside as we get busy with our practical adult lives. We get to know ourselves better and get to know others in a profound way through the exploration of great books and the other arts.

We both open and exercise our minds as we try to understand what a particular writer is trying to say and then to determine whether we agree with it. We experience noncompetitive conviviality and make lasting friendships based on a shared interest in questions of meaning. We exercise our ability to take part in civic discourse and continue that at home. We reexamine some of the assumptions and decisions that are guiding our lives. Without trying to sound too high and mighty about it, I think that we benefit by becoming more fully human.

To what do you attribute the success of Classical Pursuits?

The recognition that there are a lot of people who, like me, seek to know, to experience, to share, to feel, to understand. A combination of great books, great conversation, and great places seems to fit the bill.

ElderTreks

Nineteen-year-old ElderTreks is the world's first adventure travel company designed exclusively for people fifty and over; it provides exciting small-group activities on the land and sea in more than eighty countries. Excursions focus on adventure, indigenous cultures, and nature. Check out the wildlife in Tanzania, scour the Gobi Desert in Mongolia on a camel, witness the awesome spectacles of Angkor Wat in Thailand, and even visit the seventh continent of Antarctica. All of these adventures and more are possible when you travel with ElderTreks.

Boasting an itinerary designed with you in mind, ElderTreks also welcome companions of any age. ElderTreks guides are veterans of adventure travel excursions, and trips are kept to a maximum of sixteen participants.

Seaborne trips occur on actual expedition ships, not cruise liners. The smaller adventure boats enhance personal interaction and simultaneously reduce environmental impact on the sites they visit. Activities are rated on a scale ranging from easy to heart-pumping. In other words, there's always something for everyone.

ElderTreks activities are all-inclusive. All meals, all accommodations, all domestic transportation and domestic departure taxes, all entrance fees, and tips at hotels and restaurants are included in the price of the trip. On the off chance there are exceptions, it will be duly noted in the travel brochures and literature.

The ease with which you can embark with ElderTreks enhances their attractiveness. There are no mandatory group flights. If you want to use your frequent-flier miles, enjoy a stopover or two, extend your stay, or arrive early, that's entirely up to you. ElderTreks does their absolute best to ensure that they answer all your questions and make your experience with them as utterly satisfying as is possible. No rigid itineraries need apply; ElderTreks is in business to bring you a truly one-of-a-kind experience you won't get anywhere else.

As part of their desire to give something back, ElderTreks also supports a number of development projects throughout the world, and they make sure you have close contact with local people. During the course of their trips, you will have the opportunity to visit schools and orphanages. They select hotels based on comfort, location, and charm, with private washrooms. Shared facilities are only used where there is no alternative, and such exceptions are clearly noted.

ElderTrek's many repeat travelers and the high marks they score on their comment forms demonstrate that they consistently deliver high-caliber programs at an affordable price. You will find their programs eventful, stimulating, and a great value. For more information, visit their website at *www.eldertreks.com*.

Examples of ElderTreks Educational Travel Programs

Canadian Rockies

(Reprinted with permission, 2004 ElderTreks)

Journey into the heart of Canada's Rocky Mountains and witness the pristine beauty of snow-capped mountains, the stillness of crystal blue lakes, and marvel at the depth of the gorges and canyons—this is Canada's unspoiled wonderland!

Travel back in time along the twisting canyons, known as the Drumheller Badlands, to the domain of the dinosaur. View ancient treasures at the world famous Royal Tyrrell Museum of Paleontology. Experience the vibrant dancing, drumming and singing of the Native American culture at an Aboriginal PowWow and Rodeo. Enjoy a taste of the back-country on our overnight horseback (or wagon) excursion, keeping an eye out for elk, big horn sheep, bears and coyote. Relax by a campfire under the stars—Western Canada awaits you!

A helicopter flight takes you over spectacular glaciers, waterfalls and alpine lakes, to the starting point of our mountain hike. Expert guides show you the way, pointing out unique flora and fauna, as you explore the Rockies from high above. Avid hikers have the opportunity for an additional optional heli-hiking excursion, later in the trip.

Your journey stops in the historic mountain towns of Banff, Lake Louise and Jasper, each situated within the boundaries of two of Canada's most picturesque national parks—Banff and Jasper. Nestled between the rolling hills of Calgary and Banff and surrounded by spectacular landscape and an abundance of wildlife, Rafter Six Lodge provides the perfect home base for your Western Canada adventure.

Your adventure ends in Calgary, but those wishing to continue their journey westward, can board the Rocky Mountaineer, a uniquely designed train that only travels in daylight hours.

Queen Charlotte Islands: Canada's Galapagos

Known to the native Haida people as Gwaii Haanas, "Place of Wonder," the Queen Charlotte Islands of the South Moresby archipelago contain 130 spectacular islands. The delicate ecological balance of indigenous flora and fauna has earned these isolated islands the title Canada's Galapagos.

Aboard the sailboat Ocean Light II, sail southward from Camp Moresby along the eastern coast and around small islands to see tufted puffins, anklets, herons, bald eagles, seals and whales. Stop at Hotsprings Island for a therapeutic warm bath before traveling onward to explore the history of the Haida Indian nation.

See the UNESCO World Heritage Site—Ninstints—boasting the best original standing totem poles in the world, surrounded by a towering temperate rainforest.

Senior Summer School, Inc.

Based in Deerfield Beach, Florida, Senior Summer School offers adventurous older adults an affordable opportunity to enhance their summer through leisure, education, and discovery. Campuses are located at a number of locations across the United States and Canada, including Flagstaff, Arizona; Madison, Wisconsin; Boston, Massachusetts; Los Angeles, California; Boone, North Carolina; Greensburg, Pennsylvania; and New Brunswick, Canada.

The program itself is designed for independent, active, and healthy seniors who want to experience today's college life. Programs last anywhere from two to six weeks during the summer months. While each campus is independently owned and operated, all locations offer the highest-quality learning environment.

Among the many activities offered by Senior Summer School are local sight-seeing trips, private exploration time, leisure activities, and extended day and weekend field trips. Students are encouraged to be independent, to go off and explore the many sights and sounds of campus life and the surrounding environs.

Accommodations include private residence hall suites, hotels, university dormitories, and private apartments. All accommodations are in modern buildings featuring elevator service, housekeeping, common TV areas, and laundry and vending services. Private rooms are also wired for individual TV/phone service. In addition to computer access, all campuses feature recreational areas with tennis courts, swimming pools, and golf courses. Most locations will even arrange to pick up participants who arrive by plane.

Meals are prepared fresh each day by a team of professionals and served cafeteria-style, with unlimited helpings. Each meal is carefully designed to include a selection of hot entrees, as well as salads and a great variety of drinks and desserts.

Class programs are entirely optional and are an extension of each university. Courses on a wide variety of topics are taught by seasoned instructors, eager to introduce and immerse you in their field of study. There are no grades or mandatory attendance requirements. As with other lifelong learning programs, you only need a desire to experience something new. Your classmates will range from those who never attended college to those with college and advanced degrees. Visit the Senior Summer School website at *www.seniorsummerschool.com.*

Examples of Senior Summer School Educational Travel Programs

At Appalachian State University, Boone, North Carolina

(Reprinted with permission, 2004 Senior Summer School)

The Broyhill Inn on the Appalachian State University Campus will house Senior Summer School participants for sessions of two or four weeks long. Your room, available for single or double occupancy, will provide a comfortable bed, color television with cable and telephone with free local calls. Appalachian State University, rated as one of best undergraduate universities by *Time* magazine, is where over 12,000 students seek degrees in a wide variety of fields. Since its founding in 1899, the university serves as a center of cultural and professional activity within the state and region.

Meals will be catered by the hotel. Three meals daily: Breakfast, Lunch, and Dinner. The hotel's meal service is known to be among the finest in the high country area.

Classes and lectures will be offered on site in the hotel's conference center. Classes will feature instructors from Appalachian State University and local professionals. There will be at least two morning classes and one afternoon class offered during the session.

Sample Classes and Lectures offered one, two, three, or five times a week include Contemporary Legal Issues—Ethics/Current Events—Biblical Narratives—Memory—Judaism in the South—Literature (Select Writers/Short Stories)—Folk Dancing—Body Shaping (Fitness)—Political Science/American Politics—Nutrition—Criminal Justice and Health Topics.

Historic and scenic opportunities are available at local attractions such as the Appalachian Cultural Museum, the Daniel Boone Native Gardens, Grandfather Mountain, Linville Caverns, and Hickory Ridge Homestead. The performing arts can be seen in theatre and concerts with the Appalachian Summer Festival, Concerts on the Lawn, and Horn of the West as well as local professional theatre companies. Weekend sight-seeing will explore the region further with visits to Asheville, NC home of George Vanderbilt mansion, the Biltmore; Charlotte, NC, the Queen City; and Winston-Salem, NC another university city, rich in history. There will be one local tour included as part of the program each week. Weekend excursions and theatre outings will be at an additional fee.

At Mt. Allison University, Sackville, New Brunswick, Canada

Situated at the headwaters of the Bay of Fundy, Sackville is noted as one of the top ten towns in Canada. The area is abundant with unusual flora and fauna; and the much celebrated and nationally recognized Waterfowl Park exemplifies the area's commitment to environmental conservation. There are many beautiful examples of Victorian architecture throughout the community.

The streets of historic Sackville are lined with maple and elm trees, with the homes reflecting the styles and values of a community where, for more than two centuries, people have settled, prospered, and lived well. Sackville has many local businesses and quality retail stores, as well as a modern hospital providing quality medical treatment.

Mt. Allison University has been rated Number One Undergraduate University in Canada for seven consecutive years. It's known for its fine arts, music, and commerce departments, and quaint campus with elegant ivy-covered, sandstone buildings.

Although Mount Allison University is located in the small town of Sackville, many of the opportunities of larger urban areas are offered.

There are many nearby attractions rich with history and natural beauty to explore; Sackville has become known for its abundance and variety of wildlife and birds, and the Waterfowl Park on the renowned Tantramar Marshes. The university, established in 1839, combines a strong sense of history and tradition with a modern approach to its senior summer programs. The program opportunities offered at Mt. Allison are designed and recommended for active and adventurous senior participants. Every year rugged and adventuresome seniors prepare to learn and be challenged at Mt. Allison University. American currency is widely accepted in the area, and you will be able to enjoy the benefits of the increased value of the American dollar at the local shops and attractions.

Meals are served cafeteria style, offering regional dishes that the area is famed for. Scheduled meals are three meals Sunday through Thursday, breakfast and lunch Friday, brunch on Saturdays. Friday dinners will be on your own allowing you to experience the tastes of local restaurants. Saturday night dinners will be available during the planned Saturday excursions.

Mt. Allison University classes will be taught by highly qualified instructors and university professors. In the past, each week concentrated on a particular theme. Topics include the town of Sackville, the history of the university and surrounding area. Other sessions may be art workshops with varying mediums such as drawing, painting and printmaking, Acadian culture, Canadian history and culture, government structure, native and aboriginal issues, computer classes as well as current social topics.

Extensive sightseeing and travel is a large part of the Mount Allison program. An attempt is made to travel twice a week, usually on Tuesday and Thursdays. Included in the program fee is a visit to the world's highest tides at the Bay of Fundy, the Hopewell Cape Rocks, the Jost Winery in Nova Scotia, a trip to the famous Acadian village Le Pays de la Saquine, to Fundy Geological Museum, and to Dorchester Cape to witness the famous Sand Piper ballet. Optional sightseeing trips are offered on the weekend at an additional cost to Prince Edward Island and the city of Halifax in Nova Scotia, our two most popular destinations.

Seniors enjoy interesting activities such as tie dying (for that special souvenir), visits to Live Bait Theatre, and dinners at quality restaurants in nearby towns or cities. You may even learn how to prepare local seafood.

Other options include relaxing during an evening movie or trying your luck at a game of bridge or canasta. Computer facilities are fully available to seniors, so bring your email addresses!

Mount Allison provides a relaxing environment that promotes a well rounded Maritime experience, through classes, discussions, fine arts, travel, and physical and social activity.

Interview with an Expert—Seth Wirshba

Seth Wirshba is president of Senior Summer School, an education and travel program for seniors. He also serves on the board of the Loggers' Run Community Middle School in Boca Raton, Florida.

How long has Senior Summer school been offering programs for older adults?

In the summer of 2006 we will be celebrating our twentieth season.

Approximately how many older adults participate in your programs?

We usually have one thousand participants in the summer and a few hundred during our New Year's Eve programs.

What are the most popular subjects studied?

Senior Summer School offers such a wide variety of subjects it is hard to say which are the most popular. However, we always try to include the following at all locations: politics, history, current events, music, art, local issues for the area, and health. All sessions include a wide variety of subjects with four to five different classes each day.

Is there any difference between your program now and when it first started?

Yes, seniors today tend to go for shorter time periods then in years past. We started as an eight-week program and now most of the sessions are two weeks.

What benefits do you feel older adults get from attending your programs?

Seniors get a lot from our programs! They meet people from all over the country; discover new areas; listen to talented teachers, professors, and professionals; visit museums and points of interest; and also escape the summer heat.

To what do you attribute the success of Senior Summer School?

Making our program affordable to all.

As was stated earlier in this chapter, listed here are just six of the many, many educational travel opportunities available for older adults. An Internet search using any combination of words, such as *educational travel* or *mature educational travel*, will yield many intriguing prospects for continuing your lifelong learning adventure.

It's up to you to decide how much educational travel can fit into your schedule and your budget. Although some of the programs—international ones, for instance—can be more expensive, there are many that are not. Educational travel adds a whole new dimension to your after-fifty years. Try it once and you'll wonder how you ever got along without it.

Up Close and Personal

Nancy Merz Nordstrom

Sitting in a terminal at Logan International Airport in Boston, surrounded by strangers, I couldn't help wondering how, at age fifty-one and after being a widow for three years, I was about to take my first solo trip—to Europe, no less. I'd never been out of the United States except for short trips to Canada and Bermuda with my family; I'd never even owned a passport. Yet here I was waiting to board a SwissAir flight to Zürich. To say I was having second thoughts was putting it mildly.

After twenty-nine years of marriage—my entire adulthood, really—being a single, mid-life woman was still not a comfortable place for me. And in the last three years, I had become very aware of how our society seemed fixated on couplehood, especially when it came to marketing vacations. I realized that traveling solo was going to be a real challenge—a challenge made even more difficult by that ubiquitous single supplement extra cost, a practice by hotels that in effect penalizes anyone who is unattached. So it was with great interest that I had read an article earlier in the year about Interhostel, an educational travel company for older adults, based at the University of New Hampshire in Durham.

The article talked about how their programs were perfect for solo travelers. It went on to say that traveling with Interhostel groups was fun, educational, and safe for singles, especially single women. A bonus was that many of the programs did not have that infamous single supplement. I was very interested.

So here I was, five months later, about to leave for Innsbruck, Austria, and the Northern Tyrolean section of Italy. As a child I had loved the story of *Heidi*, so a trip to the Austrian and Italian Alps seemed like a good fit. A plus was that program participants would be staying in single dorm rooms, with private baths, at the University of Innsbruck.

In the weeks prior to departure, I received lots of information about our program, some of it from the travel company handling the flight arrangements, some from the Interhostel representative who would be traveling with us, and some from Interhostel itself. I read everything thoroughly, including books from the suggested reading list. We were told about our accommodations, what to pack, what type of clothing to bring, and our day-to-day itineraries. I was well prepared.

When I walked into the airport terminal on the night of my departure, I was greeted by an "Interhostel" sign wielded by a representative from the company who had made the travel arrangements, as well as by Luzi, the guide from Interhostel who would be traveling with us. Both women helped usher me through the check-in process and then directed me to where the other group members were sitting.

They all seemed friendly as we introduced ourselves—a nice mix of couples and single women, with a few single men. There were several fifty-somethings in the group, with the rest in their sixties and seventies. I was promptly christened the baby of the group, since I was only fifty-one.

To participate in an Interhostel program, one had to be at least fifty. My research after I learned about Interhostel, and educational travel in general, had made me aware of Elderhostel as well, but their minimum age at the time was fifty-five, and I didn't want to wait four more years for this first travel experience.

Our overnight flight to Zürich was, for the most part, uneventful. The only excitement occurred when one of my seatmates lost his teeth. The airline had seated me next to a British couple who were vegetarians. I too had requested a vegetarian dinner after reading that vegetarian selections were easier to digest, especially when one is eating dinner at 11 p.m.

Sometime during the night, my neighbor had taken his dentures out, and while he was sleeping, he had lost them. After a flurry of activity in the early morning, sun-drenched cabin, the missing teeth were located on the floor under my seat. How they got there remains a mystery to this day.

Five hours after leaving Boston we landed in Zürich. We regrouped and walked over to the departure gate for our Munich-bound plane. A one-hour flight put us on the ground, where a young Austrian guide named Irene joined us. She would stay with us throughout the entire program, and having studied in the United States, she spoke flawless English.

We then boarded the bus we would use throughout our program. Hans, our bus driver, would also stay with us the entire time. So a pattern of consistency and familiarity was immediately established, in that we had Luzi, Irene, Hans, and the same traveling vehicle. Very reassuring.

The two-hour ride to Innsbruck, down the Autobahn through the wide-open farmlands of southern Germany, was quite comfortable. Most of us were operating on very little sleep, so some of the group took the opportunity to nap. Never having been in this part of the world before, however, I didn't want to miss a thing. The red-orange-tiled roofs of all the farmhouses along the way were quite eye-catching, but the scent that wafted through the air was less than wonderful. *Freshlander air* was what the Germans called the after-effects of fertilizing the fields with processed sewage.

Check-in at the Studentenhaus (University of Innsbruck dorms) was quick and easy—pick up the key and go. No time-consuming forms to fill out. We each had our own room—Spartan but utilitarian and very clean. The view looked down upon the River Inn and old-world buildings on the opposite bank. I was awestruck.

After a short settling in, we all boarded the bus for a trip to the nearby mountain village of Lanz, where our introductory dinner in an inn built in 1313 awaited us. Roast lamb and warm apple strudel! It was delicious.

What's interesting to note is that in Europe, one has to ask for water and has to pay for plain bread and you only get butter for breakfast. Bread and water are not part of the usual table setting like in the United States. Anticipating our wants, however, wherever we went during our program, Interhostel had arranged for us to always find pitchers of water waiting on our tables.

Leaving the inn after dinner, we were greeted by oom-pah-pah music from across the street—a very nice surprise that set the tone for our entire program. They drove us back to Innsbruck through picture-perfect mountain villages that looked like they belonged on postcards. What a wonderful beginning.

The next morning, our program began in earnest. While we were in Innsbruck, our breakfasts would all be taken in the student cafeteria in our building. There was a wonderful buffet every morning from which to select. Muesli cereal with warm, creamy milk quickly became my favorite choice.

Our first excursion found us at the site of the 1964 and 1976 Olympics. We toured the area, including hiking up to the ski jump site, and listened to the tales of our guide. Other tour groups were there, too (none from the

United States), and I found it interesting that the women in those groups were much more dressed up than we were, complete with sandals or heels. No jeans, sneakers, or walking shoes were anywhere to be seen.

Later in the morning, we took a walking tour of the Old City of Innsbruck, with Irene as our guide. The buildings were incredible and so ancient. Fifteenth-century frescoes abounded, and everything was bedecked with the most gorgeous flower boxes I have ever seen. Being in buildings so old makes one realize how young the United States actually is.

After lunch in the downtown student cafeteria, called a *Mensa* (Latin for table), we found our classroom at the university for our first lecture on the history of Austria. The professor spoke perfect, but accented, English, and he gave a thoroughly enjoyable talk that really helped set the program in perspective. There was a lot of give and take between him and the audience, especially with those who were old enough to have lived through World War II. No one hesitated to speak their minds about the thorny issues of that war, and he retained his good humor through it all.

That evening, we walked over to a local beer garden for dinner, where we were wined and dined in typical Austrian style. Free time after dinner gave me the opportunity to walk back to the Old City, find an outdoor café, and settle in for a musical evening of Tyrolean entertainment, complete with costumed singers and dancers. Other members of the group had the same idea, however, and we soon found ourselves together again, enjoying a wonderful, picturesque evening.

Later, back at the Studentenhaus, one of the women produced a bottle of wine, and late evening saw four of us sitting on a balcony overlooking the night-darkened city while we became better acquainted. A very nice ending to our first day.

Lectures on Austrian music and the history of the Hapsburgs, one of the great ruling families of Europe, started the next day. A bit of free time followed and then lunch at the Mensa again.

In the afternoon, we traveled to Schloss Ambras, a magnificent castle just outside Innsbruck that had once been home to the Hapsburgs. What an incredible place—beautiful grounds, great collections, and medieval armor everywhere. Again, the sheer age of the castle, in comparison to buildings in the United States, took my breath away.

That evening, we took a long walk through Innsbruck to a vegetarian restaurant where we all dined on lasagna. The walk to and from the restaurant gave us a wonderful chance to see more of the city. Along the way, Irene pointed out items of interest and local history, and she told fascinating stories.

The next morning, in preparation for our trip to Italy and the South Tyrol, our lecturer took us through several hundred years of the history of that region, focusing specifically on the treaty after World War I in 1918 that took South Tyrol away from Austria and made it Italian. Since he blamed President Woodrow Wilson for that, things got a bit sticky between him and some of our group who also knew their history. But it certainly made for a fascinating two and a half hours, which flew by. It's always interesting and very educational to learn about other points of view.

Since we had some free time after the lecture, some of us went to a flea market that was held every Saturday. It was fascinating. So many people speak English that communicating is not a problem. We then strolled down to the main shopping district, but most of the stores were closed since it was a Saturday afternoon. But we did manage to find an outdoor café and indulged in coffee and pastry.

While we were sitting at the café, we heard people chanting and were very surprised to see a large human-rights demonstration coming down Maria Theresien Strasse, the main street of Innsbruck. They were Turkish patriots and sympathizers protesting the death of one of their leaders. They carried signs, banners, and coffins as they surged down the street.

Now, that street—Maria Theresien Strasse—is the very same street that I had seen in a film the day before as part of the lecture on the history of Austria. In that film, the street was once again the scene of a big parade, but the parade—if you want to call it that—was not made up of human rights activists, but rather of Nazis during World War II. What the film showed was the taking over of Austria by Hitler and the Nazis marching in to take possession of the city of Innsbruck.

It was sobering and kind of eerie to sit there and watch this modern-day demonstration, since in my mind's eye I saw the Nazis instead. I couldn't help wondering how many people around me were seeing the same thing. I'm sure it brought back a lot of memories for some.

Later that day, our bus took us up into the mountains for an easy two-hour hike to the Hinterhorn Alm. The weather was gorgeous and the scenery spectacular, and I really felt like I was in a scene from *Heidi*. Once we got to the top, we stopped at a small family-run farm that provides refreshment to hikers. I sat outside with a bottle of water, gazing at the scenery with the sound of cowbells in the air.

After we hiked back down, we went to a picturesque restaurant at the base of the mountain where we had a grillfest consisting of chicken, sausage, veal, potato salad, and coleslaw. Quite delicious after all that fresh air.

Early the next morning, we were traveling along the Autobahn for the four-hour trip to Italy. We stopped at the Brenner Pass in the Austrian/Italian Alps for refreshments and to change some money into liras. The only money we had needed on this trip was for incidentals, gifts, and snacks at the wonderful Austrian cafés. But everyone wanted to have some liras for just such items.

We drove through the Italian countryside, dotted with vineyards, and then on into Verona, our first stop. We ate lunch at a trattoria, where we had bruschetta, pasta with mushrooms, and a fruit cup with sorbet. After lunch, we checked into our small pensione, which had very comfortable single accommodations.

At dinner in a local ristorante that evening, we were treated to a short discourse on the opera *Aida*, which we were seeing later in an outdoor, one-thousand-year-old Roman amphitheatre! The amphitheatre held twenty thousand Italians, who took their opera very seriously. Once the opera began, you could hear a pin drop, the audience was that quiet. The performance was spectacular, complete with live animals, a cast of two hundred, and a full moon that bathed the entire area in a golden glow.

Although the opera was thoroughly enjoyable and I loved every minute of it, what I found most interesting was that it did not start until 9:15 p.m. and ended at 1:30 a.m.! And then, as if 1:30 a.m. wasn't late enough, after the performance all the opera-goers made a mad dash for the outdoor cafés that ringed the amphitheatre area. They were not ready to call it a night by any means. I wondered how everyone would be able to get up the next morning, since this was Sunday night—or technically Monday morning. Turns out none of the stores and shops open on Monday until 3:30 p.m. during opera season! Everyone sleeps in.

Not us, however. We were up and out for a 10:30 a.m. walking tour of Verona. I noticed that the buildings in Italy seem old and dirty in comparison to the pristine condition and whiteness of Austrian buildings (which are also accented by incredible flower boxes). It's quite a contrast. As the tour continued, however, the beauty of Verona came through, and I soon forgot to make comparisons.

We had some free time and then lunch on our own in Verona before the bus departed mid-afternoon for the drive to the village of Dorf Tyrol in the Italian Alps. Three hours later, we came to the outskirts of the town. The bus was unable to continue up the narrow hill road, so we disembarked and hiked up the rest of the way. Our luggage was loaded onto a motorized cart and taken up for us.

Dorf Tyrol was beautiful—a perfect little Tyrolean village with signs in both German and Italian. We already knew about the dual signage because of the lecture we had listened to before leaving Innsbruck. Sentiment about the Austrian loss of the South Tyrol in 1918 still ran deep in the villagers, and even today unrest often simmers in these northern Italian mountains.

The views from my balcony were spectacular—the mountains and the valleys were beyond belief! After dinner, we sat in an outdoor café at the hotel, drinking in both the wine and the night views, with the lights of tiny villages blinking on the distant mountainsides.

During the night, a terrific hailstorm blew through the town, and the large ice crystals covered my balcony. There was severe damage to the vineyards and to the apple and grape crops, the main sources of income in the area. Tree limbs were down everywhere, yet once the sun rose into a cloudless morning sky, everyone took to the outdoors. The cleanup began immediately, and as I strolled through the town after an early breakfast, I saw women descend on the local cemetery to begin cleaning up there even before tackling their own homes.

All during the stormy night, I had heard bells tolling. Turns out they were ringing to "keep the lightning away." Folklore or superstition, no doubt, but very interesting.

Mid-morning found us walking down the mountain to Brunnenburg, the castle home of the late poet Ezra Pound. His grandson now lives there, and he has established a Tyrolean lifestyle museum. Pound's grandson gave us a very special guided tour and a lecture on the life and times of the controversial poet. The castle maintains a small vineyard (we all bought a bottle of wine), and it also houses American students who come to study in the area.

After lunch, we took a cable car up to the top of the nearest mountain, where we found spectacular views, a restaurant, a gift shop, and walking trails. When we were back on level ground, it was time for our tour of Meran, complete with a lecture on the bus as we rode. We spent the later afternoon exploring the wonderful churches, parks, and hidden gems of this medium-sized city. While we were resting at one point on a shady park bench, we heard beautiful music coming from behind us.

Turning around, we saw the open door of an elegant old cathedral. We entered and sat down in the darkened church to listen to a wonderful soprano practicing for a Brahms concert later that evening. In was truly an unexpected pleasure.

Early the next morning, we departed for Brixen, Italy, via the rugged, spectacularly beautiful, and incredibly steep Dolomite Mountains. To this day, I wonder how our bus managed to make it around some of the hairpin curves and turns that we encountered. When we arrived in Brixen, we all clapped and congratulated Hans for his outstanding job in piloting the bus.

As we made our way toward Brixen, we saw people hiking, rock-climbing, and camping all over the mountains. There were even traffic jams because of the crowds. Without a doubt, people in this area certainly take advantage of this natural resource. We also passed an Italian racing team, as well as other bikers, chugging their way up the mountains on their multispeed bicycles.

Once in Brixen, we had lunch in an inn built in 1661. Later, we took a guided walk around the town that was supplemented by a local guide who gave us an excellent overview of the history, art, and architecture of this medieval city. The frescoes and the ancient cathedrals were amazing. While we were there, the bells began tolling all over town, and one could very easily imagine being back in the Middle Ages. It was quite special.

From Brixen, we headed back to Innsbruck and our rooms at the Studentenhaus. We were due to go back to the vegetarian restaurant for dinner that evening, but some of us opted out and decided to make it potluck instead. It was surprising how much food we were able to round up in a short time. Using the student kitchen on the dorm floor, and supplementing the food with some of the wine we bought, we had a great time. We were all very tired, though, and glad for an early lights out.

Having opted out of a lecture on Austrian art the next morning, I spent two hours sitting by the river in back of my room, reading and writing. It was shady and cool and very refreshing. From there, I strolled down to the Mensa for lunch and then boarded the bus for the ride to the old walled city of Hall.

Along the way, our guide talked about medieval walled cities—their significance and their importance. We spent several hours in the old city with a very knowledgeable guide and even visited the mint where the Hapsburgs minted their money. We each got to use the old press.

Our next stop was the Castle Tratzberg. The bus could not make it up the hill, so we got out and walked for about twenty-five minutes to get to the castle. Once we refreshed ourselves, we were given audiotapes in English to use as we went from room to room. I thoroughly enjoyed the tour and learned a lot. In the gift shop, a very nice man helped us all find souvenirs. Only later did we learn that the nice man was actually Count Ensignburg, a Hapsburg descendant and owner of the castle. Seems he, his wife, and two children still live there!

Back in Innsbruck, we had dinner in an outdoor café—cheese spaetzle, a salad, and blueberry cheesecake with vanilla sauce. The high point of the dinner, however, wasn't the food, but the toilet. One of our group came back from the restroom laughing and quite excited. Seems this restaurant had the latest in modern plumbing—a self-cleaning toilet, complete with a mechanical arm that came out, clamped itself on the seat (which was rotating), and proceeding to wash it off. We all had to go in to see it. Austrian hygiene and efficiency at its best.

After dinner, our hosts took us to a large beer hall for an evening of Tyrolean entertainment. We sat at long tables, drank beer, and watched a great show. The hall was very crowded and full of tourists. Toward the end of the evening, the performers sang snatches of songs from at least a dozen different countries. As each country's song was sung, anyone there from that country would stand and sing along. It was very moving.

The United States seemed to have the most people in attendance, due in large part to a huge group of students from the University of New Orleans. They were staying in the Studentenhaus with us. The University of New Orleans and the University of Innsbruck are sister schools, and student exchanges between the two are very common.

The next day was completely free. I went off on my own to explore and find local artisan shops. I bought earrings for my daughters and some pottery for myself, along with coffee beans. I bought coffee beans in Italy, too, and in several places in Austria because it was so delicious.

After lunch at the Mensa, a few of us in the group went off to check out a local secondhand shop someone had learned about. From there, it was back to my room for a brief rest and some reading. We were on our own for dinner and opted to reprise the potluck of the other night, since we had leftovers. Everyone turned in early, since we were leaving at the crack of dawn for the glaciers high up in the mountains.

Early the next morning, in the rain, we headed for the Stubai Valley area. We were hoping that the weather would clear by the time we arrived, and it did. We traveled through picturesque towns of incredible beauty. Each one was nicer than the last. All along the way, we saw evidence of the most popular tourist attractions in the area—alpine and cross-country skiing areas. This is where the Austrian Olympic ski teams come to practice and perform.

We ate lunch in a quaint little alpine restaurant and finally arrived at the base of the glacier mountain. We took a funicular (cable railway) up to the base camp, or first level, where we found a cozy restaurant and ski lodge. Some of the group, including me, opted to go no further.

By this time, the weather had turned nasty again, although that didn't deter some of the more intrepid members of our group. They climbed aboard a second enclosed lift and went to the top of the glacier. They didn't stay long, however, because it was so murky up there. They couldn't see a thing. While they were stumbling around on the glacier, the rest of us were in the warm restaurant drinking cappuccino and having a great time.

On the way back to Innsbruck, we drove through villages even prettier than those we encountered on our trip out. We stopped several times to take pictures and ate dinner at another wonderful restaurant in a small alpine village.

I woke up the next day to another misty morning. A choir from the University of South Carolina was in town for a series of concerts. Since it was Sunday, we went to a high Mass at the Cathedral of St. Jakob to hear them sing. After the Mass was over, the choir came down to the front of the church to sing some songs, including Black spirituals. They were great.

The rest of the day was free, and in the evening we went back to our favorite café—the home of the amazing revolving toilet—for dinner.

The last day of our program dawned sunny and clear. We visited the oldest bell foundry in Europe, built in 1599. It has been run by the same family for fourteen generations.

Bells were an integral part of my travel experience. Whether it was the bells ringing to keep the lightning away in Dorf Tyrol or the tolling of the bells from the many churches in the medieval city of Brixen, or the bells in Innsbruck calling everyone to Sunday services, their lyrical sound was part of the landscape of these wonderful countries.

After touring one last rococo cathedral (we saw so many ornate churches that I lost count), we all went over to the Folk Art Museum for a special docent-guided tour. Entire rooms from old Tyrolean homes had been transported there and reconstructed. They certainly gave us a sense of what it was like to live in the area two hundred, three hundred, and even five hundred years ago.

We emerged to find ourselves gathered up into a festival of some sort in the park next door—an unexpected event that gave us a chance for a last sampling of some of the tasty treats of Austria.

I spied a horse-drawn carriage across the street and indulged in a tour around Innsbruck. As I rode through the streets, I let myself sink back in the carriage and soak in the sights and sounds of this remarkable city while the driver pointed out sights of interest. I felt as though my first educational travel adventure had been an unqualified success.

That evening, our delicious farewell dinner was held at the oldest inn in Innsbruck, the Goldener Adler. Our souvenir menus told us we were having warm duck breast salad, steak with vegetables, unlimited wine, and sacher torte for dessert. We had a great time recapping the many interesting things we had learned, the places we visited, and all the highlights of the program. There were stories, laughter, picture taking, and even a lengthy limerick by one of the more poetically inclined members of our group. Musical entertainment was provided by a Tyrolean zither player. The evening was a fitting finale to an outstanding program.

The trip home was uneventful but long. When we touched down at Logan Airport, everyone clapped. In the terminal, there was more exchanging of phone numbers and addresses. It's too bad that email wasn't as prevalent then as it is today. But some of us vowed to keep in touch.

Even today, ten years later, I consider this trip a personal achievement for me. It was really a journey of self-discovery, albeit one that was so far out of my comfort zone that it didn't even register on the scale, so to speak.

A program like this might also be out of your comfort zone. If so, you can rest assured that educational travel programs are the perfect way to begin stepping out of that comfort zone. You are safe, well cared for, and guided the entire way. Within a few days, the group becomes a surrogate family, watching out for each other and providing support when it is needed.

For me, being back in a classroom after more than twenty-five years was invigorating. Thanks to this program, I realized that I wanted to return to school, which I did that fall. I also came home feeling more secure about being a single woman and realized that life could be fulfilling no matter what one's marital status.

Programs like this are also just plain fun! And they are the perfect way to begin incorporating lifelong learning into your life. So take that first step and look into educational travel. It's the experience of a lifetime!

Unfortunately, Interhostel, the educational travel organization that produced the above program, was disbanded by the University of New Hampshire in 2005.

Educational Travel—A Lesson in Values

Keith Schiager

Keith Schiager lives in Salt Lake City, Utah.

We have traveled in several third-world countries where the poverty is overwhelming, but one experience in Nepal stands out in my memory.

On a river rafting trip, we camped overnight on the riverbank in a remote area. The next day, our guide took us on a trail to a village that had no access to the outside world other than foot trails or small boats. Village children greeted us shyly: "Namaste." As we looked around the poor village, we saw shacks with no walls, people in rags, and a few pigs and water buffalos. The only "store" was a shed about the size of a closet. Water for all purposes was provided by one hose running into town from a mountain spring.

Along the trail we had seen bananas growing wild, so one woman in our group asked (through our guide) if they had any bananas for sale. The storekeeper went behind the shed and returned with a large bunch of very small bananas. "How much does he want for the whole bunch?"

"One dollar!"

"I'll buy the bunch," she said, taking the bananas and passing some around our group so all could taste.

There were enough bananas for two or three for every member of our group, but as I started on my second, I noticed the way the children were staring at us. Their eyes were big and wistful, and it was obvious that they envied us. We all had thought they must have so many bananas that they wouldn't think them special, and our group member had bought them mainly as a way of interacting with the villagers.

As our guide explained, the wild bananas were about the only cash crop for the village, so they very rarely ate any themselves. After learning the facts, we bought another bunch (for considerably more cash) and distributed them to the children of the village. What a pleasure for us to see their big smiles and hear their laughter.

Life lesson: Value, like beauty, is in the eye of the beholder!

MY QUEST

Joan Bonagura

Joan Bonagura is a member of QUEST: A Community for Lifelong Learning, sponsored by the City College of New York, Center for Worker Education, in New York City.

The Robust
boldly unearth mysteries
embrace passions
infuse pleasure
and dramatize the hidden

The Guest Speakers
capture the elusive
resurrect the past
interpret the present
and forecast the future

The Creative
reconstruct images
imagine serenity
define cruelty
and illumine beauty

The Lunch Crowd
share humor and experience
treasure moments together
present observations
and discuss personal views

The Analytical
don't hesitate to
witness shadows receding
present exalted discourse
that gives us impetus to blossom.

LEARNING LATER, LIVING GREATER
MY WAY!

Patricia E. Stevens

Patricia E. Stevens is a member of the Osher Lifelong Learning Institute, sponsored by the University of Southern Maine, Gorham.

After taking an American history course on Thomas Jefferson at my local lifelong learning program in Gorham, Maine, it did not take me long to make up my mind where I wanted to go on "vacation."

Monticello, Jefferson's home in Virginia, was my destination. Forty years in the building, this historic homestead is a piece of Americana, based on Paladin architecture. A visit to this home, and the area too, would be a fitting finale to my course.

You see, the class facilitator, a local professor, had made the Revolutionary period come alive for us twenty-first-century patriots. We had learned about Jefferson's democratic ideology, his family life, and the politics of the Revolutionary period. This background made my adventure to Monticello seem like a field trip. I felt I already knew this man Jefferson and what he stood for. In preparation for my trip, I also read *In Pursuit of Reason: The Life of Thomas Jefferson*, by Noble E. Cunningham, Jr.

At Monticello, a beautiful home with wonderful views of the lower Blue Ridge Mountains, we listened to guides tell the story of this home—the day-to-day life, the slaves, the politics. We visited the cellar kitchens and saw extensive gardens. Nearby were the battlefields of Culpepper and Manassas, remnants of another, later war. Armed with the knowledge from my Jefferson course, I enjoyed my visit to the fullest.

On the advice of the professor who taught my Jefferson course, I visited the University of Virginia in Charlottesville to revel in the architecture of their old, historic buildings, as well as to appreciate Jefferson's dedication to education. My teacher also suggested a visit to Michie Tavern for a delicious meal, with servers garbed in colonial dress—a wonderful way to get the flavor of the era.

Intent on continuing my field trip about Thomas Jefferson and the era, my next stop was colonial Williamsburg, 120 miles away. There I was fortunate to listen to a re-enactor in the guise of Jefferson who said it took Jefferson five to ten days to make the same trip that had just taken me but two hours. As a representative of the new colonial government, Jefferson took every opportunity to return home to Monticello when he was done with government business in Williamsburg.

At his request, nothing on Jefferson's headstone says he was president of the United States. Instead it simply says, "Here was buried Thomas Jefferson, Author of the Declaration of American Independence, of the Statute of Virginia for Religious Freedom, and the Father of the University of Virginia."

My "vacation" was an educational, interesting, and informative experience, full of art, architecture, history, and government. I was inspired by and thoroughly enjoyed my Jefferson course at the Osher Lifelong Learning Institute and look forward to taking many more courses.

Charting My Journey

· · · ·

Charting My Journey

••••

PART FIVE

Rebels
with a
Cause

Chapter Eleven

The Connection between Lifelong Learning and Community Service

Dedicate some of your life to others. Your dedication will not be a sacrifice. It will be an exhilarating experience because it is an intense effort applied toward a meaningful end.
—Dr. Tom Dooley

The coming wave of boomers are the rebels with a cause who brought enormous change to society in the 1960s and 1970s. Many of them, it is expected, will look to continue their pioneering social efforts into their later years. And the current population of older adults, most from the Greatest Generation, are already demonstrating their strong commitment to society by engaging in a wide range of civic endeavors. It's quite obvious that older adults, no matter what the generation, can be and are a great asset to our society. So with that being said, we'll now examine the connection between lifelong learning and meaningful community service—how lifelong learners get involved and help society better serve us all.

In earlier chapters, we talked about how becoming involved in lifelong learning can lead to other things. Meaningful community service is one of those other things. Lifelong learning, combined with meaningful community service, so engages all your senses that it produces a natural high, a feeling so unique and exquisite that you will find yourself looking for other ways to keep that exuberance a permanent fixture in your after-fifty years.

Meaningful community service is different for each person. It's about engaging in whatever endeavor makes you feel complete and useful. It's about whatever activity enriches and stimulates your life. For some, meaningful community service might mean getting involved at higher levels with volunteer organizations. For others, it might mean something entirely different.

> Volunteering is one of the best ways people over sixty can contribute to their own well-being.
> —Linda Fried, Johns Hopkins University

Whatever it means to you, however, you can be sure that by using your wisdom and experience, you can soar to greater heights and deliver even greater impact in whatever project you undertake. Those who are involved in their communities routinely encounter new perspectives and ideas that challenge as much as they enlighten. Your involvement in meaningful community service will help add yet another facet to your lifelong learning quest.

According to *The Wall Street Journal*, however, a growing number of mature volunteers are seeking positions that offer something more—more influence, more authority, more power. They are taking leadership positions in volunteer organizations, ensuring that their skills, wisdom, and knowledge are being utilized to the fullest. [1]

A 2004 estimate by the Independent Sector says that the dollar value for volunteer work is $17.55 an hour. [2] Given that number, can you imagine what a significant resource the more than seventy-six million baby boomers will be to our society, even if only a modest number of them engage in community service work? If that's the case, then what this generation of older adults will give back to society far outweighs what they will take out, thereby negating the doomsday economic predictions of what the retirement of the baby boomers might mean to our society.

Lifelong learners who are already offering their skills to the public sector, however, have set a notable example for the coming wave of older adults on how to engage in community service. To set the stage for the further exploration of community service, we'll give you some concrete examples of how these current-day lifelong learners engage in meaningful volunteerism. Then, in the next chapter, we'll talk about the many aspects of community service; and Chapter 13 will give you resources to help you decide how community service can fit into your life and your goal of being a complete lifelong learner.

Lifelong Learners and Community Service

The Institute for Continuing Learning (ICL) at Young Harris College in Georgia is an excellent example of an organization that combines lifelong learning and community service. The following excerpt is taken from an article, written by Lucy Scofield, in their spring 2004 newsletter.

Almost all ICL members are great volunteers. They all have causes and they give freely of their time and enthusiasm. With most, it has been a way of life ever since we sold Girl Scout cookies and such when we were young.

ICL itself is non-profit and totally dependent upon the active support of its membership. We teach, organize, keep books, publish bulletins of course schedules and write this quarterly newsletter to the membership. This is necessary for the group's survival.

However, there is another side to the lives of ICL members. We participate in so many different activities that it is impossible to name them all in this space. But here is a sampling of activities in which members have recently participated.

- Working with the American Cancer Society
- Activities in Habitat for Humanity
- Involvement in the Friends of the Library
- Volunteers at the Union County Nursing Home
- Active in the Hiwassee River Watershed Coalition
- Volunteering at the Union County Chamber of Commerce
- Teaching reading and math to detainees at the Colwell Detention Center
- Delivering Meals on Wheels
- Giving of time and talent to SAFE, the shelter for abused women and families
- Hospice volunteers
- Devoting time to the Mountain Shelter's Humane Society of Union and Towns Counties

The level of meaningful community service by the members of ICL is not unusual. Here are some other examples of how lifelong learners at other programs around the country give back to their communities:

The Academy for Lifelong Learning (ALL) at Carnegie Mellon University has been providing tutors for the last six years to a local elementary school. ALL members work with students who need help with reading and math. The academy also donated a new fax machine to the school.

The Center for Learning in Retirement at Rock Valley College, in Rockford, Illinois, offers its members the chance to learn how to teach reading to adults. Once they complete the course, members can become volunteer tutors in their community.

Members of the Duke University Institute for Learning in Retirement in Durham, North Carolina, are very active in several different volunteer projects. The program adopted a local elementary school in 1993, and since then, interested members have been spending two hours per week there as tutors and classroom assistants. Other members support the Children's Hospital/Children's Miracle Network, which raises money for sick children in the area. Still other members volunteer for studies at the Center for Aging, while others work with international students and faculty at Duke.

The Renaissance Institute at the College of Notre Dame in Maryland is committed to taking part in service and intergenerational programs. In the Freshman Interviews program, members are interviewed by students from the Perspectives on Education and Culture course. Along with that program, a six-week Service Learning program has been started for members who are interested in finding out just what service learning is all about. They will then use this knowledge to identify community outreach initiatives.

Members of the Seniors' Education Centre at the University of Regina in Saskatchewan have a chance to participate in the Outreach and Applied Research Projects that take place at the university. Among the projects currently under way are Rural Education Outreach, Intercultural Grandmothers, and Older Adult Literacy.

Members of the Senior College at Lewiston-Auburn College in Maine are involved in a unique service program entitled Franco-American Architecture in Lewiston. They do cultural fieldwork and develop an exhibit around this theme. Course activity includes oral history, geography, genealogy, archaeology, and archival research.

Members of the Academy for Learning in Retirement at Saratoga Springs, New York, sit on boards of local organizations, work in soup kitchens and food pantries, volunteer at hospices, and work in museums and churches.

Members of the Adult Learning Program at the University of Connecticut in Hartford volunteer at the Athenaeum, and do volunteer teaching at the local high schools.

The Academy of Senior Professionals (ASPEC) at Eckerd College in St. Petersburg, Florida, says its membership volunteers their time at 110 nonprofit agencies in the area. A few of the wide-ranging activities include fund-raising for the local orchestra, docent activities at museums, working at a spouse abuse center, sitting on boards, teaching courses at local schools, providing low-income tax assistance, and working in churches.

The membership of the Berkshire Institute for Lifetime Learning at Berkshire Community College in Massachusetts are deeply involved in volunteering for the many cultural activities in the area. They also volunteer to read for the blind and dyslexic, construct housing for the homeless, work at various libraries, and work at local hospitals and hospices.

A sampling of volunteer activities from the Lifelong Learning Institute at Caldwell College in New Jersey includes establishment of a computer science curriculum in grades K–8 at two local schools and serving on the educational advisory boards and on various committees at these schools.

This list could go on and on. What is clear, however, is that these activities demonstrate the link between lifelong learning and community service. The two just naturally go together.

Intergenerational Mentoring

In reading through the above list, you can tell that mentoring is one of the favorite ways lifelong learners give back to their communities. It has been said that one generation's philosophy becomes the common sense of the next. That being the case, helping younger generations is one of the more valuable roles older lifelong learners can play in our society.

Older adults who belong to Lifelong Learning Institutes often work with college undergraduate and graduate students. They also reach out into the community to work with elementary and high school students as mentors. Older learners many times initiate such programs, working together with community agencies and organizations.

When older adults are matched with schoolchildren, these two generations share activities and in the process many stereotypes are broken down. Older adults benefit from this work in that they develop a greater sense of purpose and more self-esteem. Being so involved in the community also leads to more life satisfaction. At the same time, the students learn more about getting older while increasing their own self-esteem, knowledge, skills, and motivation. And they also gain role models with valuable experience who can guide them into maturity.

Intergenerational programs also benefit the entire community. Participants pool resources and engage in creative problem solving to tackle social issues. Along the way, they find that respect for diversity and each other's generational traditions have been growing.

Intergenerational community service work is so valuable to our society that the Center for Intergenerational Learning at Temple University seeks candidates to be trained to join its new Intergenerational Training Experts Network (ITEN). The goal of the network will be to help build the capacity of nonprofit organizations to infuse intergenerational approaches into their programs and to engage more older adults in meaningful volunteer roles. If this sounds interesting, check out their website at *templecil.org/ITEN*.

Mentoring can take place almost anywhere—in the home (children often listen to their grandparents more than to their parents), in the workplace through in-house workshops run by experienced coworkers, and in the schools. There is a desperate need for school mentors in all grades. In fact, this type of mentoring has become very popular.

The role of a mentor is not to impose your thoughts and beliefs on the person you are mentoring. Instead, the goal is to get them to reveal their own thoughts and beliefs, by using gentle encouragement throughout the process. Successful mentors point out the importance of developing the ability to listen while they are using appropriate questions to further aid the process. This approach ensures both the mentor and the mentored are on the same wavelength and that both will benefit from the exchange of ideas. Mentors gain an infusion of vitality and energy from the youth they are mentoring, while the mentored gain valuable perspective and knowledge about the larger world they may not have had the chance to explore yet.

Successful mentors don't try to impress, nor do they impose their own belief systems. Instead, they try to bring out the mentored's own innate sense of knowledge. Respect the fact that they are unique individuals with as much right to their own beliefs as you. Remember to listen to their concerns before you attempt to share your wisdom. Recognize that successful mentoring takes time.

Make sure you ask yourself some important question before you embark on this adventure. Why do you want to be a mentor? What knowledge do you want to pass on? Prepare an inventory of your skills, knowledge, and life experiences. Determine who would most benefit from your experience. When you have these answers, then you can begin to make a difference in someone's life.

> Studies have shown that older adults who volunteer live longer than their peers who don't volunteer.
> —*Mayo Clinic Health Letter* (August 2001)

Intergenerational mentoring is truly one of the most valuable methods of community engagement. Mentoring helps combat family dysfunction, drug addiction, and abuse. It's a wonderful feeling knowing you've helped the next generation.

School Volunteers

Although school volunteers are similar to mentors, the educational tasks they undertake with their young charges can be quite varied. We used to think that school volunteers automatically meant parents, and mothers in particular, since they were the ones usually at home during the day. Not anymore. Today, school volunteers come from all levels of society, be it stay-at-home mothers or fathers, staff from large corporations, and especially older adults who no longer work full time. Although there is more variety in who becomes a school volunteer, the numbers of actual participants has dropped because more people are employed full time. Consequently, schools are beginning to look more and more toward the experience, knowledge, and wisdom that can be found right in their own communities among the older adult population.

School volunteering is the perfect venue for the assets that older adults have amassed over a lifetime. Today, the United States is fortunate to have the world's largest number of healthy, well-educated retired adults. And, as we mentioned earlier, by 2030 there will be about sixty-five million older persons—20 percent of the population. What a huge resource!

To say that this resource of older adults can make a major difference to school districts caught in budget crunches, teacher shortages, and increasing enrollments is an understatement. School volunteers can help ease teacher stress and make up the shortfall when classroom aides and specialists are cut from tightened budgets.[3]

All across the country, teachers are utilizing older volunteers in their classrooms and winning support for school district activities among mature adults. The Agelink Project, an intergenerational child-care program for school-age children, provides after-school services linking children with volunteer older adults in North Carolina. The Senior Motivators in Learning and Educational Services (SMILES) program in Salt Lake City recruits and trains older adults and places them in district schools, where they help with activities such as story reading, field trips, tutoring, arts and crafts, and sports. Many SMILES volunteers work in resource rooms with special education students.[4]

Older volunteers perk up the class day for students by offering new and unique viewpoints. Experts in a wide variety of skills and talents, they share their perspectives on many different topics. The volunteers also find that they too benefit—the intergenerational contact is priceless.

With the decline in the extended family, intergenerational programs become even more valuable as older adults are called on to be surrogate grandparents. In addition, intergenerational programs can help dispel some of the negative stereotypes each generation has about the other.

How's this for a factoid? When the 2005 school year ended in June, 1,800 Experience Corps members had put in approximately 446,000 hours helping 13,250 students develop the confidence and skills they'll need to succeed in school and in life. What's that worth? As was previously mentioned, the Independent Sector puts the dollar value of each volunteer hour at $17.55. Add it up, and you'll see that Experience Corps members provided tutoring and mentoring services worth $7.8 million dollars ($7,827,300) this school year alone.[5]

Older Peace Corps Volunteers

The link between lifelong learning and the Peace Corps is very strong. Put simply, the primary job of Peace Corps volunteers is to teach. What's especially nice is that older Americans are contributing to Peace Corps programs all over the globe, and, in the process, they are finding their age to be an asset. The organization recognizes that no group has more to offer in terms of experience, maturity, and demonstrated ability. There is no upper age limit to join the Peace Corps. In fact, volunteers who are well into their eighties have served and continue to serve. For more information on the Peace Corps, check out their website at *www.peacecorps.gov/index.cfm?shell=learn.whovol.older*.

Support for Older Adult Volunteer Projects

Nothing speaks more to the viability of a project than the willingness of an organization or foundation to provide the necessary funds. Here are some examples from Civic Ventures of volunteer projects for older adults that have been recently funded. Each of these projects has a strong connection between lifelong learning and community service.[6]

- In Arizona, the Piper Foundation announced $1.6 million in grants to support the development of four Next Chapter centers in Maricopa County. The centers are designed to help older adults to explore opportunities for volunteer and paid service, as well as options related to health, wellness, and education. *www.civicventures.com/310.html*.

- In Ohio, the Cleveland Foundation provided $360,000 in grants to support projects that will expand paid employment and unpaid service opportunities for older adults in that community. *www.civicventures.org/294.html*.

- The Gerontological Society of America (GSA) inaugurated a project called Civic Engagement in an Older America that will promote research on programs and public policies likely to increase civic participation among older adults. *www.civicventures.org/290.html*.

- The National Council on the Aging launched RespectAbility, an initiative designed to help community organizations and decision makers enhance civic participation by older Americans. The project includes research with leaders of nonprofit organizations to identify barriers to engaging older adults, a national public awareness campaign, and preparation by veteran journalists of news articles on engagement by older adults. *www.civicventures.org/277.html*.

- The Harvard School of Public Health–MetLife Foundation

Initiative on Retirement and Civic Engagement released a new report on "Reinventing Aging: Baby Boomers and Civic Engagement." Last fall, the initiative announced the launching of its second phase, which will include a number of activities intended to expand public awareness of the value of older adults as a social resource. *www.civicventures.org/291.html.*

- Researchers at Johns Hopkins Medicine published research based on the Experience Corps program which showed that older adults who volunteer in troubled urban schools not only improve the educational experience of the children, but also realize meaningful improvements in their own mental and physical health. *www.civicventures.org/news_2004.html.*

Lifelong learning and community service go hand-in-hand. If you truly desire to make your later life more complete, then meaningful community service—service that engages both your mind and your heart—should be a part of that plan as well. There are too many benefits to be gained and given from engaging in community service for it to be ignored. Take the opportunity to use your hard-earned wisdom and life experience for the benefit of younger generations. You'll make a lasting impact on them for years to come. It's a great feeling.

INTERVIEW WITH AN EXPERT

Jane McBride

Jane McBride has, for the last five years, chaired an ASPEC special interest group with the goal of developing understanding of all aspects and resources within the community. Representatives from the community meet with ASPEC members at bimonthly meetings to present information, describe volunteer opportunities, and answer questions. Jane has been an ASPEC senator for four years and is currently president of the ASPEC Senate. Since she joined ASPEC in 1996, Jane has volunteered in her adopted community of St. Petersburg at a children's center and has been a member of the Juvenile Welfare Board of the South County Council. ASPEC is sponsored by Eckerd College, in St. Petersburg, Florida.

The Academy of Senior Professionals at Eckerd College (ASPEC) is very much involved in community outreach. Can you give us some examples of the community service that members undertake?

Members serve their churches in a variety of ways—in choirs, as deacons, in social service activities, and so on. They are involved in the arts — in museums as docents and receptionists and at gift shops, special events, and fund-raisers. They volunteer in child care centers, schools, the free clinic, child abuse, hospices, and other places. They serve on boards and are very hands-on workers.

How do ASPEC members select their community service?

They choose what interests them and where they feel they can use their talents and skills to the most advantage.

Would you say that being involved in lifelong learning through the ASPEC program has led to greater community involvement among your members?

Yes, absolutely. ASPEC is built upon four pillars: intergenerational, social, community, and peer-led interest groups., Community, to us, means reaching out to others, learning about our (usually adopted) community, and doing what we feel will give added meaning to our lives.

Does ASPEC *have any plans for new outreach?*

We are always looking for ways in which we can be involved and for where our interests and skills may benefit others

Do you have a favorite story about community outreach and an ASPEC *member?*

I like the way Nita and Vera used their library experiences to provide parents in a children's center with a book and activities to encourage reading at home and to ask for feedback, or the way Jan used her experience as a florist to design an arrangement for Arts in Bloom at the Museum of Fine Arts. Then there was Ann, who used her experience as a therapist with disabled children to work at a center for mentally retarded adults, and had her husband, Eric, help them with their finances. I like the way Paula sponsored educational programs at the Holocaust museum, and the way a group of members used their expertise to consult on a local water project. I could go on and on. Our members are very involved in the community.

The members of ASPEC *certainly epitomize the axiom by Henry van Dyke:*

> Use what talent you possess!
> The woods would be very silent if no birds
> sang except those that sang best.

Learning Later, Living Greater My Way!

Alfred Bernstein

Alfred Bernstein is a member of the Omnilore program sponsored by The California State University, Dominguez Hills.

The goal of the Pursuit of Wisdom discussion group at the Omnilore program was to appreciate and understand wisdom and apply these concepts to one's own life. Who would have thought that an old curmudgeon like me could change his well-ordered life? I proved that it is never too late to become wiser.

This transformation happened as a direct result of my being exposed to ideas from my fellow group members. I am now a volunteer tutor in the Walteria Elementary School. I help individuals and small groups of students in the first through third grades improve their skills in reading and arithmetic. It is truly a rewarding experience for me, and maybe a bit of a help for the children.

The spontaneity of the children revitalizes me every time I tutor. Some children have even shown progress in their endeavors. My life has gained greater purpose, and my heart is fuller.

Charting My Journey

• • • •

Charting My Journey

••••

Chapter Twelve

Lifelong Learning through Community Service

*Service to others is the rent we pay for
the privilege of living on this earth.*
—Pierre Teilhard de Chardin

"Mentors, mediators, monitors, motivators, and mobilizers"—those are the community roles the late Maggie Kuhn (founder of the Gray Panthers) thought should be filled by those who no longer hold full-time paying jobs. Filling these roles is an ambitious undertaking. But thanks to millions of older adults who already offer their time and expertise, and the estimated seventy-six million plus of us who will be leaving the full-time workforce over the coming years, we can do it. With the knowledge, skills, and wisdom we have developed over a lifetime of full-time work and personal experience, we are well positioned to take on the roles Kuhn envisioned.

We will use our talents to find ways to meld old and new interests into civic activities that will give us a renewed sense of purpose and usefulness. At the same time, we will be engaging in lifelong learning because all our senses are involved in helping to enhance our society and make it a better place to live for all generations. And when we do so, the later years of our lives will be greatly enriched.

Let's now take a look at the many aspects of community service.

Facts about Community Service

All of us have volunteered at some point in our lives. Helping out at our child's school, a place of worship, or a community event was volunteering, whether or not we thought of it that way. Here are some interesting facts about older adults and community service in the United States:

- President Jimmy Carter's mother was eighty-three when she joined the Peace Corps.

- Mature Americans are the most active and well informed citizens when it comes to both politics and current affairs, so they are the ones who are often seen as the community leaders and activists.

- A recent study indicated that 40 percent of Americans between the ages of fifty and seventy-five said they were "very interested" or "fairly interested" in half-time community service roles after they no longer worked full time.

- More than twelve thousand older volunteer executives offer advice and assistance to more than three hundred thousand small businesses through SCORE.

- The experiential knowledge of mature adults is of tremendous value to our society.

- Mature volunteers are contributing more in terms of dollar value to our society than the amount older Americans are getting back in support.

- An estimated twenty-four million adults over the age of fifty-five are serving as volunteers in our society, and more would if they were asked.

- Despite the multitude of people who share their time and talents, the needs of our communities far outweigh the work that is already being done.

Community Service Venues

Where in their communities are all these people volunteering? Here's a short list:

- Day care centers

I am eighty-five years old, and I'm still learning. As a volunteer, I work with the disadvantaged from all ages and races and walks of life. It has opened my eyes and my mind, making me more aware of the problems of others.

—Shirley Newmark, Beachwood, Ohio

- Neighborhood watches
- Public schools and colleges
- Halfway houses
- Community theatres
- Drug rehabilitation centers
- Fraternal organizations and civic clubs
- Retirement centers and homes for the elderly
- Meals on Wheels
- Church- or community-sponsored soup kitchens or food pantries
- Museums, art galleries, and monuments
- Community choirs, bands, and orchestras
- Prisons
- Neighborhood parks
- Youth organizations, sports teams, and after-school programs
- Shelters for battered women and children
- Historical sites, battlefields, and national parks

Examples of Community Service Activities

Looking for some examples of how you can give some time within your community? Here are some things you may find interesting, depending on your talents, skills, and time:

- Provide one-on-one tutoring to local school children, especially in reading, English, and math.
- Sit on boards of local organizations.
- Work in churches or synagogues.
- Volunteer at hospices or hospitals.
- Be a docent at local museums.
- Work in soup kitchens or food pantries.
- Be a mentor or a mock job interviewer to graduating students.
- Serve as a subject control for studies at local universities or colleges.

- Be a volunteer teacher at local schools.
- Be a fund-raiser for local nonprofits.
- Work at spouse abuse centers.
- Provide low-income tax assistance.
- Volunteer to usher at local cultural events.
- Read for the blind and dyslexic.
- Construct housing for the homeless.
- Work at libraries.
- Teach reading to adults.
- Answer local help lines.
- Be a court volunteer.
- Work in police departments.
- Be a friend to international students.
- Serve as Red Cross bloodmobile workers.
- Be part of disaster recovery teams.
- Drive those needing medical treatment.
- Take part in city beautification projects.
- Volunteer in local environmental programs.
- Act as a judge at student Model UN programs.
- Counsel people wanting to start their own businesses.
- Participate in food drives.
- Take part in drug awareness programs.
- Answer phones during local PBS membership drives.
- Join a women's club to provide assistance to local communities.
- Serve lunch to shut-ins.
- Volunteer at local botanical gardens.
- Serve on local town/city councils.
- Sit on leadership committees.
- Get involved in local crime prevention programs.
- Work in Goodwill/Salvation Army thrift stores.
- Take part in health screening registration drives.

- Serve on educational advisory boards.
- Volunteer at children's centers and nursing homes.
- Serve on the boards of science and governmental institutions.
- Travel to remote countries to promote various types of education.
- Do cultural fieldwork.
- Work for local chambers of commerce.
- Take part in rural outreach programs.

Finding the Right Opportunity

There are literally millions of ways to volunteer. But how do you harness them into the right opportunity for you? How do you find the opportunity that fits your lifestyle? Here are some suggestions:

- Look for causes and groups that work with issues you feel strongly about.
- Make a list of your skills. You'll then need only a minimum of training, and those skills can be applied for the benefit of others.
- Or take the opportunity to learn something new through community service.
- Look for opportunities that will help you combine your other goals in life.
- Review your schedule so you don't overcommit. No one wins if that happens. Take into account your other life commitments.
- Look at opportunities you can take on as a team with your spouse.
- "Virtual volunteer" if you love working on a computer. There are more than one hundred organizations that use online volunteers.

After so many years of volunteer work, I felt there were many projects that I just wanted to see some younger people take over. But now I have found something new, where I can make a real contribution for the benefit of others, while at the same time deriving a great deal of joy myself.

—Gretchen Lankford, Pittsburgh, Pennsylvania

- Think about new and different venues where volunteers might be useful.

- Find out how much time is required; how much, if any, of your own funds will be used; and whether expenses are reimbursed.

Benefits of Community Service

There are many life-enriching benefits to be gained from community service. Here are just a few:

- Community service produces the halo effect. By helping out, you not only help make the world a better place, but also enrich your own life.

- Community service gives you the opportunity to fulfill your dreams. Perhaps our career paths took us in a different direction than the one we secretly dream about. So instead of finding a project that is a continuation of that career, find one that fulfills the inner you. Engage in that fantasy!

- Most people can physically, mentally, and emotionally benefit from a moderate amount of service work.

- Being a volunteer enhances the control you feel over your own life.

- A measure of status and identity is conferred when you contribute and work in a volunteer capacity.

- You feel fulfilled with a new sense of purpose.

- Community service boosts character, and it builds strong minds that can reason, think critically, negotiate, and solve problems.

- You will be intellectually challenged.

- Giving back promises greater meaning and stimulation and the chance to make a difference in others' lives.

- People who have found a valued role in life live longer.

- You develop a new perspective on life, making material things less important.

- You will come away feeling valued and needed.

- You make new contacts, which might lead to a second career, full time or part time.

- Social interaction increases as you meet new people.
- Finally, community service enables you to leave a legacy. Erik Erikson's idea that "we are what survives of us" speaks to how we can leave society better than we found it. And that's what we'll be remembered for!

If you have already left the full-time workforce, why not investigate the many community service options available in your community? You will soon find one or more that fit your experience and interests.

If you are still working and free time is at a premium, tuck this away until you are ready to leave the world of full-time work. Then bring it back out and begin to think about how to continue to be involved in lifelong learning through community service.

If you see a need that isn't being met, think about how you can meet that need. If necessary, think big. Start a new organization if that's what it takes to fill the gap. Let your imagination guide you. There's always a need for meaningful community service. It takes only one person to get the ball rolling. That person can be you!

Community service is:

- an opportunity to fill your later years with joy and stimulation
- an opportunity to help change the stereotypical views of older adults
- an opportunity to leave a lasting legacy for the next generation

Learning Later, Living Greater My Way!

Shirley Newmark

Shirley Newmark is a member of the Rose Institute for Lifelong Learning in Beachwood, Ohio.

I have been attending many lectures and classes here at the Rose Institute for Lifelong Learning. Thanks to these classes, I have learned things such as how wise our forefathers were and what a wonderful legacy they left us. I have also learned how influential the wives of presidents were and how they made deep impressions on presidential decisions. These classes have given me an opportunity to listen and learn, and also to form new opinions. I find that experience also plays a large part in developing new ideas.

I did not complete my college education until I was sixty-eight years old. As a young woman, I attended Miami University, in Oxford, Ohio, for just two years. When I was sixty-four, I went back to school and finally graduated from Cleveland State University.

Being back in school was very different than it had been in the 1930s. I found the students to be more outgoing, but thanks to that, I too found myself becoming more outgoing and assertive.

There were some benefits to being an older student. For instance, I did not hesitate to talk with the professors when I was having trouble with sign language. My problem was easily straightened out.

The students were also very helpful. They worked with me around the modern equipment. There was so much more automation than in the late thirties. I was treated with a great deal of respect by the undergraduates.

I have changed my attitude concerning young people. I thought they did not understand the trials and problems of the elderly. But to some degree, they do. I realize we do not think as quickly and are much more hesitant about making decisions than those who are younger. But at the same time, I have also learned that I do not always understand their problems either.

There are more advantages today for them than there were when I was young. However, with the advantages, there are more risks and more problems, too. I am concerned about the future we have given our children. Although we have given them advances in science, they still have much to learn, as do we all.

Over the years, I have also been a volunteer, working with the disadvantaged. It opened my eyes and made me more aware of the problems of others. This work was instrumental in focusing my children. Consequently, they are now involved in volunteer work, too.

I am now eighty-five years old, and I am still learning. I try to take advantage of all the opportunities offered here at the Rose Lifelong Learning program. I have met my contemporaries, who are very alert and anxious to learn, too.

I hope to continue to learn with an open mind and to take advantage of the opportunities given me. Living at Rose is special. I am learning something new every day.

Charting My Journey

••••

Charting My Journey

• • • •

Chapter Thirteen

Service Opportunities in the Community

> *Nothing is more pleasing and engaging*
> *than the sense of having conferred benefits.*
> *Not even the gratification of receiving them.*
> —Ellis Peters

In this chapter, we'll take a look at just some of the many organizations within the community that actively recruit and need older adults interested in meaningful community service. You might be surprised at the extensive list, which is so wide-ranging that there is sure to be something of interest to you.

How to Find Community Service Opportunities

The first thing you need to do in order to find a service opportunity that's right for you is define your parameters. A wealth of exciting, challenging, and stimulating opportunities await you. In fact, narrowing down your selection may be the most difficult part, there is so much to choose from.

A recent search on Google for volunteer organizations netted 28,800,000 results, far too many to sift through—you'd be straining your eyes for days poring over the results. Obviously, when you do decide to begin your search, you will need to be rather specific. Define your interests, skills, and abilities first. Then decide if you want to volunteer locally in your community or state, nationally, or even internationally. This bit of homework will also help when you finally contact an organization. You will be able to provide them with a good overview of what you are looking for and what you can provide for them.

We suggest that you begin by reviewing what your own state has to offer. From there, you can narrow it down to your city or town. The Internet and the phone book are the most useful tools. Try looking under Volunteer Organizations in the phone book, or search by *(your state) volunteer organizations* on the Internet. This way, you can acquaint yourself with the options that are available to you. The Resources section of this book has some good places to help you get started.

> If we look carefully, we cannot help realizing that virtually all the activities that make a town or part of a city into a community depend in one way or another on volunteers.
>
> —Margaret Mead

If during your working career you belonged, and perhaps still do, to a national trade or professional organization, that's a great place to start your search. Check out their websites. Most will have ways for you to volunteer your time and expertise. For instance, all of the building and home maintenance trades are needed in such organizations as Habitat for Humanity. Doctors and nurses are needed both in this country and abroad. Whatever you did in your working life can be translated into meaningful community service in your later years.

Another way to begin your search is by specific interest. Is that interest terminology or education? If so, Net Day Compass, at *www.netdaycompass.org*, is the place to start. If literacy is your passion, try *literacy volunteer opportunities (your state)*.

And don't forget the library. Tell your local librarian what you want to do; he or she should be able to provide you with plenty of information.

Other sources include your local church or temple, and the local Rotary, Lions, Kiwanis, and Optimist clubs. These organizations do a lot of international work and have connections overseas, too.

Civic Ventures

Before we go any further, we need to talk about Civic Ventures, a San Francisco–based, national, nonprofit organization that is at the forefront of redefining our later years as they relate to community service. If you expect to leave work over the next twenty to thirty years, and you plan to make those years the best years of your life, then you should know about Civic Ventures.

Civic Ventures, according to their website (*www.civicventures.org*), creates ideas and invents programs to help society achieve the greatest return on experience.[1] With the first of the more than seventy-six million baby boomers turning sixty in 2006, this coming wave of older adults, Civic Ventures goes on to say, "are on the front edge of the largest, healthiest, best educated population of Americans ever to move through and beyond their fifties. They are pioneers in a new stage spanning the decades between middle and late life. Neither young nor old, they represent an extraordinary pool of social and human capital."[2]

Civic Ventures focuses on the "vanguard of a new movement made up of a growing number of Americans who are redefining the second half of life. These people are not just extending their years on the job; they are doing work that adds meaning to these years. They want to share their experience while acquiring new experiences. They are inventors, organizers, leaders, activists, teachers, and entrepreneurs who attach deep meaning to the notion of giving back." They create better opportunities for aging Americans to use their time, talent, and experience in areas that need these assets—areas such as education, health care, and the nonprofit sector.[3]

Civic Ventures also played a key role in creating Experience Corps, a national service program that mobilizes Americans fifty-five and up to help improve urban elementary schools. Experience Corps is the largest AmeriCorps program engaging older Americans. It is a wonderful example of how the generations can be brought together for mutual benefit. See *www.experiencecorps.org*.[4]

Now, Civic Ventures is creating The Next Chapter programs to help individuals nearing retirement answer the question, "What's next?" They will provide "directions and connections" that enable people to clarify their vision, then develop a practical plan for realizing that vision.[5] Encouraging continued contributions to one's community is a vital element of The Next Chapter initiative. We will talk more about The Next Chapter program in the upcoming chapter.

Spending some time on the Civic Ventures website will help you clarify your thinking about community service and give you helpful direction as you take this next step in your life.

Opportunities within Your Community

Community-level agencies and organizations welcome the talents of mature adults. Many communities have volunteer centers that offer information about the types of volunteer opportunities that are available and the agencies and organizations that are seeking volunteer assistance. Volunteer centers refer an estimated eight hundred thousand new volunteers each year.

Volunteers assist a wide variety of community organizations, which provide services to such populations as the elderly, youth, people with AIDS, and the homeless. Opportunities are also available in areas such as the arts and the environment.

To locate the volunteer center in your community, check the telephone book under Volunteer Center, Voluntary Action Center, Volunteer Bureau, or United Way (volunteer centers are sometimes part of the local United Way, many of which maintain extensive databases on volunteer opportunities) or call 1-800-595-4448.

Examples of Local, State, and National Volunteer Agencies and Programs

Network for Good. Network for Good is a nonprofit organization that connects individuals with their favorite charities. Find them at *www.networkforgood.org*.

Volunteer.Org. Volunteer.Org is a resource for people who want to use their skills and talents to really make a difference. Find them at *www.1-800-volunteer.org*.

AARP. AARP, the nation's oldest and largest organization for older adults, maintains an information center to help you find places to volunteer. Find them at *www.aarp.org*.

Environmental Alliance for Senior Involvement. This organization is dedicated to building, promoting, and utilizing the environmental expertise and intense commitment of older persons. Find them at *www.easi.org*.

Executive Service Corps (ESC). This is an organization of retired businessmen and -women who volunteer their expertise to nonprofit and public service organizations. Find them at *www.iesc.org*.

National Retiree Volunteer Coalition. This program is part of Volunteers of America; it takes the skills and talents of older adults and transforms them into useful tools for community leadership and service. Find them at *www.nrvc.org.*

Seniors Community on MSN. This is a member-to-member computer discussion group. If you are an active computer user, this is your chance to help and teach other older adults who may not be as well versed in the current technology. Find them at *communities.msn.com/seniors/.*

Examples of Federal Volunteer Programs and Resources

Another route to take is to look into federal volunteer programs. These are administered by government agencies and have a tremendous impact on our society in all fifty states. Here are a few examples:

Older Americans Act Programs. Volunteers work through state and territorial units on aging, area agencies on aging, and more than twenty thousand local organizations that offer opportunities and services to active older persons as well as those elderly who need help.

Here are just a few of their activities:

- Assisting at group meal sites
- Delivering meals to the homebound
- Escorting frail older persons to health care services, shopping errands, and other services
- Visiting homebound older persons
- Providing telephone reassurance
- Repairing and weatherizing homes
- Counseling older persons in a variety of areas
- Serving as nursing home ombudsmen
- Providing homemaking assistance
- Assisting in senior centers and other group programs

If you are interested in volunteering in Older Americans Act programs, contact your area agency on aging, which is listed in the yellow pages or under county government listings, or call the Eldercare Locator at 1-800-677-1116.

The National Senior Service Corps (Senior Corps). Senior Corps, a part of the federally funded Corporation for National and Community Service, is a network of federally supported programs that help people aged fifty-five and older find service opportunities in their communities. Senior Corps involves mature adults in three types of services:

- *Foster Grandparents*: Low-income individuals aged sixty and over who carry out the challenging and rewarding work of helping special and exceptional needs children.

- *Senior Companions*: Low-income adults who serve as companions for two to four older clients who need help. (Both Foster Grandparents and Senior Companions must serve twenty hours per week and receive a small stipend.)

- *Retired and Senior Volunteer Program*: This program involves adults aged fifty-five and older in service that matches their personal interests and makes use of their skills and lifelong experiences. You can work as little or as much as you want. You do not receive a stipend.

For information on Senior Corps programs, contact the Corporation for National and Community Service at 1-800-424-8867 or visit *www.seniorcorps.org.* This website tells how to become involved and has resources for persons participating in the program.

Service Corps of Retired Executives (SCORE). SCORE is made up of retired executives and small-business owners. SCORE volunteers provide counseling to small-business owners free of charge. Teams of volunteer counselors also assist small-business owners in the areas of planning and management, and they offer seminars and workshops on major considerations in running a business. To locate the SCORE office nearest you, call 1-800-634-0245 or contact your nearest Small Business Administration (SBA) office. Some information is also available at *www.score.org/.*

Volunteers in Parks (VIP). Older adults with an interest in history and the great outdoors can volunteer their time with the National Park Service's Volunteers in Parks program. In 1995, more than seventy-seven thousand people volunteered in almost every park in the system. Their website is located at *www.nps.gov/volunteer/*.

Literacy Volunteers of America (LVA). Literacy Volunteers of America is a national network of local, state, and regional literacy providers who give adults and their families the opportunity to acquire skills to be effective in their roles as members of their families, communities, and workplaces. Their website—*www.literacyvolunteers.org*—contains a U.S. map that allows you to click on your state to find out what volunteer options are available to you.

> Older adults are America's only increasing natural resource.
> —Marc Freedman

AmeriCorps. AmeriCorps has service programs in which volunteers tutor and mentor youth, build affordable housing, teach computer skills, clean parks and streams, run after-school programs, and help communities respond to disasters. Information can be found at their website, at *www.americorps.org/*.

Citizen Corps. The Citizen Corps website, at *www.citizencorps.gov/*, has information about Citizen Corps and its programs, which engage Americans in specific homeland security efforts in communities throughout the country.

Learn and Serve America. The website of this organization, at *www.learnandserve.org/*, offers information about this program and has resources for educators and others involved in developing and managing service-learning projects.

National Aging Information Center. A service of the Administration on Aging, this site is full of information on older adults and community service. An excellent starting point can be found at *www.aoa.gov*.

Volunteer Friends. Ask a Friend is a nationwide campaign developed by Senior Corps, which taps the experience, skills, and talents of volunteers over fifty-five to meet a wide range of community challenges. Find this site at *www.volunteerfriends.org*.

Future Possibilities. Future Possibilities is a not-for-profit organization that delivers life skills coaching and personal development programs to children ages seven through twelve. Their website is located at *www.futurepossibilities.org*.

Habitat for Humanity. Habitat for Humanity International is a non-profit, ecumenical Christian housing ministry. Habitat has built more than 175,000 houses around the world, providing more than 750,000 people in more than 3,000 communities with safe, decent, and affordable shelter. Its website is located at *www.habitatforhumanity.org*.

Examples of International Volunteer Organizations

If going global is more your style, many international organizations seek your help. To see a lengthy list, be sure to refer to the Resources section of this book. There, you will find some of the largest volunteer organizations, which support millions of volunteers all around the world. Here are two examples:

Idealist.org (Action without Borders)—www.idealist.org. Action without Borders is independent of any government, political ideology, or religious creed. Its work is guided by the common desire of its members and supporters to find practical solutions to social and environmental problems, in a spirit of generosity and mutual respect. This website maintains an extensive list of volunteer options organized by country or state. Searching for *Massachusetts*, for example, yielded 380 organizations offering all kinds of volunteer opportunities.

Volunteers for Peace (VFP)—*www.vfp.org*. This is a nonprofit membership organization that has been placing American volunteers in overseas workcamps since 1981. For a membership fee of fifteen dollars, VFP will send you, in early April, its annual VFP *International Workcamp Directory*, which lists detailed information on over eight hundred workcamps in more than sixty countries worldwide.

The registration fee of $225 per workcamp covers everything. (Many volunteers take part in multiple workcamps in a season.) VFP works directly with the host organizations to arrange for your participation. Volunteers are responsible for getting to the site. You can contact them at Volunteers for Peace, 43 Tiffany Road, Belmont, VT 05730, by phone at 1-802-259-2759, and by email at *vfp@vfp.org*.

Virtual Volunteering

Strange as it might sound, online, or virtual, volunteering is becoming a very recognized way to give some of your time to worthy projects. Many people actively search for volunteer opportunities they can participate in through home or work computers because of time constraints, personal preference, a disability, or a home-based obligation that prevents them from commuting to a volunteer locale.

Volunteering via computer allows anyone to contribute time and expertise to nonprofit organizations, schools, government offices, and other agencies that utilize volunteer services. Agencies benefit, too, in that they can then use more volunteers, further cultivate community support, and augment staff resources and existing volunteer programs.

Virtual volunteering is also known as online volunteering, cyber service, online mentoring, teletutoring, and various other names. To get more information about virtual volunteering, go to *www.serviceleader.org/vv*.

Community Service Vacations

Want to spend your vacation doing good for others? If so, then community service vacations are the perfect venue for you. Type the term *volunteer vacations* into Google, and you'll get over half a million hits. This is an overwhelming number to be sure, but cruising through a few of them will give you an excellent idea of what's out there to pick from both nationally and internationally. If this avenue interests you, then do a little homework and spend some time surfing the sites. In the interests of saving space, I will discuss just a few.

One of the best sites is Volunteer America, a portal site that provides anyone, no matter what your age, with opportunities for volunteer vacations on public lands all across America. This site offers information on organizations and service programs designed to combine good works with having fun. Their extensive website can be found at *www.volunteeramerica.net/vacations.htm*. Here are just a few examples of service vacations:

American Hiking Society (AHS). Create and maintain hiking trails. Find out more on their site at *www.americanhiking.org*.

Wilderness Volunteers. Work with public land agencies, including the National Park Service, the Forest Service, the Bureau of Land Management, and the U.S. Fish and Wildlife Service. Find out more at *www.wildernessvolunteers.org*.

Passport in Time (PIT). Work with professional archaeologists and historians on projects including archaeological excavation, surveys, archival research, historic structure restoration, gathering oral histories, or writing interpretive brochures. Find them at *www.passportintime.com*.

Sierra Club. Working on projects related to the conservation efforts of the club gives participants a sense of ownership of the land. Their site is located at *www.sierraclub.org*.

Investigating the local, state, national, governmental, and international organizations discussed in this chapter will give you a helpful overview of the myriad of opportunities out there for becoming involved in community service. And remember, by doing so, you will also continue to learn and grow, enriching and enhancing your later years. Community service is too good an opportunity to pass up!

Up Close and Personal

Teri Baker

(Excerpted from "The Third Age," May 2003 issue, and reprinted here with permission.)

Once a teacher, always a teacher. If you are as gifted as John Terrey, that's a good thing.

So say John's fellow older adults at Edmonds Community College's Creative Retirement Institute (CRI), which he helped found twelve years ago. John, who has volunteered nearly two hundred hours of teaching to CRI, says that what he gets back is priceless. "They bring so much with them," he says, "like the Harvard graduate, an outstanding engineer, who can now study what he wants to."

Being around people who, no matter what their level of formal education, want to learn keeps John, now seventy-nine, excited about teaching. Over his working career, John has taught high school through graduate school, and he has been praised as a key force in establishing and expanding Washington State's renowned community college system.

At CRI, he has taught poetry, philosophy, Shakespeare, and other courses. Whether in the classroom or in ordinary conversation, John provokes people to think. "When you finish the book, you're half finished," he says. "Now you have to reflect. What is the foundation of his argument?"

He shares another insight: "Poetry is a participatory activity. Poets say little and mean much. Your job is to find out the much." John is also willing to learn from others, not only in the classes he takes at CRI, but also in those he teaches. He says, "Their questions are more important than my notes."

Although he has won an array of impressive awards (the list of his published articles fills two full pages), and the Everett Community College Media Center is named for him, John's ego does not get in his way. He speaks of a senior who wanted to talk about economist John Maynard Kanes. "This man, who drives down from Arlington for class, had more to offer than I did, so I let him become the primary teacher that day."

An innate sense of humor helps make John a popular teacher. He quotes a bit of his own poetry, laughs, and says, "When I first wrote that, two people knew what I meant—myself and God. And I have since forgotten." Rather than focusing on his considerable accomplishments, he would rather talk about lifelong learning. "That," he says, "is why it is a real joy to be with CRI."

Over the years, John has taught thousands of students and is still in touch with some of them. He was delighted and surprised to discover a student he taught at Bellevue High in one of his CRI classes forty years later. "I still love to see the bond between teacher and student," he says. "And I loved it when one of my CRI students explained why she was taking classes. She quoted Socrates by replying, 'I am here to enlarge my mind.'"

This teacher, who loves literature, poetry, art, and philosophy, was once a school dropout. Born into a poor, motherless family with a father who was an alcoholic, he and his seven siblings were left to their own resources during the depths of the Depression.

After frequent moves, John came to Seattle, where an aunt and uncle lived. Under their aegis and on the condition that he return to school, he lived with them. His school experiences before that had not been happy ones, but under the tutelage of school staff, he began to excel.

On his seventeenth birthday, however, he dropped out to join the U.S. Marines and was sent to the South Pacific. During his time with the Marines, he discovered poetry, thanks to *101 Famous Poems* sent to him by his high school English teacher.

John, as part of the Marine Raiders, a group that was the first ashore during battles for the beachheads, fought at Beaugainville, New Caledonia, Guam, Guadalcanal, and Okinawa. He contracted malaria and dengue fever and was wounded four times. He came home on a hospital ship and spent six months in the hospital.

Once he was home for good, he decided to finish his education and took the bus to the local high school to ask about night classes. "Somebody gave me an English test," he recalls. "Then they kept bringing me more and more tests about every subject. This went on for two or three hours, and I began to wonder just what it was going to take to get into school." He did not realize he was taking the test for a general education degree. He had just finished high school—and with terrific grades!

John went to Western Washington University via Public Law 16, which provided education funds for people disabled in the war. He graduated and spent the next fifteen years teaching high school. Along the way, he picked up a master's degree in education.

The early 1960s were busy years for John. In addition to teaching, he was president of the Washington Education Association for two years, earned his doctorate at Washington State University, and was involved in crafting legislation to establish independent community colleges throughout the state.

In 1964, he joined Tacoma Community College when "it was just a piece of paper" and helped raise the million dollars necessary for it to open. "I taught the first class there," he says, eyes twinkling. "That's because all the other classes started at eight, and I started mine at ten to eight."

Nearly half of John's thirty-eight-year career in public education was devoted to the community college system, which served 100,307 students in 1969, when he became its deputy director. By the time he retired as executive director seventeen years later, enrollment was nearly 160,000.

John worked with the legislature, served on many of the state's education boards and commissions, and is still a member of the College Planning Network. An adjunct professor of higher education at UW since 1974, he has been named a distinguished alumnus of WWU and WSU; in 1997, he received the Washington Commission for the Humanities Award.

The humanities—those branches of knowledge, such as literature and art, that are concerned with human thought and culture—are important to John. He says, "The humanities are at their best when they become an integral part of one's value system which is devoted to the enlargement of the human spirit. The highest expression of the humanities is found in the work an individual does in his daily life."

John's daily life involves community service work. Besides CRI, he is involved in the Lutheran Alliance To Create Housing (LATCH), which he helped found in 1990 to provide homes for people with low incomes. Says John, "One of the beauties of it is...tenants govern themselves. They form committees for playgrounds, maintenance, and so forth, and learn to work things out together. I can't take credit for the concept, but I know a great idea when I see it."

Retirement is not all work for John. He and his wife travel and spend time with the nieces and nephews. John sees the retirement years as a great opportunity to learn things you always wanted to know, but didn't have time to pursue. "I have been blessed to enjoy what I do."

Note that he says, *do*, not *did*. Always a teacher, ever a learner—that's John's secret to happy retirement.

Learning Later, Living Greater
My Way!

Sam Rifman

Sam Rifman is a member of the Omnilore program sponsored by California State University, Dominguez Hills.

What a surprise it was for me to find more than I was looking for in the study/discussion group Pursuit of Wisdom. Alfred and I learned during one class about the opportunity to be a child advocate—but it didn't work out. What did work out was a lead to RSVP, the Retired and Senior Volunteer Program. The helpful staff identified an opportunity for me to participate in a math clinic at the Hermosa Valley School. As a retired engineer, I felt this was perfect.

But what was even better than playing a small role in assisting sixth- to eighth-graders with math problems was the reward I got one day.

One little girl asked me if it was true I wasn't being paid to help out. I told her I wasn't being paid, but if she gave me a smile, I would consider it reward enough. And so she gave me the most glorious smile anyone could hope to receive in this lifetime, a moment I will never forget. My pursuit of wisdom led me to a reward far greater than any dollar amount. Maybe others will find their payoff—as I found mine!

Charting My Journey

• • • •

Charting My Journey

••••

PART SIX

Reprise—
To Boldly Go

Chapter Fourteen

What's on the Horizon?

*Whether sixty or sixteen, there is in every human heart
the lure of wonder, the unfailing childlike appetite
of what's next and the joy of the game of living...*
—Samuel Ullman

Up to this point, we have discussed programs and opportunities for engaging in lifelong learning that already exist; they've been up and running for some time. Now we're going to take a quick peek at some of the new and innovative ideas that are being developed and put in place for the twenty-first century.

The goal of this chapter is to help you realize that many new options to enhance and enrich your third age will be presenting themselves to you in the coming decades. With over 76 million adults reaching fifty and beyond in the next twenty to thirty years, new opportunities will be almost limitless. So keep your ears and eyes open for ways to ensure a vibrant, alert mind, no matter what your age. You will be pleasantly surprised. As Bob Dylan said, "The times they are a-changin'."

Already, exciting new opportunities are on the horizon. Here are some of them:

The Next Chapter

In Part 5, we talked in depth about Civic Ventures, the San Francisco–based organization that serves as a catalyst and incubator of both ideas and programs that help America achieve an "experience dividend."[1]

They have now developed The Next Chapter initiative to help communities create places and programs that provide older adults with direction and connection as they begin the next chapter of their lives. The Next Chapter concept is based on the premise that access to meaningful choices for work, service, learning, and social connections plays a crucial role in the vitality of older adults and will enrich the life of the community.[2]

The Next Chapter program envisions community places or programs that offer older adults:

- Life planning programs—to help them assess their current status and strengths, explore and envision future possibilities, and make choices by setting goals and plans.

- Meaningful engagement through work and service—to encourage and help them navigate opportunities to take on public service roles, through paid work and volunteer service.

- Continued learning for new directions—to provide a broad range of learning options that enrich their lives and help them retool for new careers.

- Peer and community connections—provide places and programs that foster connections to people of all ages in the community.[3]

In more than twenty communities throughout America, this concept is being turned into tangible programs. Here are some examples:[4]

Chicago Life Opportunities Initiative, Council for Jewish Elderly, Chicago, Illinois—www.cje.net/future

As part of the Chicago Life Opportunities Initiative, the Council for Jewish Elderly, in conjunction with the Loyola University Chicago School of Social Work, created an assessment tool called Mapping Your Future Your Way. This tool can be used online or in a printed version. Mapping Your Future helps people understand the need for planning and begin to explore their interests in five areas—health, work and leisure, finances, housing, and relationships. For each topic, the tool provides a framework of issues to think about, and the online version provides links to other websites with related information.

Pathways to Vital Living: A Curriculum for Midlife and Beyond, Senior Resource Alliance, Winter Park, Florida—www.wppl.org/institute/programs.htm

The Pathways to Vital Living curriculum was developed by the Senior Resource Alliance, the Area Agency on Aging of Central Florida, in collaboration with the Winter Park Health Foundation. It provides a planning and program kit for conducting twelve workshops on varied topics, such as relationship transitions, intentional recreation, meaningful service, mental vitality, and spiritual development. It uses interactive, experiential learning to help older adults assess and explore nine key areas to help them make important life choices.

What's Next!, Fairhill Center, Cleveland, Ohio—www.fairhillcenter.org/ WhatsNext

As part of The Cleveland Foundation's Successful Aging Initiative, the What's Next! program at the Fairhill Center offers a seminar series where older adults meet in two-hour, weekly sessions to dream, discover, share, and plan for the years ahead, and to develop a lifelong learning plan that encompasses wellness, creativity, values, and spirituality. Facilitators assist participants in taking stock of personal resources, and they provide guidance to a vast array of course offerings and learning opportunities.

Cleveland Metroparks Emerald Necklace O.W.L.S., Cleveland, Ohio— www.clemetparks.com/volunteer/index.asp

The Emerald Necklace O.W.L.S. (Older Workers Leading Success) offers intergenerational opportunities and increased participation of adults fifty years and older as employees, volunteers, and participants in public park programs and facilities. It includes three components: (1) older adult volunteer mentors and tutors working with students as part of a park intern program; (2) a volunteer corps to monitor trails; and (3) older-adult employment, including recruitment and job sharing. This project is supported through the Elder Engagement component of The Cleveland Foundation's Successful Aging Initiative.

Retired Social Workers—An Untapped Resource, National Association of Social Workers Illinois Chapter, Chicago, Illinois— www.naswil.affiniscape.com/ displaycommon.cfm?an=1&subarticlenbr=20

The Retired Social Workers, sponsored by the National Association of Social Workers, encourages retired social workers to return to social work to serve older adults as paid professionals. The program includes two key components: (1) professional development to reorient retired social workers to current conditions, agency changes, and present senior issues and attitudes; and (2) placement into positions—as part-time, intermittent, or full-time workers—to provide services and support for older adults. As one of its many programs, the Retired Social Workers received a grant from the Chicago Community Trust to place and pay retired social workers for the Chicago Life Opportunities Initiative.

Wisdom Works!, MetroHealth System, Cleveland, Ohio—www.successfulaging.org/page7787.cfm

MetroHealth's Wisdom Works! program is designed to help retain mature, experienced nurses in paid and volunteer positions to maintain access to care for vulnerable members of the community. In addition to identifying nursing roles appropriate for older nurses, the program identifies workplace modifications needed to keep older nurses and share best practices in retaining an older nursing workforce. This project is being expanded through a grant from the Elder Engagement component of The Cleveland Foundation's Successful Aging Initiative.

Allegheny County Library Association, Pittsburgh, Pennsylvania— www.einetwork.net/acla

The Allegheny County Library Association has organized partnerships to expand the educational options for older adults. Through the Third Age Learning Community, the University of Pittsburgh brings noncredit university-level classes to local libraries. The Senior Center Library Connection works with fifteen Pittsburgh-area senior resource centers to offer book discussion groups, which are held alternative months at the centers and libraries. One Book One Community, in which residents read and discuss the same book at the same time, has worked well to engage older adults in learning and libraries.

OASIS without Walls, Parma, Ohio—www.oasisnet/org/cleveland

OASIS is a national education organization aimed at enriching the lives of adults fifty and over. It offers creative lifelong learning classes in arts and humanities, wellness, life coaching, technology, and other subjects. Through support from The Cleveland Foundation's Successful Aging Initiative, programming at its Parma center in Cleveland has been expanded through OASIS without Walls, which takes lifelong learning activities into the community—everywhere from community and recreation centers to churches and libraries.

Tempe Connections, Tempe, Arizona—www. civicventures.org/185.html

Tempe Connections is part of the Maricopa County Next Chapter Initiative. It was developed under the leadership of the City of Tempe's public library and social services division. It creates a new physical space within the library that houses a café and program space. The café, called Connections Café, acts as a focal point for Next Chapter activities.

> I believe strongly that our members find personal growth from the social aspects of our program as well as from the academic.
> —Gretchen Lankford, Pittsburgh, Pennsylvania

Connected to the café are meeting rooms reserved specifically for Tempe Connections participants. A concierge is available to assist with questions.

Boomerang, Chandler Public Library, Chandler, Arizona—www.my-boomerang.org

Chandler's Boomerang project is part of the Maricopa County Next Chapter Initiative. It was developed under the leadership of the Chandler Public Library, and it is a community project, not a single physical center. The project is implemented through multiple points of entry, including community forums, six centers based at libraries and community colleges, and a website. Its website is the primary information source and a resource navigation tool, with links to project partners, available programs and services, and other relevant information sources—not only within the local community, but also on a regional, state, and national level.

Lehigh Valley Alliance on Aging, United Way of the Lehigh Valley, Pennsylvania—www.lvagingmatters.org

The website of the Lehigh Valley Alliance on Aging provides a comprehensive one-stop source of information for the region's older adults and the professionals who serve them. The website incorporates a Benefits CheckUp, a benefits finder tool, life planning information, resources for financial planning, lifelong learning, volunteering and social connections, a directory of local services, rights and benefits, and resources and a listserve for professionals serving older adults.

Mather's—More Than a Café, Chicago, Illinois—www.matherlifeways. com

Mather's—More Than a Café was conceived of as a Starbucks for seniors. It combines a restaurant, a gathering place, and an educational center under one roof. The three Chicago-area Mather's Cafés primarily serve active, independent older adults in their neighborhoods. Programs and classes on exercise, computers, and art supplement the restaurant. Day trips, monthly parties, and community events encourage new relationships and social interaction. Social workers and health care professionals are available to provide individual consultations and referrals. Connections with other senior groups and health care providers ensure strong support networks for those involved. The Mather's Cafés are operated by the non-profit Mather LifeWays.

For more information on the far-reaching and innovative work of Civic Ventures, be sure to visit their website at *www.civicventures.org*.

Libraries for the Future

Libraries for the Future (LFF) is the program division of the Americans for Libraries Council. LFF provides programs at the national, state, and local levels, typically in partnership with libraries, library systems, foundations, and community-based organizations. They currently operate in more than one hundred communities in twenty states. Their signature programs include Family Place, a national initiative that transforms libraries into centers for healthy child development and family literacy, and EqualAccess Libraries, a model program that helps libraries animate new technologies and enhance their capacities as centers for information and education.[5]

As part of Libraries for the Future's Lifelong Access Libraries—Centers for Lifelong Learning and Civic Engagement initiative, libraries in seven states are receiving training and technical assistance to support their development of Lifelong Access centers.

These centers are library-community collaborations, a new library services model for working with older adults that fosters successful aging through an emphasis on learning, social connections, life planning, and community engagement. In Pennsylvania, Arizona, Connecticut, and Massachusetts, Lifelong Access Libraries are working with older-adult advisory councils to develop innovative programs—creating welcoming spaces to foster social connections, and reorganizing and expanding information resources to support learning and community connections.

Lifelong Access reflects the Access philosophy of community collaboration and stakeholder involvement. Library staff develop partnerships with community colleges, senior centers, health organizations, workforce agencies, and volunteer centers in order to maximize community resources. Together, these community collaborations work to:

- Promote coordination of programs and services.
- Engage older adults in the design and delivery of services.
- Share resources and expertise to provide life planning counseling and opportunities for lifelong learning.
- Provide options for meaningful work or community service.
- Provide information and assistance with resource navigation.
- Develop community space or spaces that foster social exchange and connections across generations and cultural groups.

Libraries are natural partners for promoting productive aging, with spaces, learning programs, service opportunities, and community information. Training in Lifelong Access helps librarians build on these assets for the benefit of older adults and the rest of the community.[6]

Campus Living

It was Isaac Asimov who said, "An aging problem? No problem. Put senior citizens back in college. Under such conditions, accustomed to lifelong learning, why shouldn't they remain creative and innovative to very nearly the end of their lives?"

Today, there are older adults who espouse this same philosophy, and they are moving into communities on or near college campuses in order to avail themselves of the educational opportunities (both for credit and non-credit) and cultural opportunities that abound in towns that host colleges and universities. They are also looking for personal growth and intellectual stimulation.

For those of us who are interested in lifelong learning, this idea holds great appeal. Since our expectations about what our after-fifty years should look like are higher, we are searching for more meaning and value for our

> My ninety-two-year-old mother and I take classes and go on field trips together—mother and daughter, side-by-side!
>
> —Judith Adler, Larchmont, New York

later years. That being the case, for some of us, the idea of returning to the stimulating academic environment we enjoyed years earlier makes perfect sense.

Colleges and universities are taking note of this trend. They are catering to those in their after-fifty years with a broad array of academic programs, cultural offerings, community service initiatives, and even housing options.

The benefits for the academic institutions that sponsor such communities are many. Administrators say that having a more diverse campus population has many intergenerational benefits. The older adults not only take courses, they teach them. Schools with research components find a willing audience of volunteers, interested in taking part in all manner of studies. Many schools like this concept of nearby living because it offers housing for alumni and retired professors. It can also provide housing for the parents of faculty.

Support for the college or university among the older adults is also high. They take part in social and cultural events, lend their expertise and community contacts to fund-raising, and are often generous donors themselves. The high-energy feeling of a college campus is also very appealing to older adults. Being back in that atmosphere usually makes anyone over fifty feel younger, more vigorous, and recharged.

The Internet can help you find more information on this subject. One good site with lots of information is Campus Continuum, at *www.campuscontinuum.com/resources.htm*.

If the idea of living near or on a college campus in your third age years appeals to you, here are just a few of the universities and colleges that sponsor such communities:

- Cornell University (New York)—The Kendall at Ithaca
- Ithaca College (New York)—Longview
- Dartmouth College (New Hampshire)—The Kendall at Hanover
- Oberlin College (Ohio)—The Kendall at Oberlin
- West Chester University (Pennsylvania)—The Kendall at

Longwood

- Lasell College (Massachusetts)—Lasell Village
- Indiana University (Indiana)—Meadowood
- Iowa State University(Iowa)—Green Hills
- Penn State (Pennsylvania)—The Village at Penn State
- University of Florida (Florida)—Oak Hammock
- University of Arizona (Arizona)—Arizona Senior Academy
- University of Virginia (Virginia)—The Colonnades
- Haverford and Swarthmore Colleges (Pennsylvania)—Quadrangle
- Notre Dame (Indiana)—Holy Cross Village
- University of Michigan (Michigan)—University Commons
- Davidson College (North Carolina)—The Pines at Davidson
- Eckerd College (Florida)—College Harbor Retirement Community
- University of Central Arkansas (Arkansas)—College Square
- Benedictine University (Illinois)—Villa St. Benedict
- Stanford University (California)—University Retirement Community
- Messiah College (Pennsylvania)—Messiah Village

Virtual Communities

Yet another new concept that includes lifelong learning through classroom study, educational travel, and community service is the idea of a "virtual retirement community."

A virtual retirement community is best explained by offering this example:

In Boston, when they were faced with the prospect of leaving their longtime homes and neighborhood in order to obtain the services of a retirement community, a group of neighbors got together and created an alternative to that prospect—Beacon Hill Village (BHV), a virtual retirement community.

Beacon Hill Village partnered with service providers with proven track records and thereby was able to offer its members excellent access to all the things a normal retirement community member would enjoy. Social services, exercises facilities, cultural events, home maintenance services, and medical and assisted living services were just a few of the things they were able to provide. Beacon Hill Village further enhanced their status by becoming a nonprofit organization, which enabled them to offer their programs at reduced rates.[7]

Nowadays, Beacon Hill Village residents are able to participate in all manner of travel, adventure, social events, seminars, educational classes in their own homes, and rapid access to medical services such as doctor visits, exercise programs, and much more.

In the words of Judy Willet, director of Beacon Hill Village,

Forget moving into a retirement community; stay in your home and have the services come to you. Beacon Hill Village, a nonprofit organization, enhances the lives of people fifty and over in central Boston.

The Village offers an alternative for people who want to stay in their homes and the neighborhoods they love for the rest of their lives. Started by a group of Beacon Hill people in 2002, The Village now has over three hundred members, sixty of whom are people of modest means who pay one hundred dollars through The Village's Membership Plus Program, instead of the annual fee of $550.

The Village is a one-stop-shopping concept. Members call BHV for anything large or small. "This is an absolutely marvelous invention. It is allowing my mother to live independently, as she approaches her ninety-second birthday," says Robert Kuttner, *The Boston Globe* columnist. Our services range from personalized concierge services, referrals with discounts to electricians, plumbers, and restaurants, to services for home care. Members take advantage of trips, free grocery shopping, personal trainers, Tai Chi classes, massage therapists, patient advocates, geriatric care managers—you name it, they do it!

This pioneering program is a one of a kind across the nation. Many communities have called The Village to get information to start a similar program in their cities. People want to stay in their own homes and in their communities as they age, with the services and programs that offer them safety and peace of mind. Beacon Hill Village is a lifestyle solution that makes "city living easier" for many elders in Boston.

For more information on this new and innovative concept, be sure to visit their website at *www.beaconhillvillage.org*.

Active Adult Communities

In the past, these communities were dedicated to bingo, shuffleboard, golf, and easy living. Not anymore. Today, such communities are changing— morphing into active adult campuses full of lifelong learning possibilities. Not only are they providing resources for the body, but they are also beginning to provide resources that feed the mind and soul.

Walking, jogging, and biking paths are replacing the shuffleboard courts. State-of-the-art gyms and pools offer residents multiple ways to stay physically fit. Bingo rooms are gone, replaced by classrooms offering all kinds of classes, courses, and workshops. Smart homes, wired for the technology of today and the future, complete with home offices, are becoming the norm.

The tastes of home buyers who are interested in living in active adult communities are also changing. Today, the trend is toward smaller, more active communities, closer to people's homes. They want to stay near families, friends, churches, and all the other community resources they have developed over the years. Here is a sampling of what active adult communities are offering in the way of lifelong learning for their residents.

Del Webb/Pulte Homes

Del Webb/Pulte Homes is the nation's largest home builder, and a pioneer and established leader in a communities for active adults in nineteen different states: Arizona, California, Colorado, Connecticut, Florida, Georgia, Illinois, Indiana, Maryland, Massachusetts, Michigan, Nevada, New Jersey, North Carolina, Ohio, Pennsylvania, South Carolina, Texas, and Virginia.

Thanks to a series of surveys done by the company, which showed that baby boomers plan to continue their education as they transition out of the workplace and into retirement, the company is looking at a variety of ways to incorporate lifelong learning into their communities. Here is just one example:

Sun City Grand in Arizona has partnered with Arizona State University (ASU) to offer residents a wide variety of classes. The curriculum includes courses in business, philosophy, management, sociology, literature, finance, history, environment, music, astronomy, speech, religion, health, home repair, and meteorology. The ASU Lifelong Learning Academy is housed in the student union–like Chaparral Center, which is part of the Sun City Grand retirement community.

Lennar Corporation/U.S. Home

The Lennar Corporation/U.S. Home is one of the nation's leading builders of active-adult communities. With over forty-five active communities across the nation, they are setting the standard for buyers looking for the very best activities and amenities for their active lifestyles. Golf courses, clubhouses, greenbelt trails, hobby centers, classrooms, and computer labs are all part of the lifestyle offered to today's buyers.

Jensen's Residential Communities

Jensen's Residential Communities offer twenty-eight residential communities for older adults in the eastern United States—New Hampshire, Connecticut, New Jersey, Maryland, North Carolina, South Carolina, and Georgia. They are dedicated to providing to their residents the best community environment at a reasonable cost. Social activities and recreational amenities abound, including lifelong learning opportunities.

The Kendal Corporation

The Kendal Corporation is nationally recognized as a leader in serving older adults throughout the Northeast. Their philosophy is based on the idea that growing older can bring new opportunities for growth and development. To that end, their communities offer lifelong learning and community service opportunities to their residents. They often collaborate with colleges and universities to build continuing care communities near a local campus.

They have communities near Dartmouth College in New Hampshire, others near both Dennison and Oberlin Colleges in Ohio, yet another near Ithaca and Cornell Colleges in New York, another near Washington and

Lee University in Virginia, and still another near the five colleges (UMass, and Smith, Holyoke, Hampshire, and Amherst Colleges) in western Massachusetts.

So if you are interested in moving to an active-adult community, you don't have to worry about giving up your interest in lifelong learning. In fact, such a move is likely to enhance it. More and more active-adult communities are offering their residents ways to stay connected with life and society in general, ways to keep learning, and ways to keep both their minds and their bodies active.

The Internet can help you learn more about active-adult communities. There are a host of sites that can help you begin your search. See the Resources section for some of them.

Miscellaneous Initiatives

Here are just a few of the miscellaneous new programs and initiatives being developed around the country, all of which will help you continue your lifelong learning quest during the after-fifty years. Thanks to Civic Ventures *Blueprint for the Next Chapter* for this list.[8]

The Senior Companion Program is part of Senior Corps, a network of national service programs that provides older Americans with the opportunity to apply their life experiences to meeting community needs. Senior Companions serve one-on-one with the frail elderly and other homebound persons who have difficulty completing everyday tasks.

The Third Age Initiative of Leadership Greater Hartford provides leadership training for older adults and helps connect them with leadership roles in the community.

The Discovering What's Next program in Newton, Massachusetts, partners with the Newton Community Education program to offer deeper exploration of topics touched on in library forums. A two-part seminar, Life Planning for Couples in the Second Half of Life, identified major lifestyle changes couples face and engaged participants in a process of exploration and conversation about the implications for their relationships.

The *Transition Talks, Discovering What's Next: Re-Vitalizing Retirement* workshops and forums in Newton, Massachusetts, were extremely popular, and participants expressed a desire to continue meeting in smaller groups. As a result, Transition Talks was developed—informal drop-in conversation groups held at local Starbucks stores and the public library to discuss topics related to retirement and aging.

Cleveland's *oasis without Walls* program conducted focus groups of baby boomers in their effort to attract younger members. The responses of the participants led program planners to offer a series of courses related to spirituality and inner explorations, including Inner Peace by Meditation, the Seven Chakras, Peaceful Practices, and Sage-ing Circles.

Cleveland's *LifeLearn* program at the Goodrich-Gannett Neighborhood Center offers computer classes and incorporates computer and technology features into lifelong learning programs. Older-adult participants are able to apply and advance their computer skills to specific topics they explored in classes or discussions.

The *Seniors Connect@Cleveland Pubic Library* initiative is sponsoring senior health and legal information fairs as part of its overall program to promote health and wellness. Libraries across the country are becoming key gateways to health information and are offering programs on health and wellness for active adults.

We've presented just a few of the many innovative and exciting ideas being developed to help keep older adults active, engaged, and contributing members of society. All of these ideas have a lifelong learning component, a valuable ingredient needed to reach that goal.

Along with that, the aging of the baby boomer generation and what that will mean for our society is a hot topic right now as, indeed, it should be. In fact, the White House Conference on Aging, which is held only once every ten years, dedicated its entire agenda at the December 2005 conference to how society can best meet the needs of the aging baby boomers. Let's show them how to do that!

Interview with an Expert

Judy Goggin

Judy Goggin has worked in the field of aging and lifelong learning for more than twenty-five years. Since 2001, Judy has been a senior vice president of Civic Ventures. a national nonprofit organization that works to expand the contributions of older Americans to society, and to help transform the aging of American society into a source of individual and social renewal. She is currently leading the development of the Civic Ventures Next Chapter initiative. The Next Chapter initiative provides individuals who are moving beyond the middle years with direction and connections for the next chapter in their lives.

Can you give us a short overview of the Next Chapter concept?

The Next Chapter programs help individuals nearing retirement answer the question "What's next?" by providing "directions and connections" that enable them to clarify their vision and then develop a practical plan for realizing that vision. Encouraging continued contributions to one's community is a vital element of the Next Chapter initiative.

How many programs are up and running now in 2005?

As of 2005, over twenty Next Chapter and similar programs were in development in Arizona (seven), California (two), Connecticut (three), Florida (two), Illinois (three), Massachusetts (four), Minnesota (one), New York (four), North Carolina (one), Ohio (seven), Oregon (one), Pennsylvania (two), and Virginia (one).

All of these programs reflect Next Chapter principles and practices. Some have been developed in conjunction with the Civic Ventures' national initiative. Others have been created independently but share at least some of the principles and elements of the Next Chapter concept. To review current programs and to learn more about the Next Chapter initiative, visit the Civic Ventures website at *www.civicventures.org*.

What do you envision for the future of the Next Chapter initiative?

The model will evolve as local projects experiment with it. More projects will appear across the country. Baby boomers will have a big influence in designing and leading these efforts in their local communities. An important area to develop is to expand the opportunities for baby boomers to find "good work"—both paid and unpaid—that uses their talents and experience to tackle important social problems. Health care, education, social services, and nonprofit organizations generally need to adapt existing programs and create new ones that will be flexible and meaningful and will integrated these resources into their workforce.

What is the Civic Ventures philosophy in regard to the baby boomers?

It's dangerous to think of baby boomers as a single group. Their cohort spans seventeen years and represents millions of individuals. We have to be careful about generalizing. But we think that the leading-edge baby boomers who came of age in the sixties and heard JFK's call to "Ask not what you country can do for you; ask what you can do for your country" may be inclined toward revisiting that idealism now that they are reaching a time when they may have more time to devote to serving their communities—in either paid or unpaid positions.

LEARNING LATER, LIVING GREATER MY WAY!

Trish O'Leary

Trish O'Leary is a member of the Institute for Learning in Retirement sponsored by Albertus Magnus College in Connecticut.

As a child and young adult, I loved classes and learning. The start of a new school year or semester always felt to me like my own personal celebration of a New Year's Day, a fresh beginning. When I began working in the business world, I had to leave that enjoyment behind.

Sometimes I would find a night course to take, first in Chicago at The Newberry Library and then later in the 1970s, when I moved to Boston, at the Boston Center for Adult Education. Often, though, the people taking the same class didn't have much opportunity to get to know each other. Instead of forming a community of learning, as had happened in my college experience, the night school students I met were separate individuals occupying the same space but without a sense of kinship.

I first heard about the Institute for Learning in Retirement shortly after I moved to the New Haven, Connecticut, area in 1988. A storytelling friend, Bobby Steward, told me how much she was enjoying her course on The Good Life and a course from a graphic artist who guided the class members into making and embellishing their own boxes. Following Bobby's example, I signed up.

The first course I took, Writing Nonfiction, was taught by a lively Ph.D. named Laura Rees, a member of the faculty of Albertus Magnus, our host college. She said she enjoyed the receptivity of her study group members. The next semester, I took another writing course from the same teacher, as well as a course on Indian and Irish women writers. We read Arundhati Roys *The God of Small Things* and then Irish women poets. That course unveiled for me a piece of my Irish heritage I did not know existed: female poets who knew their craft. Reading the works of poets like

Kathleen Raines and Eavan Boland was like being introduced to interesting relatives I'd never before laid eyes on.

This exposure to poetry led me to sign up for another poetry course. It, in turn, made me aware of contemporary poets. When our program needed more literature courses the following term, I volunteered to lead a poetry course that would combine reading great poets with writing some poetry of our own—following the maxim that imitation is the sincerest form of flattery.

At the last session of the class, each person brought in copies of a favorite poem to share. Before they read or recited from memory a favorite poem, each class member would briefly explain what had drawn them to that poem. (A few years ago, when Roger Housden's *Ten Poems To Change Your Life* appeared in the bookstore, it was fun to compare his selections with those from our group.)

In fall 2001, I started teaching Memoirs and Family Stories. This course, which I've now led seven times, has provided an opportunity not only to share the writings of powerful memoirists but also to learn about the remarkable lives of many of the program participants—whether in terms of their breadth of travel, their overcoming of hardships and persecution, or their devotion to families and service to the community.

After I had been a member of the Institute for Learning in Retirement for a few years, I was given the opportunity to join the curriculum committee, the group that plans courses for our program in the spring and fall. To me, a woman who once read course catalogs for enjoyment, matching study group leaders with course content is as much fun as fixing dates was for Dolly Levi.

This year, I'm the president of our institute. I plan to again teach memoirs in order to keep on encouraging those wonderful stories people have to share, and I look forward to seeing the friends I have made in classes over the last several years. Our program has helped me recapture the satisfaction of learning and teaching—parts of myself that I had lost track of. It is truly a double "bonus" for me and a wonderful way to "make our bonus years count!"

Charting My Journey

• • • •

Charting My Journey

• • • •

Chapter Fifteen

Reprise— To Boldly Go

Don't be afraid to take a big step.
You can't cross a chasm in two small jumps.
—David Lloyd George

Well, a lot of new ideas and concepts have been thrown at you in the earlier chapters of this book. It might seem a bit overwhelming—but it really isn't. If you break it all down, it looks something like this:

Part 1, "To Boldly Go," talked about the ability of aging generations to effect change in our society, and how we now stand on the threshold of doing it again—changing societal views about getting older. This section also introduced you to the concept of lifelong learning. The deliberate inclusion of lifelong learning in your after-fifty years may be an entirely new idea for many of you.

Part 2, "It Ain't Over Till It's Over," went into some detail about the importance of keeping your brain active and alert as you age. In order to enhance and enrich your after-fifty years, you must challenge and stimulate your brain. This part also discussed the mind/body connection and how the two can work in tandem to make your later years the very best they can be.

Part 3, "Health Clubs for the Brain," introduced you to the concept of lifelong learning in the classroom. We talked about the different types of lifelong learning programs in your community and the many benefits to be gained when you join one of these programs.

Part 4, "Up, Up, and Away!," opened the door to educational travel programs and showed you how lifelong learning can take place anywhere in the world. After you read this section, you probably were ready to pack

> What could be better in our retirement years than finding a source of enriched learning experiences among satisfying friendships?
> —Marilee Martin, St. Louis, Missouri

your bags and take off!

Part 5, "Rebels with a Cause," discussed the opportunities community service can give you to incorporate lifelong learning into your life while you help improve the quality of life within our society. Being involved in service work is one of the most important activities we can undertake as we age.

This now brings us to Part 6, "Reprise—To Boldly Go." and this section is just that, a summary that brings everything in the book into focus for you and points the way to that next step on your journey to make your after-fifty years the very best they can be.

An Assignment

In the next chapter, you will find the exercise Charting My Journey. It's designed to build on the notes you've jotted down at the end of each chapter, making it easier to organize your thoughts about the material in this book.

Set aside some quiet time to begin the exercise. It's okay if you don't do it all at once. In fact, it might be better to complete it over several days or weeks rather than rushing it. You want to build in time to think about your answers and to change and rework them as necessary to make them relevant for you. When you are done, you should have a clearer idea of why you want to engage in lifelong learning in your after-fifty years and how to make it happen. Good luck!

A Word about Change

There's no doubt that as you move into your after-fifty years, you will undergo significant change. Change is very challenging. A host of books have been written about how to effect successful change. Therefore, we won't go into a lot of detail here about how to do that. Suffice to say that you must step outside your comfort zone. How to do that is the challenge we all face.

Here are a few helpful hints:

- Give yourself time to adapt to your changed life. Don't jump right in the Monday after you leave your full-time job. Give yourself time to reflect, unwind, and relax. If necessary, sit on an empty beach and watch the waves lapping on the shore. Let your mind wander. Take time to be by yourself. Answers will come.

- Make only one or two changes at a time. The faster a change comes, the more difficult it is to adapt to it. Take your time. You have to crawl before you can walk.

- Take control of your life. The greater your involvement in making changes, the more likely you will view the changes as opportunities. Don't let people around you dictate what you should or should not do. Think about what is right for *you*.

- Think of this new chapter in your life in a positive way. A positive mind-set will go a long way toward creating an environment conducive to successful change.

- Create a vision and a strategy for yourself. Jot down the ideas you have and figure out ways to make them happen. Make a "to do" list and start working your way through it. Before you know it, you'll be well on your way toward a new and exciting life.[1]

Change is transformation. You can transform your life through lifelong learning. Pursuing this path helps you decide what kind of future you want, how self-fulfilled you want to be, and how engaged you want to be in your community and your family.

A Word about Motivation

Motivation is that something we all wish we had more of, that special something we need in order to create an outstanding life.

Again, hundreds of books have been written on this subject. Everyone is always looking for the magic bullet that will make one truly motivated. Unfortunately, it doesn't work that way. Being motivated to make change is hard work. But getting motivated is vital to enhancing and enriching your after-fifty years, so here are a few tips to get you going.

- Visualize and brainstorm. Picture yourself doing what you've

> Now that I have time to learn, it's as though I rode my bicycle very fast to win some race and then circled back to learn where I had been and what I missed—and, of course, where I was going.
>
> —Shirley Guralnik, Beachwood, Ohio

always dreamed of doing once you had more time.

• Organize your home. Now that you're no longer working full time, you have the perfect opportunity to tackle all those projects you've been putting off. An organized home equals an organized mind.

• Search out a role model. Know someone whose after-fifty years are fantastic? Talk to them. Ask questions. Use what you've learned to begin to build your own successful after-fifty life.

• Build in quiet time. Just as quiet time is necessary for change, so too it is necessary to get motivated. You need time to just sit and think. Be sure to get enough sleep, too. Rest is critical to clear thinking.

• Read and learn. Hit the bookstore or library. Read stories about how others have overcome inertia and gone on to develop their motivation.

• Set goals. Make an action plan and a to-do list. If you don't plan for yourself, someone else will.

• Challenge yourself. Goals that are too easy sap your motivation. Constructive goals take hard work and stepping outside your comfort zone. But be sure to make them achievable. Don't set yourself up for failure by setting unattainable goals.

• Start small. When we are creating a new plan for ourselves, we all tend to hit the ground running—and then burn out after a short time. So start small and take baby steps. Again, you have to crawl before you can walk.

• Create a positive atmosphere. Just like with change, thinking positive is essential to success. A negative atmosphere will sink you every time. So ignore those little voices in your head that say you can't do it. Post positive affirmations if necessary. Do whatever it takes to keep a positive mind-set.

• Reward yourself. For every little step that you successfully complete on your path to motivation, give yourself a treat. It doesn't have to be much. Even setting aside a half hour to listen to a favorite music piece in the midst of a busy day can be rewarding.[2]

Consider this book food for thought. Think about how you want to spend your third age. Think about what's important to you once a job no longer consumes most of your time and mental energy. And think about what you want to leave as a legacy to future generations.

This book is also a guide—a resource—to help you begin your journey of discovery into the next phase of your life. Contained within these pages is the information you need to take the first step in that journey.

We hope you will engage in lifelong learning because you are excited by it, because you understand its value in your later life, and because it's one sure way to make your after-fifty years the very best they can be. So get out there! Grab life! They say you don't get a second chance, but in the words of Kahlil Gibran, "To be able to look back upon one's life in satisfaction, is to live twice!"

LEARNING LATER, LIVING GREATER MY WAY!

Patricia Edie

Patricia Edie is a member of the Omnilore program sponsored by California State University in Dominguez Hills

As a child, I was often asked, "What do you want to be when you grow up?" I would look into my distant future and think... teacher?... mother?... nurse? "What do you want to be when you grow up?" I would ask my grandson as I looked at his little face and dreamed of his distant future. Somehow that question always conjures up possibilities for the young as they consider their...distant future. How energizing it is to realize that for me as a sixty-three-year-old woman, the distant future is now and I am still able to ask myself that question!

I have always been at home in an educational setting, and throughout my professional careers in education and business, I took advantage of courses and seminars that helped me to stay at the cutting edge of my professions. Over the years, there were often other things I wanted to learn—things unrelated to my work—that I would put on the back burner and say, "Someday...."

When I retired, I realized that for the first time in my life, I truly owned my life. Each day was one of choice for me. No one else owned my time. How was I going to choose to spend it? I wanted to grow, to enlarge myself. What did I want to be? One of the greatest surprises for me upon retirement was the realization that a large slate of educational opportunities was open to me.

I am fortunate to share my life with a man who loves learning as much as I do. We set out to sign up for classes at the local community college, and we took a series of interesting courses and one-day seminars. We were challenged by the new ideas and actually came to have limited fluency in a foreign language. We began to travel, and when we prepared for a trip, we would read anything we could find on the culture, politics, history, and people of our destination country.

While we had each other to talk to—to discuss our new concepts and ideas—over time, we began to realize that something was missing. We seemed to be isolated and wished we had other like-minded people with whom to discuss our new knowledge. One day, I noticed a small paragraph in a local newspaper telling of an orientation for a group called Omnilore, an organization for "minds not ready for retirement." Thus began our entry into the world of learning in retirement. We found that this particular group is an "active" learning program based on peer-directed learning.

Groups of members get together to teach each other specific topics. As members, we are required to do research on some related aspect of a topic, to teach it to the others in the group, and then to participate in lively discussions of the concepts with the other members. This approach was quite different from attending lectures, where we, as learners, received the knowledge from a professional teacher. Here, we were learners who, when our turns came, became the teachers. What a concept!

We dove into this new experience. It was a chance to broaden our knowledge. One class we signed up for was on the music of Bach. I had minimal exposure to or appreciation for classical music and wondered what all the fuss was about. I chose the concept of "counterpoint as used in Bach's fugues" for my research topic.

As I read and listened, I slowly began to understand the concept and recognize the patterns. The greatest aspect of the experience was that when the day for my presentation arrived, I had an audience—a group of people who shared my interest and enthusiasm, and who wanted to hear what I had to say. In teaching them what I had learned, it became even clearer in my own mind. Stephen Covey says that if you want to learn something, teach it to someone else.

In addition to classical music, I have researched evolutionary psychology in a class on Darwin; the Role of Women in Renaissance Florence; Sufism in a class on Islam; U.S. Immigration Policies; Social Network Analysis; Genetic Screening; Chinese Religions; and The Unification of Italy, to name a few.

As a result of this experience, my sense of myself has changed. I am more than the roles I filled during my working years. I have expanded my boundaries. I find I am able to listen more critically to conversations, and I have knowledgeable opinions to offer in most discussions. I am more aware, noticing things in the news or in my community. I feel more defined and alive. My adult children listen to my comments and say things like, "How do you know all that?" I have a life that continues to enrich me and give me meaning and purpose.

What do I want to be when I grow up? I want to be a student, continually questioning and learning.

.

Charting My Journey

• • • •

Charting My Journey

• • • •

PART SEVEN

Resources

Charting
My Journey

Knowledge prolongs life itself and enlarges the sphere of existence.
—John Quincy Adams

The object of this appendix is to help you decide if you want to incorporate lifelong learning into your after-fifty years, and if so, how. In *Learning Later, Living Greater*, we have discussed three ways in which you can do that: in the classroom, through educational travel, and through meaningful community service work. Using the notes you jotted down at the end of each chapter, you can now begin to pull your thoughts together and start to think about the role lifelong learning will play in your later years.

This exercise is by no means a scientific one; consider it as something designed to help you organize your thoughts about these new endeavors. Take your time completing it—it doesn't have to be done in a day. Reflect. Get comfortable with the possibility of incorporating lifelong learning into your life. As you begin reflecting, you will discover new insights about yourself. This reflection is really planning for the next phase of your life. By giving yourself the time to plan properly, you are ensuring that the years ahead will be the most exciting and enriching possible.

Oh, by the way, while you're busy planning for those years, be sure to include some leisure time into your day—time for reflection, time for yourself, time to call your own. Deliberately creating leisure time is not natural in our society, so it has to be developed, cultivated, and allowed to grow.

In the words of Johann Wolfgang von Goethe, "One ought, every day at least, to hear a little song, read a good poem, see a fine picture, and if it were possible, to speak a few reasonable words."

Getting Organized

Begin with six pieces of paper, and write the title of each of the following six parts of this book across the top (one piece of paper for each part).

To Boldly Go
It Ain't Over Till It's Over
Health Clubs for the Brain
Up, Up, and Away!
Rebels with a Cause
Reprise—To Boldly Go

Go through your chapter notes (the things you wrote down on the "Charting My Journey" pages), pick out what you consider to be the most important ones, and jot them down on the paper that corresponds to that part. Each part has two or three chapters.

Can you think of anything else you'd like to add? If so, jot it down in the appropriate place.

Do you have any questions that need answering? List them where appropriate.

The following questions should be answered specifically for Part 3 ("Health Clubs for the Brain"), Part 4 ("Up, Up, and Away!"), and Part 5 ("Rebels with a Cause")

Ask yourself the following: How much do I enjoy interacting with other people? A lot? Occasionally? Never? Make a note of your answer for each of the three parts.

Think about how much of your after-fifty time you would like to devote to each of these three parts. Jot that time down on the appropriate pages.

Think about your budget for after you leave full-time work. Can you afford to devote a few hundred dollars (approximately) a year to lifelong learning in the classroom? A few thousand dollars (approximately) a year to educational travel? Some pin money for traveling to and from meaningful community service work? Jot your answers down on the appropriate pages.

Making Sense of It All

A Little Introspection

1. Take a new piece of paper. Write a paragraph, or as much as you need, about what you envision as the perfect life in your after-fifty years. Let yourself daydream a bit, but be practical, too. Winning the lottery and living the life of the rich and famous isn't very realistic.

2. Make a list of the most important things to come out of this writing exercise—the things you *have* to have in your after-fifty years. Make sure they're attainable, even if you have to work a bit for them.

3. Put this page aside. You will use it soon.

Pulling It All Together

1. At this point, you should have seven pieces of paper—six from your book notes and one from your writing exercise.

2. Now, pick out and highlight what you consider to be the most important points from each of the six parts. You will find yourself highlighting two, three, or more items on each page.

3. Now look at the most important things that you listed from your writing exercise. Can you see any similarities with the first list? Make a note of them.

4. These similarities are what appeal to you the most about lifelong learning. This is your Similarity List. They may not be an exact match, just similar. That's okay.

5. Using the Similarity List, rate the three opportunities for lifelong learning from one to three—with one having the least similarities and three the most:
    *   in the classroom
    *   through educational travel
    *   through meaningful community service

6. Review your ratings. Do they make sense to you? If not, go back and revisit where necessary.

7. How does the winner(s) fit in with your time? With your budget? Do you think this is doable in your after-fifty years?

8. Now make a list of the questions you need answers to. Do you need to do some research? Make some phone calls? Surf the Internet? Visit your library? Make a plan of action to get your questions answered so you can make intelligent and informed decisions.

9. Once your research is completed, you're ready to make an Action Plan based on what you've discovered about how you want to live in your after-fifty years. The steps of your Action Plan should be readily apparent to you, based on your current circumstances.

10. That's it! Congratulations! You are on your way to creating an enhanced and enriched life in your later years. From time to time, as your life changes, revisit this exercise and tweak it as necessary.

Some Additional Help

Not sure you're a lifelong learner? Answering yes to just a few of these questions will help convince you.[1]

- Do you like to make things happen instead of waiting to react to situations?

- Would you describe yourself as someone who obtained a significant portion of your knowledge outside of a formal classroom?

- Are there always things you'd love to know more about or wish you could appreciate more deeply?

- Do you experience positive feelings about yourself when you learn something new?

- Can you identify certain personal life experiences as times of immense learning even though they probably wouldn't be defined as classes or courses?

- Are you open to new ideas and experiences?

- Do you enjoy gaining the perspectives and wisdom of others?

- Are you awed by the infinite nature of knowledge—that you could never possibly know everything you want to know in life?

Some general tips for those who want to become lifelong learners, or better lifelong learners: [2]

- Know what you want and what you are looking for. Is it self-enrichment? A new direction?

- Remember that adults learn in different ways than children. We have different reasons for learning, driven by a unique sense of ourselves and our time.

- Design your learning to suit your convenience and style. No particular way of learning is better than another.

- Take time to appreciate the experience of learning about something you love. Pushing too hard wastes energy.

- The most important lesson? Learning should be fun!

Resources

Chapter 5—Lifelong Learning in the After-Fifty Years

- The Minnesota Learning in Retirement Network (LIRN), a statewide association of university- and community-based senior learning organizations. Find them at *www.minnesotahumanities.org*.

- The Bernard Osher Foundation is a charitable foundation that has benefited a wide range of educational, cultural, and other non-profit organizations. In 2001, the foundation began to consider older-adult programs, and since then has funded more than seventy Lifelong Learning Institutes across the United States. The contact is Dr. Mary G.F. Bitterman, Director, Osher Lifelong Learning Institutes, One Ferry Building, Suite 225, San Francisco, CA 94111—*mbitterman@osherlli.org*.

- The Senior Citizen's Guide is designed to help older adults and those with aging parents or spouses find housing, health, financial, travel, entertainment, consumer services, and other senior-related resources within specific regions or cities in the United States. Find them at *www.seniorcitizensguide.com*.

Chapter 6—Lifelong Learning in the Classroom

- Elderhostel, Inc., a not-for-profit organization, is the nation's first and the world's largest educational travel organization for older adults. Since 1975, they have been offering exceptional learning opportunities at remarkable values. Find them at *www.elderhostel.org*.

- The Elderhostel Institute Network (EIN) is North America's largest and most respected educational network for older adults. It is a resource and communications network for Lifelong Learning Institutes across North America. Listed on their website are the locations and all the contact information for the more than 350 Lifelong Learning Institutes that belong to the network. Find them at *www.elderhostel.org/ein/intro.asp.*

- The Association of Learning in Retirement Organizations of the West (ALIROW) is an association of independent learning in retirement (LIR) associations located on campuses of sponsoring universities and colleges in the western United States. Find them at *www.alirow.org.*

Chapter 7—Other Types of Community-Based Learning Programs

- OASIS is a national nonprofit educational organization for older adults. Find them and a list of their programs across the United States at *www.oasisnet.org.*

- The Shepherd's Centers of America (SCA) is a network of community learning and volunteer organizations that serve the needs of older adults. Find them and a list of their programs across the United States at *www.shepherdcenters.org.*

- SeniorNet is a nonprofit organization of computer-using adults, aged fifty and older, that provides older adults education for and access to computer technologies. Find them at *www.seniornet.org.*

- The Public Broadcasting Service (PBS) has an entire section devoted to lifelong learning. The PBS campus offers more than 120 courses through TV and the Internet for pleasure or a degree. Find them at *www.pbs.org.*

- P.O.V., the award-winning PBS series, offers unique ways to interact with their programming. Community Engagement campaigns are designed to build audiences, inspire civic dialogue, and, when possible, foster ongoing community involvement around issues raised in selected programs. Check them out at *www.pbs.org/pov/*.

- **The Great Lecture Library** comprises lectures and sermons that have taken place at the Chautauqua Institution, renowned as a center for education, the arts, religion, and recreation. They offer a comprehensive online library of over 1,200 lectures and sermons in forty-five major categories of interest. Check them out at *www.greatlecturelibrary.com*.

- **Book-Clubs-Resource.com** is a complete guide to book clubs and reading groups, with an outstanding collection of links and information for readers, including information about saving with discount book clubs. Find them at *www.book-clubs-resource.com/*.

- **Yahoo Reading Groups** is found online within Yahoo Clubs at *www.clubs.yahoo.com*.

- **The Great Decisions Global Affairs Education Program** includes the annual Briefing Book, Great Decisions TV, the National Opinion Ballot Report, discussion groups across the country, and the *GD Online* newsletter. Find them at *www.great-decisions.org*.

- **The Great Books Foundation** is dedicated to helping people learn how to think and share ideas by educating them to become participants in, leaders of, and advocates for Shared Inquiry. Find them at *www.greatbooks.com*.

- **The Teaching Company** brings engaging professors into your home or car through courses on DVD, audio CD, and other formats, with over two hundred courses for lifelong learners. Visit them at *www.teach12.com*.

- **Senior Theatre** companies range from amateur to professional and are sponsored by educational institutions, retirement communities, senior centers, and community theatre groups. Find out more at *www.seniortheatre.com*.

- **Study Circles** are a simple yet powerful method for learning using the skills, knowledge, and experience of its members. Learn more at *www.studycircles.org*.

- **Autodidactic Press** feels that self-education is the essence of genuine learning. Find out more at *www.autodidactic.com*.

- **The Smithsonian Associates (TSA)** is a public education and membership unit of the Smithsonian. Participants of all ages explore the best in scientific, historic, artistic, and cultural expression in America and abroad through a diversified program of performing arts, films, lectures, seminars, courses, and special events developed from Smithsonian and related resources. Find out more at *www.smithsonianassociates.org*.

Chapter 8—The International Perspective

- To see the global impact of lifelong learning, check out the U3A website at *www.worldu3a.org*.

- Another excellent site that contains a substantial list of several hundred links to websites in the United Kingdom and abroad in no fewer than twenty-eight countries is the U3A website WWW Links at *www.harrowu3a.co.uk/u3a_sites.html*.

- **The International Association of Universities of the Third Age (AIUTA)** is an international organization of UTAs and U3As around the world. Find them at *www.aiuta.asso.fr/*.

- **U3A groups** around the United Kingdom are members of The Third Age Trust. Its main purpose is to encourage lifelong learning for those no longer in full-time gainful employment. Find them at *www.u3a.org.uk*.

- **TALIS, or Third Age Learning International Studies,** was created in 1990 as a forum for international older-adult learners, teachers, programmers, and researchers. Their website can be found at *www.extension.usask.ca/Talis/*.

- **CATALIST, The Canadian Network for Third Age Learning,** is a bilingual network of fifty organizations across Canada that fosters and promotes third age learning through shared knowledge, expertise, research, and resources. Check them out at *dev.www.uregina.ca/catalist/.*

- This is the first website that enables far-flung Australian citizens, many in very remote areas, to take online courses. To get an idea of what courses are being offered, check out *www.u3aonline.org.*

- Another extensive website to help distribute resources to all the far-flung Australian programs. This site can be found at *www3.griffith.edu.au/03/u3a/.*

- Lifelong learners from all around the world have listed details about their programs on this site. Be sure to check out *www.worldu3a.org/cooperation/myu3a.htm.*

- Another great site for a listing of lifelong learning links around the world is *www.harrowu3a.co.uk/index.htm.*

- Want to reminiscence? Check out *www.timewitnesses.org.*

Chapter 10—Educational Travel Organizations

- **Elderhostel,** at *www.elderhostel.org,* describes every one of its more than ten thousand programs on their easy-to-use website. Or call the registration department at 1-877-426-8056 for more information.

- To request an Elderhostel U.S./Canada, International, or Adventures Afloat catalog, please call 1-877-426-8056.

- **The Senior Summer School, Inc.,** program is designed for independent, active, and healthy seniors. Programs range from two to six weeks during the summer. Contact them at *www.seniorsummerschool.com* or by phone at 1-800-847-2466.

- **ElderTreks** is the world's first adventure travel company designed exclusively for people fifty and over. Find them at *www.eldertreks.com*, or give them a call at 1-800-741-7956.

- The Close Up Foundation works with Elderhostel to offer older Americans an opportunity to visit Washington, D.C., for an insider's view of the government at work. For more information, visit Close Up's website at *www.closeup.org* or call 1-800-Closeup. You can also find information on these Washington programs on the Elderhostel website at *www.elderhostel.org*.

- Smithsonian Journeys are not exclusively designed for just older adults, but rather for adults of all ages, however, we are including them here because of the high quality of their programs. Visit their website at *www.smithsonianjourneys.org* or call them at 1-877-EDU-TOUR (1-877-338-8687).

- Cultural heritage tours emphasize authenticity and hands-on participation, with richly orchestrated itineraries. Find out more at *www.americanpathways.com*.

- Classical Pursuits are not geared specifically toward older adults, but they still offer a variety of learning vacations for adults of all ages from all over North America. Call them at 1-877-633-2555 or visit them at *www.classicalpursuits.com*.

Chapter 11: The Connection between Lifelong Learning and Community Service

- The Center for Intergenerational Learning at Temple University seeks candidates to be trained to join its new Intergenerational Training Experts Network (ITEN). If this sounds interesting to you, check out their website at *templecil.org/ITEN/*, or contact Dr. Andrea Taylor at 1-215-204-6708 or by email at *ataylor@temple.edu*.

- The Peace Corps—Older Americans are contributing to Peace Corps programs all over the globe, and, in the process, they find their age to be an asset. For more information on the Peace Corps, check out their website at *www.peacecorps.gov.*

Intergenerational Sources

- Center for Intergenerational Learning *www.temple.edu/depart ments/CIL*
- Generations United—*www.gu.org*
- Generations Together—*www.gt.pitt.edu/*

Chapter 13—Service Opportunities in the Community

Resource Websites

- Action without Borders—*www.idealist.org*
- Corporation for National and Community Service—*www.cns.gov*
- Empower Web—*www.Sftoday.com/empower.htm*
- GuideStar—*www.guidestar.org*
- Impact Online—*www.impactonline.org*
- Network for Good—*www.nicsl.coled.umn.edu*
- Servenet—*www.servenet.org*
- ServiceLeader—*www.serviceleader.org*
- Volunteering Abroad—*www.cie.uci.edu/~cie/iop/voluntee.html*
- World Volunteer Web—*www.worldvolunteerweb.org/*
- Volunteer Vacations—*www.amizade.org/*

To locate the volunteer center in your community, check the telephone book under Volunteer Center, Voluntary Action Center, Volunteer Bureau, or United Way (volunteer centers are sometimes part of the local United Way, many of which maintain extensive databases of volunteer opportunities) or call 1-800-595-4448. Also try:

- **Senior Community Service Employment Program**—In virtually every county in the country, you can find it in your phone book or through your local department of aging.

- **The United Way**—There is a United Way in every state, listed in the phone book or on the Internet at *national.unitedway.org*. Each state agency maintains a long list of volunteer options.

  They also maintain *www.volunteersolutions.org* as an online volunteer matching tool that is managed by the local centers. Typing in your zip code will begin your search.

- Find a list of volunteer centers by state at *www.pointsoflight.org /centers/find_center.cfm*.

More Useful Websites

- Energize Inc—*www.energizeinc.com/prof/stateoffices.html*
- VolunteerMatch—*www.volunteermatch.org*.
- 1-800-Volunteer.org—*www.1-800-volunteer.org*
- AARP—*www.aarp.org*
- Environmental Alliance for Senior Involvement—*www.easi.org*
- International Executive Service Corps (IESC)—*www.iesc.org*
- National Retiree Volunteer Coalition—*www.nrvc.org*
- Seniors Community on MSN—*www.communities.msn.com/seniors*
- National Aging Information Center—*www.aoa.gov*
- Volunteer Friends—*www.volunteerfriends.org*
- Future Possibilities—*www.futurepossibilities.org*
- Habitat for Humanity—*www.habitatforhumanity.org*

International Organizations

These are just some of the largest international organizations, which support millions of volunteers around the world.

- AIESEC International—*www.aiesec.org/*
- Amnesty International—*www.amnesty.org/*
- Coordinating Committee for International Voluntary Service—*www.unesco.org/ccivs/*
- Cross-Cultural Solutions—*www.crossculturalsolutions.org*
- EarthWatch Institute—*www.earthwatch.org*

- Ecovolunteer—*www.ecovolunteer.org*
- Global Citizens Network—*www.globalcitizens.org*
- Global Health Corps—*www.globalhealthcorps.org*
- Global Service Corps—*www.globalservicecorps.org/*
- Global Volunteers—*www.globalvolunteers.org*
- Go M.A.D. (Make a Difference)—*www.go-mad.org*
- Health Volunteers Overseas—*www.hvousa.org*
- InterAction—*www.interaction.org/*
- International Association for Volunteer Effort—*www.iave.org/*
- International Federation of Red Cross and Red Crescent Societies—*www.ifrc.org/*
- International Volunteer Programs Association—*www.volunteer international.org*
- NetAid—*www.netaid.org*
- Partners of the Americas—*www.partners.net*
- Peace Corps—*www.peacecorps.gov*
- Rotary International—*www.rotary.org/*
- Service Civil International USA Branch—*www.sci-ivs.org*
- Teachers for Tomorrow—*www.teachers-for-tomorrow.org*
- United Nations Volunteers—*www.unvolunteers.org*
- United Nations Information Technology Service (UNITeS)—*www.unites.org*
- Visions in Action—*www.visionsinaction.org*
- Voluntary Service Overseas—*www.vso.org.uk*
- Volunteering in India—*www.serviceleader.org*
- Volunteers for Peace—*www.vfp.org*
- Volunteers in Asia—*www.viaprograms.org*
- Volunteers in Technical Assistance (VITA)—*www.enterprise works.org*
- World Association of Girl Guides and Girl Scouts—*www.wagggsworld.org/*

- World Organization of the Scout Movement—*www.scout.org/*
- WorldTeach—*www.worldteach.org*
- World YWCA—*www.worldywca.org/*
- Zonta International—*www.zonta.org/*
- World Council of Churches—*www.wcc-coe.org/*
- **Idealist.org (Action without Borders)**—*www.idealist.org*— Action without Borders is independent of any government, political ideology, or religious creed. Their website maintains an extensive list of volunteer options organized by country or state.

- **Volunteers for Peace (VFP)**—*www.vfp.org*—A non-profit membership organization that has been placing American volunteers in overseas work camps since 1981. Contact them at Volunteers for Peace, 43 Tiffany Road, Belmont, VT 05730, or by phone at 1-802-259-2759 and by email at *vfp@vfp.org*.

- **Older Americans Act Programs**—If you are interested in volunteering, contact your Area Agency on Aging which is listed in the yellow pages/and or under county government listings, or call the Eldercare Locator – 1-800-677-1116.

- **The National Senior Service Corps (Senior Corps)**—The Senior Corps, a part of the federally-funded Corporation for National Service, is a network of federally-supported programs that helps people age 55 and older find service opportunities in their communities. The Senior Corps involves mature adults in three types of services:

  - *Foster Grandparents*—Low income individuals age 60 and over who carry out the challenging and rewarding work of helping special and exceptional needs children.
  - *Senior Companions*—Low-income adults who serve as companions for two to four older clients who need help. (Both Foster Grandparents and Senior Companions must serve 20 hours per week and receive a small stipend.)
  - *Retired and Senior Volunteers Program (RSVP)*—This program involves adults age 55 and older in service that matches their

personal interests and makes use of their skills and lifelong experiences. You can work as little or as much as you want. You do not receive a stipend.

For information on the Senior Corps programs contact the Corporation for National Service at 1-800-424-8867 or visit *www.seniorcorps.org*. This website tells how to become involved and has resources for persons participating in the program.

- **Service Corps of Retired Executives (SCORE)**—SCORE is a 13,000-member volunteer association sponsored the U.S. Small Business Administration (SBA). To locate the SCORE office nearest you, call 1-800-634-0245 or contact your nearest SBA office. Also find them at *www.score.org*.

- **Volunteers in Parks (VIP)**—Older adults with an interest in history and the great outdoors can volunteer their time with the National Park Service's Volunteers in Parks or VIP program. Additional information on the VIP program is available from local parks or the National Park Service, P.O. Box 37127, Washington D.C. 20013-7127. Their website is located at *www.nps.gov/volunteer*.

- **Literacy Volunteers of America (LVA)**—a fully integrated national network of local, state and regional literacy providers that give adults and their families the opportunity to acquire skills to be effective in their roles as members of the families, communities and workplaces. Their Website at *www.literacyvolunteers.org* contains a U.S. map that allows you to click on your state to find out what volunteer options are available to you.

- **Americorps**—Information about AmeriCorps and its service programs in which volunteers tutor and mentor youth, build affordable housing, teach computer skills, clean parks and streams, run after-school programs, and help communities respond to disasters.can be found at *www.americorps.org*.

- **Citizen Corps**—This website at *www.citizencorps.gov* has information about Citizen Corps and its programs to engage Americans in specific homeland security efforts in communities throughout the country.

- **Learn and Serve America**—This site at *www.learnandserve.org* offers information about this program and has resources for educators and others involved in developing and managing service-learning projects.

- **Civic Ventures**—A San Francisco-based national organization that creates ideas and invents programs to help society achieve the greatest return on experience. Their website is full of invaluable information, links to volunteer opportunities, and many other resources. Visit them at *www.civicventures.org.*

- **The Experience Corps**—A national service program that mobilizes Americans 55 and up to help improve urban elementary schools. Experience Corps is the largest AmeriCorps program engaging older Americans. See *www.experiencecorps.org.*

- **Virtual Volunteering**—Also known as online volunteering, cyber service, online mentoring, teletutoring and various other names. To get more information about virtual volunteering go to *www.ser viceleader.org.*

- **Volunteer Vacations**—The Internet will give you an enormous list from which to choose. Here are just a few of the thousands of opportunities:
  - Volunteer America—*www.amazade.org*
  - American Hiking Society—*www.americanhiking.org*
  - Wilderness Volunteers—*www.wildernessvolunteers.org*
  - Passport In Time (PIT)—*www.passportintime.com*
  - Sierra Club—*www.sierraclub.org*

Chapter 14—What's on the Horizon?

Active Adult/Retirement Communities Websites

- *www.retirementliving.com*

- *www.senioroutlook.com*
- *www.retirenet.com*
- *www.wheretoliveafter50.com*
- *www.ericksoncommunities.com*
- *www.seniorresource.com*
- *www.virtual-retirement.com*
- *www.retirementhomes.com*
- *www.delweb.com*
- *www.newhomesdirectory.com*
- *www.privatecommunities.com*
- *activeadult.americanhomeguides.com/*
- *www.activeadulthousing.com*

Other Helpful Resources and Organizations

- **Chicago Life Opportunities Initiative,** Council for the Jewish Elderly, Chicago, Illinois, *www.cje.net/future.*

- **Pathways to Vital Living:** A Curriculum for Midlife and Beyond, Senior Resources Alliance, Winter Park, Florida, *www.wppl.org/institute/programs.htm.*

- **What's Next!,** Fairhill Center for Aging, Cleveland, Ohio, *www.fairhillcenter.org/WhatsNext.*

- **Cleveland Metroparks Emerald Neckland O.W.L.S.,** Cleveland, Ohio, *www.clemetparks.com/volunteer.*

- **Retired Social Workers—An Untapped Resource,** National Association of Social Workers, Illinois Chapter, Chicago, Illinois, *www.naswil.affiniscape.com.*

- **Wisdom Works!** MetroHealth System, Cleveland, Ohio, *www.successfulaging.org.*

- **Allegheny County Library Association,** Pittsburgh, Pennsylvania, *www.einetwork.net/acla.*

- **OASIS Without Walls,** Parma, Ohio, *www.oasisnet/org/cleve*

land.

- Tempe Connections, Tempe, Arizona, *www.civicventures.org.*

- Boomerang, Chandler Public Library, Chandler, Arizona, *www.myboomerang.org.*

- Lehigh Valley Alliance on Aging, United Way of the Lehigh Valley, Pennsylvania, *www.lvagingmatters.org.*

- Mather Café Plus, Chicago, Illinois, *www.matherlifeways.com.*

- Beacon Hill Village—a virtual retirement community, *www.bea conhillvillage.org.*

Chapter 15—Miscellaneous Websites

You may find these sites useful as you continue your journey to enhance and enrich your after-fifty years through lifelong learning in the classroom and the community, and through educational travel.

- A2Z Senior Supersite—*www.seniorhospitality.com*—This free, industry-wide Internet portal is designed to connect you quickly and easily to the world of Senior Hospitality, providers of senior-oriented housing, health and wellness resources, and other products and services.

- AARP—*www.aarp.org*—A nonprofit, nonpartisan membership organization dedicated to making life better for people fifty and over.

- American Society on Aging (ASA)—*www.asaging.org*—ASA is a national nonprofit organization of professionals in the field of aging.

- Baby Boomer Headquarters—*www.bbhq.com/*—All things about the 1960s.

- Baby Boomers Yahoo Directory—*dir.yahoo.com/Society_and_Culture/Cultures_and_Groups/Baby_Boomers/*—A comprehensive list of baby boomer sites.

- BenefitsCheckUp, National Council on Aging—*www.bene*

fitscheckup.org—Benefits CheckUp is a comprehensive online service to help individuals screen for federal, state, and some local private and public benefits for older adults ages fifty-five and over.

- **Boomer Café**—*www.boomercafe.com/*—An online magazine for the boomers.

- **Boomer Net**—*www.boomernet.com/*—The baby boomer surfing site.

- **BoomerWeb**—*www.boomerweb.net*—An database of nostalgia, vintage, and retro sites of the 1940s, '50s, '60s, and '70s.

- **Boomers International**—*boomersint.org/drisin.htm*—Everything for the baby boomers.

- **C-Boom**—*www.boomercafe.com/*—A site for "cool" boomers.

- **Double Nickels 55**—*www.doublenickels.com*—An electronic magazine for active adults.

- **FirstGOV for Seniors**—*www.seniors.gov*—This site links to everything that has to do with the government, from consumer protection to retirement to seniors and computers to tax assistance.

- **Go60.com**—*www.go60.com*—This is a no-nonsense, yet caring and compassionate, Internet destination devoted to helping older people improve with age.

- **Grand Times**—*www.grandtimes.com*—A unique weekly Internet magazine for older adults. Controversial, entertaining, and informative, *Grand Times* celebrates life's opportunities and examines life's challenges.

- **Ignatian Lay Volunteer Corps**—*www.ilvc.org*—The Ignatian Lay Volunteer Corps engages retired women and men aged fifty and older to work with and advocate for the poor in their communities, and to reflect on these experiences in the Jesuit tradition.

- **International Longevity Center**—*www.ilcusa.org*—This is the site for the Institute for Research and Policy on Aging.

- **Keenagers**—*www.keenagers.com*—Bringing the best of the Web to seniors.

- **League for Innovation in the Community College**—*www.league.org*—The league is an international organization dedicated to catalyzing the community college movement.

- **My Prime Time**—*www.myprimetime.com*—Advice for baby boomers about all aspects of their life.

- **The National Council on the Aging**—*www.ncoa.org*—NCOA is a national voluntary network of organizations and individuals dedicated to improving the health and independence of older persons, as well as increasing the civic contributions of older adults to their communities, society, and future generations.

- **National Education Association**—*www.nea.org/retired/*—This site, for retired educators, contains a wealth of information for members.

- **Over50s.com**—*www.over50s.com*—Another site dedicated to the over fifties and their lifestyle.

- **Points of Light Foundation**—*www.pointsoflight.org*—The Points of Light Foundation is a national nonprofit organization committed to engaging people more effectively in volunteer community service to help solve serious social problems.

- **RespectAbility, National Council on the Aging**—*www.respectability.org*—RespectAbility is a collaborative initiative designed to help community organizations and decision makers find ways to empower the growing population of older Americans to use their abilities, experience, and energy to help address community problems.

- **Retired.com**—*www.retired.com*—This site says the good life starts here. There's information on finances, travel, wellness and food, news, recreation, business, personal, shopping, organizations, entertainment, family, technology, government, etc.

- **Seniors Can**—*www.seniorscan.ca*—This site is a highly acclaimed guide for retired and older adults in Canada and offers worldwide information on a wide range of topics of interest to them.

- **SeniorCenter.com**—*www.seniorcenter.com*—Another site dedicated to providing a wealth of information dealing with health, living, travel, money, news, and shopping.

- **SeniorDiscounts.com**—*www.seniordiscounts.com*—This site strives to provide the most complete and accurate listing of all senior-related discounts for goods and services throughout the United States.

- **Senior Environmental Employment Program**—*www.epa.gov /rtp/retirement/see.htm*—This Environmental Protection Agency program draws upon the skills of retired and unemployed seniors who are interested in helping improve the natural environment.

- **SeniorLink**—*www.seniorlink.com.au/*—This is said to be Australia's favorite older-adult website.

- **Senior Resource**—*www.seniorresource.com*—This site will help older adults successfully age in place, find a retirement home, cope with aging, and understand housing options.

- **Senior Something**—*www.seniorsomething.com*—Your guide to sites for older adults, because being mature is more than just getting older.

- **Snowbird Helper**—*www.snowbirdhelper.com*—The purpose of this site is to provide as much help and information for snowbirds, potential snowbirds, retired persons, and warm-weather travelers as possible.

- **The Senior Corner**—*seniors.tcnet.org*—This site is designed for seniors in northern Michigan.

- **Troops to Teachers**—*www.proudtoserveagain.com*—Troops to Teachers is a joint program of the U.S. Department of Education and Department of Defense that helps retrain military personnel (especially those retiring) for new careers as teachers.

- **Web Wise Seniors**—*www.webwiseseniors.com*—This site is dedicated to bringing people age fifty and over the information that is critical to their needs while maintaining it in an easy-to-understand and fun format.

- **Worldwide Seniors**—*www.seniors.com*—This site is sponsored by

Arizona Senior World Newspapers.

- 2young2retire—*www.2young2retire.com*—2young2retire advocates renewal and regeneration in the after-fifty years, including meaningful work, community service, lifelong learning, and better health and relationships.

Notes

Chapter 1. To Boldly Go

1. Freedman, M. Prime Time: How Baby Boomers Will Revolutionize Retirement and Transform America. Public Affairs, Perseus Book Group. New York. 1999.

2. Ibid.

3. AARP Survey. "Baby Boomers Envision Their Retirement: An AARP Segmentation Analysis." Conducted for AARP by Roper Starch Worldwide, Inc. 1999.

4. Civic Ventures. "The New Face of Retirement: An Ongoing Survey of Attitudes on Aging." Conducted by Peter Hart. San Francisco. 2002.

5. Snowdon, D., Ph.D. *Aging With Grace: What the Nun Study Teaches Us about Leading Longer, Healthier, and More Meaningful Lives.* Bantam Books. New York. 2001.

Chapter 2. An Introduction to Lifelong Learning

1. Scheibel, A., M.D. "Good News about the Aging Brain." MetLife Foundation MindAlert Lecture Series. New Orleans. 2001.

2. Nussbaum, P., Ph.D. *Do Brain Studies Point the Way to a "Learning Vaccine?" www.paulnussbaum.com.* 2001.

3. Glass, T., et al. "Population Based Study of Social and Productive Activities as Predictors of Survival Among Elderly Americans." *British Medical Journal.* 1999.

4. Wingard, D.L. "The Sex Differential in Mortality Rates: Demographic and Behavioral Factors." *American Journal of Epidemiology*. 1982.

Chapter 3. The Latest Brain Research

1. AARP Survey on Lifelong Learning. *Learning Never Ends: Education in the 50+ Years.* Conducted for AARP by Harris Interactive Inc. New York. 2000.

2. Gage, F.H. *Functional Neurogenesis in the Adult Hippocampus.* Salk Institute. La Jolla, California. *www.salk.edu/news/releases/details.php*

3. Eriksson, P.S. *Neurogenesis in the Adult Human Hippocampus.* Goteborg University Institute of Clinical Neuroscience. Sweden.

4. Diamond, M. *Magic Trees of the Mind.* Penguin Group. 1999.

5. Nussbaum, P., Ph.D. From an address given at the American Society on Aging annual conference. Orlando, Florida. 2000.

6. Kotulak, R. *Inside the Brain: Revolutionary Discoveries of How the Mind Works.* Andrews McMeel Publishing. Kansas City, Missouri. 1997.

7. Ibid.

8. Ibid.

9. Ibid.

10. Ibid.

11. Ibid.

12. Lamdin, L., and M. Fugate. *Elderlearning: New Frontier in an Aging Society.* Oryx Press. Phoenix, Arizona. 1997.

13. Nussbaum, P., Ph.D. From an address at the American Society on Aging annual conference. Orlando, Florida. 2000.

Chapter 4. The Mind/Body Connection

1. Mind/Body Medicine. *wellfx.com/InfoBase/ther_MindBody_.html*

2. Ibid.

3. Ibid.

4. "The Mind/Body Connection: Granny Was Right After All." *www.rochester.edu/pr/Review/V59N3/feature2.html*

5. Ibid.

6. Ibid.

7. Women's Center for Mind Body Health. *womensmindbodyhealth.-info/science32.htm*

8. "The Mind/Body Connection: Granny Was Right After All." *www.rochester.edu/pr/Review/V59N3/feature2.html*

9. Consortium of Social Science Associations. COSSA Washington Update. *www.cossa.org/april32k.html*. 2000.

10. Women's Center for Mind/Body Health. *womensmindbodyhealth.-info/science32.htm*

11. Ibid.

12. Ibid.

13. Ibid.

14. Ibid.

15. Ibid.

16. Poole, M. P. *A Glass Eye at a Keyhole*. Dorrance and Company. 1938.

17. Stanley Raskin. The Value of Humor Workshop. Elderhostel Conference. 2000.

18. Optimal Cognitive Aging: Achieving and Maintaining Cerebral Fitness. *www.brainergy.com/workshops/aging.html*

Chapter 5. Lifelong Learning in the After-Fifty Years

1. Minnesota Humanities LIRN Network. *www.minnesotahumanities.org/LIRN/lirn.htm*

2. MacKay, H. "What Do You Want To Be When You Grow Up?" *www.pioneerthinking.com/beyourself.html*. 2004.

3. Timmerman, S. "Older-Adult Learning: Shifting Priorities in the 21st Century." 2003 Joint Conference of the National Council on the Aging (NCOA) and the American Society on Aging (ASA). 2003.

4. Rowe, J.W., MD., and R.L, Kahn, MD. *Successful Aging*. Dell Publishing. New York. 1998.

5. Cohen, G., MD. "The Impact of Professionally Conducted Cultural Programs on Older Adults." *www.creativeaging.org*. 2001.

Chapter 6. Lifelong Learning in the Classroom

1. "Age-Proofing Your Brain." *Consumer Reports*. August 2000.

2. CNN interview with Deanna Eversoll, Ph.D., director of the OLLI program at the University of Nebraska, Lincoln. 1999.

3. National Center for Education. *Participation Trends and Patterns in Adult Education: 1991 to 1999. nces.ed.gov/pubsearch/pubsinfo.asp*

4. ALIROW. *www.alirow.org*

5. Linnehan, M. *A Brief History of the Elderhostel Institute Network*. 1999.

6. "Participation in Lifelong Learning Institutes: What Turns Members On?" Educational Gerontology, 31: 207–224, 2005. Copyright Taylor and Francis Inc.

Chapter 7. Other Types of Community-Based Learning Programs

1. "The OASIS Mission." *www.oasisnet.org/about/index.htm*. 2005

2. The OASIS Organization. *www.oasisnet.org/about/organization.htm*

3. OASIS History. *www.oasisnet.org/about/history.htm*

4. OASIS Brochure: "Enriching the Lives of Older Adults."

5.   Shepherd's Centers of America. *www.shepherdcenters.org*

6.   Shepherd's Centers of America. Adventures in Learning. 1989.

7.   Shepherd's Centers of America. The Good Life. Fall 1999.

8.   Museums Make Education Happen. 2002 Advocacy Talking Points. *www.vamuseums.org/Happen_Education.html*

9.   U3A Sources. *Museums and Lifelong Learning*. Issue 16, June 2002.

10. SeniorNet. *www.seniornet.org*

11. Senior Living. *www.seniorliving.about.com*

12. Study Circles Resource Center. *The Study Circle Handbook*. Pomfret, Ct. 1993.

13. The Study Circles Resource Center. *www.studycircles.org*. 2005.

14. Autodidactic Press. *52 Ways to Celebrate Self-University Week*. *www.autodidactic.com/resources/selfweek.htm*. 2004.

Chapter 8. The International Perspective

1.   Swindell, R. & Thompson, J. *An International Perspective on the University of the Third Age*. Educational Gerontology. 1995.

2.   Swindell, R. & Thompson, J. *An International Perspective on the University of the Third Age*. Educational Gerontology. 1995.

3.   Rafman, C. *Sharing Knowledge, Research and Resources: A Comparison of International Networks for Third Age Learning Organizations*. McGill Institute for Learning in Retirement. 2002.

4.   Swindell, R., & Grimbeek, P. *Nine "Mini Biographies" Outlining Some Characteristics of U3A Online Participants*. U3A Online: A Virtual University. 2003. *www3.griffith.edu.au/03/u3a/*

Chapter 9. Lifelong Learning Through Educational Travel

1.   Adler, J. "Origins of Sightseeing" *Annals of Tourism Research*, 1989.

2.   Ibid.

3. Jamal, T. and Hollinshead, K. *Tourism and the Forbidden Zone: the Under Served Power of Qualitative Inquiry.* Tourism Management. 1999.

4. SeniorJournal.com. *Older Tourists Creating Boom in Heritage Tourism. www.seniorjournal.com.*

5. Ibid.

Chapter 10. Educational Travel Organizations

1. Mills, E.S. *The Story of Elderhostel.* University Press of New England. Hanover, NH. Page 32. 1993.

2. Ibid. Page 32.

3. Ibid. Page 33.

4. Ibid. Page 34.

5. Ibid. Page 38.

6. Ibid. Page 40.

7. Ibid. Page 47.

Chapter 11. The Connection Between Lifelong Learning and Community Service

1. *Wall Street Journal.* "Encore: A Guide to Life After 55." Glenn J. Ruffenach, Editor. New York City. Spring 2000 Edition.

2. Independent Sector. Value of Volunteer Time. *www.independentsector.org.* 2005.

3. ERIC. Education Resources Information Center. *Senior Citizens as School Volunteers: New Resources for the Future. www.eric.ed.gov/*

4. Experience Corps. Newsletter. April, 2005.

5. Ibid.

6. Civic Ventures. *Blueprint for The Next Chapter.* May 2005.

Chapter 13. Service Opportunities in the Community

1. Civic Ventures. *www.civicventures.org*. 2005.
2. Ibid.
3. Ibid.
4. Experience Corps *www.experiencecorps.org*
5. Civic Ventures. Blueprint for The Next Chapter. May 2005.

Chapter 14. What's on the Horizon?

1. Civic Ventures. Blueprint for The Next Chapter. May 2005.
2. Ibid.
3. Ibid.
4. Ibid.
5. Libraries for the Future. *www.lff.org*
6. Ibid.
7. Beacon Hill Village. *www.beaconhillvillage.org*.
8. Civic Ventures. Blueprint for The Next Chapter. May 2005.

Chapter 15. Reprise—To Boldly Go

1. *www.motivation123.com*
2. Ibid.

Appendix 1. Charting My Journey

1. *www.depend.com/living_well_online/health_wellness*
2. Ibid.

About the Authors

Photo: Gene Bank, Newfound Photography

Nancy Merz Nordstrom, M.Ed., directs the Elderhostel Institute Network, North America's largest educational organization for older adults. She provides resources and facilitates communication among more than 350 Lifelong Learning Institutes across the US and Canada, and develops links between these programs and similar programs in Europe, Australia, Japan, and New Zealand. She has been interviewed extensively about the learning-in-retirement movement by the media, including the *Wall Street Journal*, the *Boston Globe*, *The New York Times*, the *Washington Post*, and CNN. She lives in central New Hampshire, north of Concord. Her website is *www.learninglater.com*.

Jon F. Merz is the author of six novels, including his critically acclaimed Lawson Vampire series. Prior to embarking on a full-time writing career, he served in the United States Air Force, and worked for the US government and in private sector security. He splits his time between New York City and suburban Massachusetts, where he lives with his wife and two sons. His website is *www.jonfmerz.com*.

Sentient Publications, LLC publishes books on cultural creativity, experimental education, transformative spirituality, holistic health, new science, and ecology, approached from an integral viewpoint. Our authors are intensely interested in exploring the nature of life from fresh perspectives, addressing life's great questions, and fostering the full expression of the human potential. Sentient Publications' books arise from the spirit of inquiry and the richness of the inherent dialogue between writer and reader.

Our Culture Tools series is designed to give social catalyzers and cultural entrepreneurs the essential information, technology, and inspiration to forge a sustainable, creative, and compassionate world.

We are very interested in hearing from our readers. To direct suggestions or comments to us, or to be added to our mailing list, please contact:

SENTIENT PUBLICATIONS, LLC
1113 Spruce Street
Boulder, CO 80302
303.443.2188
contact@sentientpublications.com
www.sentientpublications.com